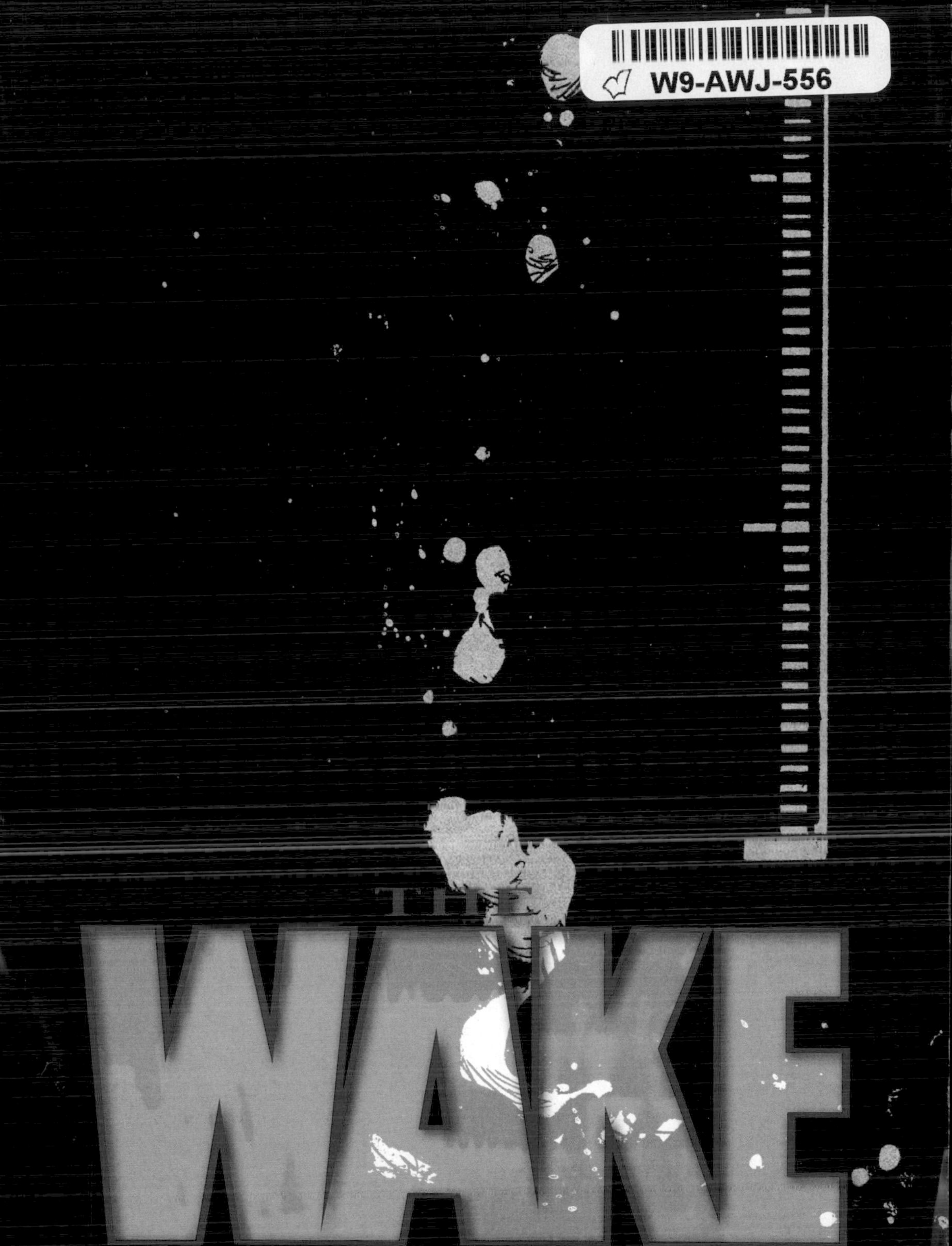
W9-AWJ-556
THE
WAKE

SCOTT
SNYDER
WRITER

SEAN
MURPHY
ARTIST

MATT
HOLLINGSWORTH
COLORIST

JARED K.
FLETCHER
LETTERER

SEAN MURPHY WITH
JORDIE BELLAIRE AND
ANDREW ROBINSON
ORIGINAL SERIES COVERS

SPECIAL THANKS TO
CHRISTIAN DIBARI

THE WAKE CREATED BY
SCOTT SNYDER AND
SEAN MURPHY

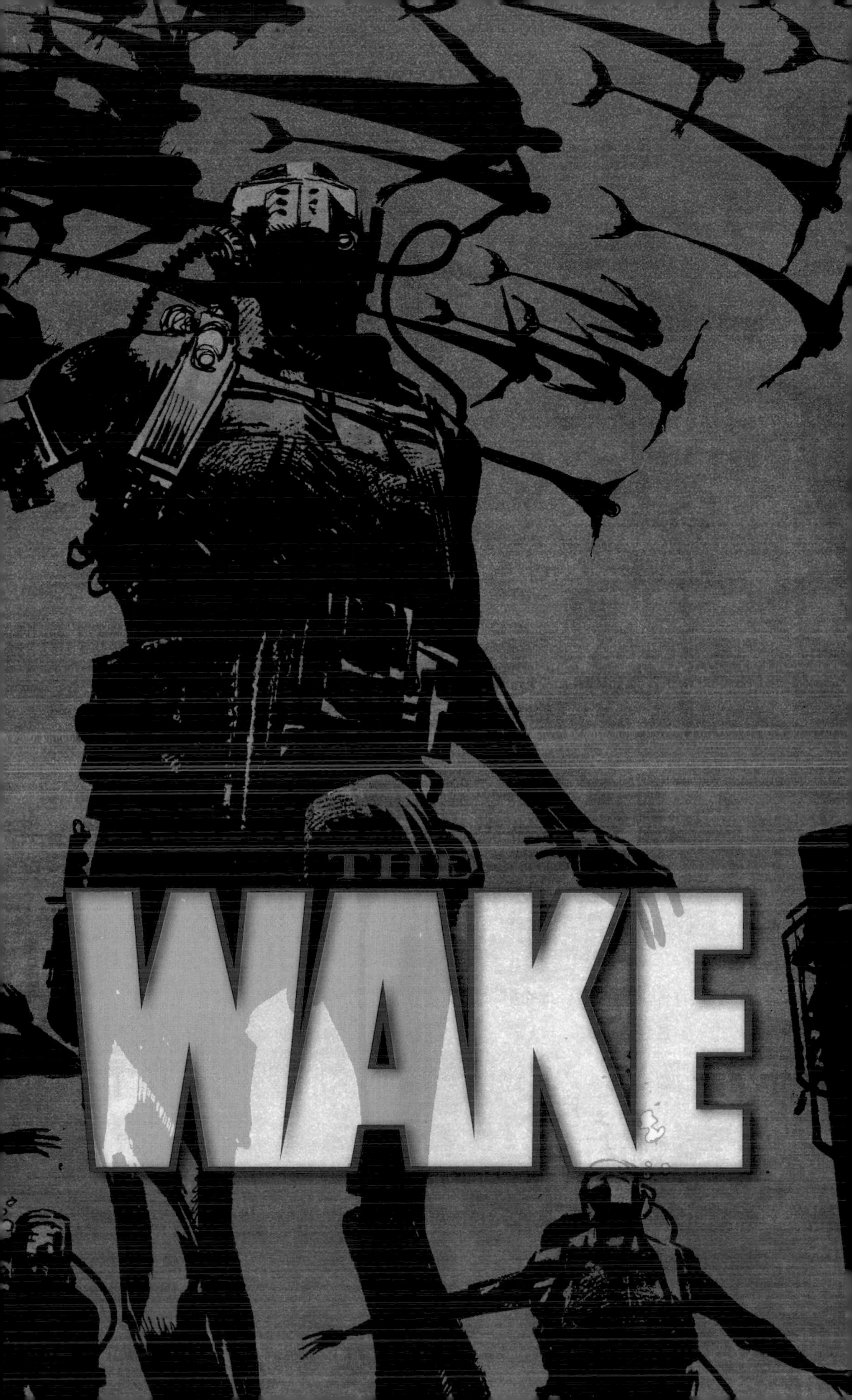
THE
WAKE

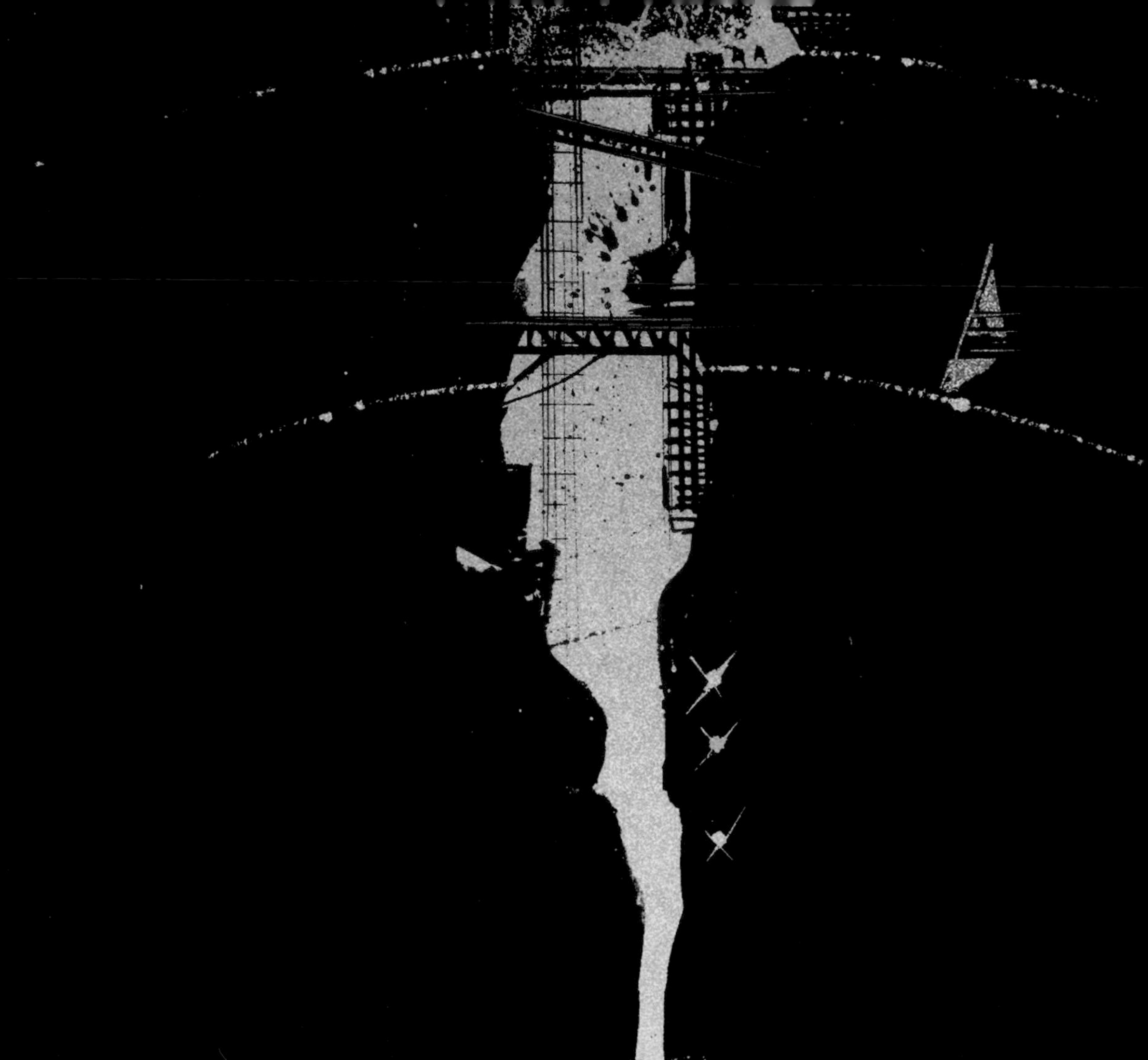

Mark Doyle Editor – Original Series
Sara Miller Assistant Editor – Original Series
Peter Hamboussi Editor
Robbin Brosterman Design Director – Books
Damian Ryland Publication Design

Shelly Bond Executive Editor – Vertigo
Hank Kanalz Senior VP – Vertigo & Integrated Publishing

Diane Nelson President
Dan DiDio and Jim Lee Co-Publishers
Geoff Johns Chief Creative Officer
Amit Desai Senior VP – Marketing & Franchise Management
Amy Genkins Senior VP – Business & Legal Affairs
Nairi Gardiner Senior VP – Finance
Jeff Boison VP – Publishing Planning
Mark Chiarello VP – Art Direction & Design
John Cunningham VP – Marketing
Terri Cunningham VP – Editorial Administration
Larry Ganem VP – Talent Relations & Services
Alison Gill Senior VP – Manufacturing & Operations
Jay Kogan VP – Business & Legal Affairs, Publishing
Jack Mahan VP – Business Affairs, Talent
Nick Napolitano VP – Manufacturing Administration
Sue Pohja VP – Book Sales
Fred Ruiz VP – Manufacturing Operations
Courtney Simmons Senior VP – Publicity
Bob Wayne Senior VP – Sales

THE WAKE

Published by DC Comics. Compilation Copyright © 2015 Scott Snyder and
Sean Murphy. All Rights Reserved.

Originally published in single magazine form as THE WAKE 1-10.
Copyright © 2013, 2014 Scott Snyder and Sean Murphy. All Rights
Reserved. All characters, their distinctive likenesses and related elements
featured in this publication are trademarks of DC Comics. VERTIGO is a
trademark of DC Comics. The stories, characters and incidents featured in
this publication are entirely fictional. DC Comics does not read or accept
unsolicited submissions of ideas, stories or artwork.

DC Comics, 4000 Warner Blvd., Burbank, CA 91522
A Warner Bros. Entertainment Company.
Printed in the USA. First Printing.
ISBN: 978-1-4012-5491-9

Snyder, Scott, author.
  The Wake / Scott Snyder, writer ; Sean Murphy, artist.
    pages cm
  ISBN 978-1-4012-5491-9
  1. Graphic novels. I. Murphy, Sean Gordon, 1980- illustrator. II. Title.

PN6727.S555W35 2014
741.5'973—dc23

2014026869

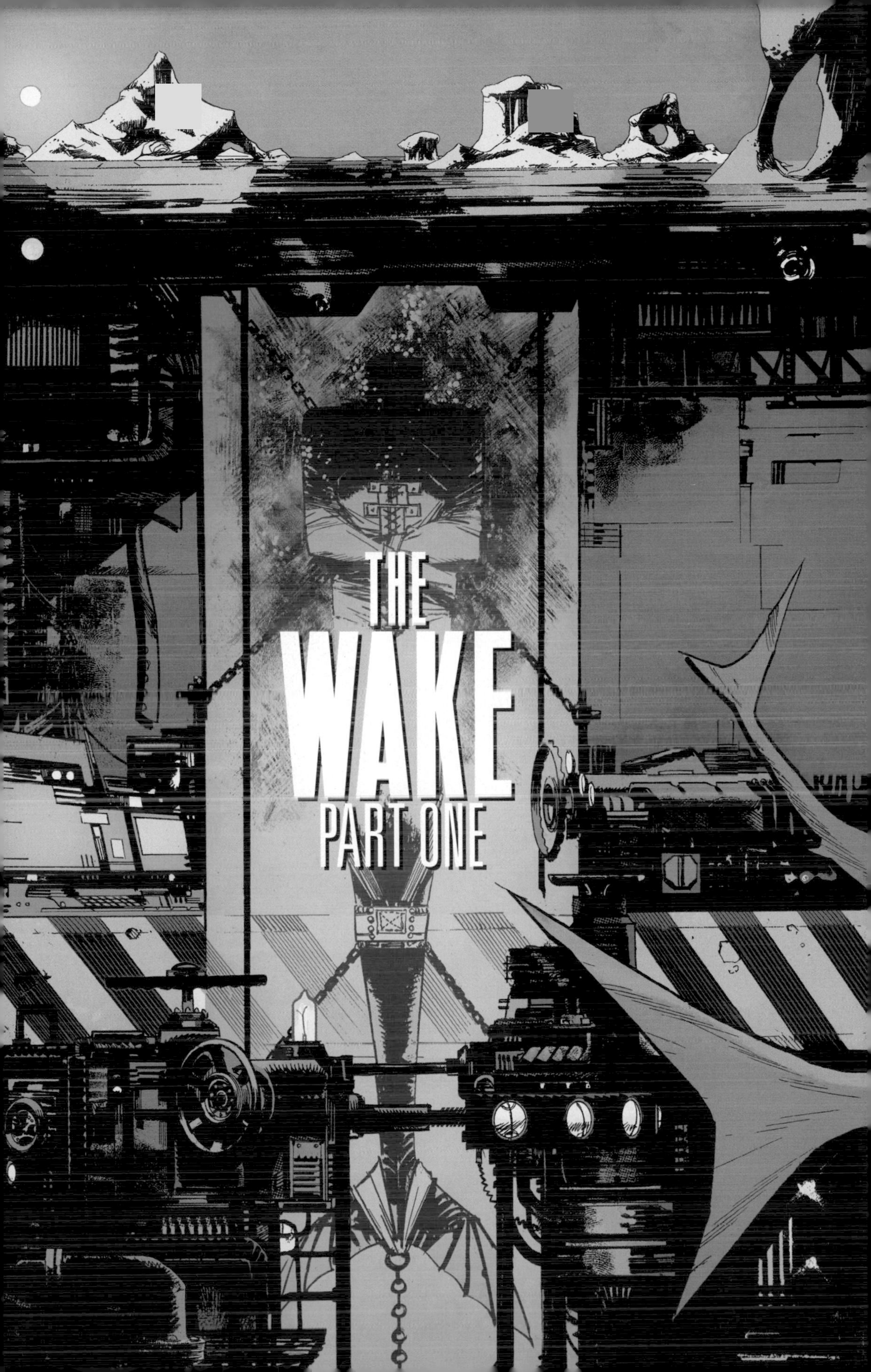
THE
WAKE
PART ONE

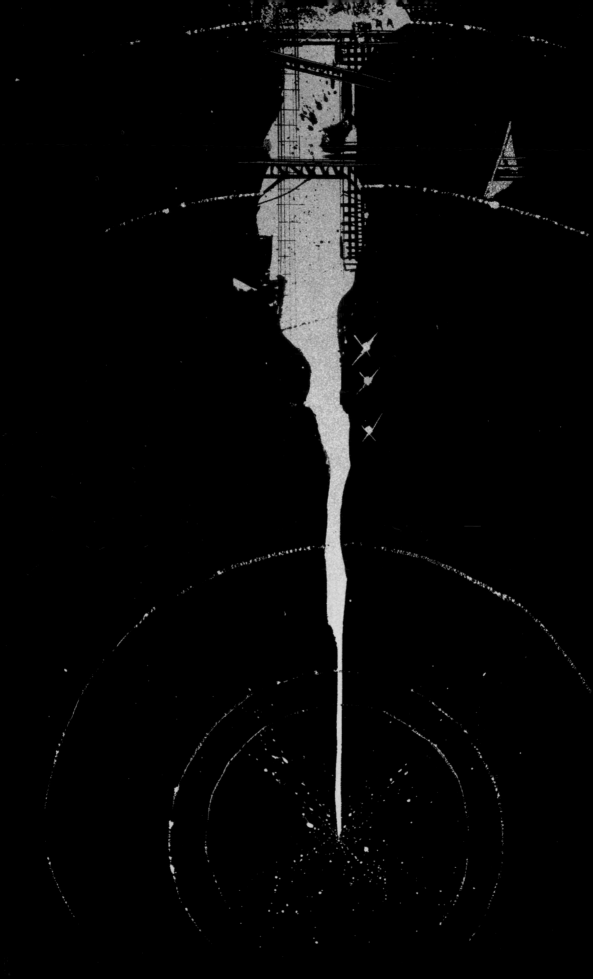

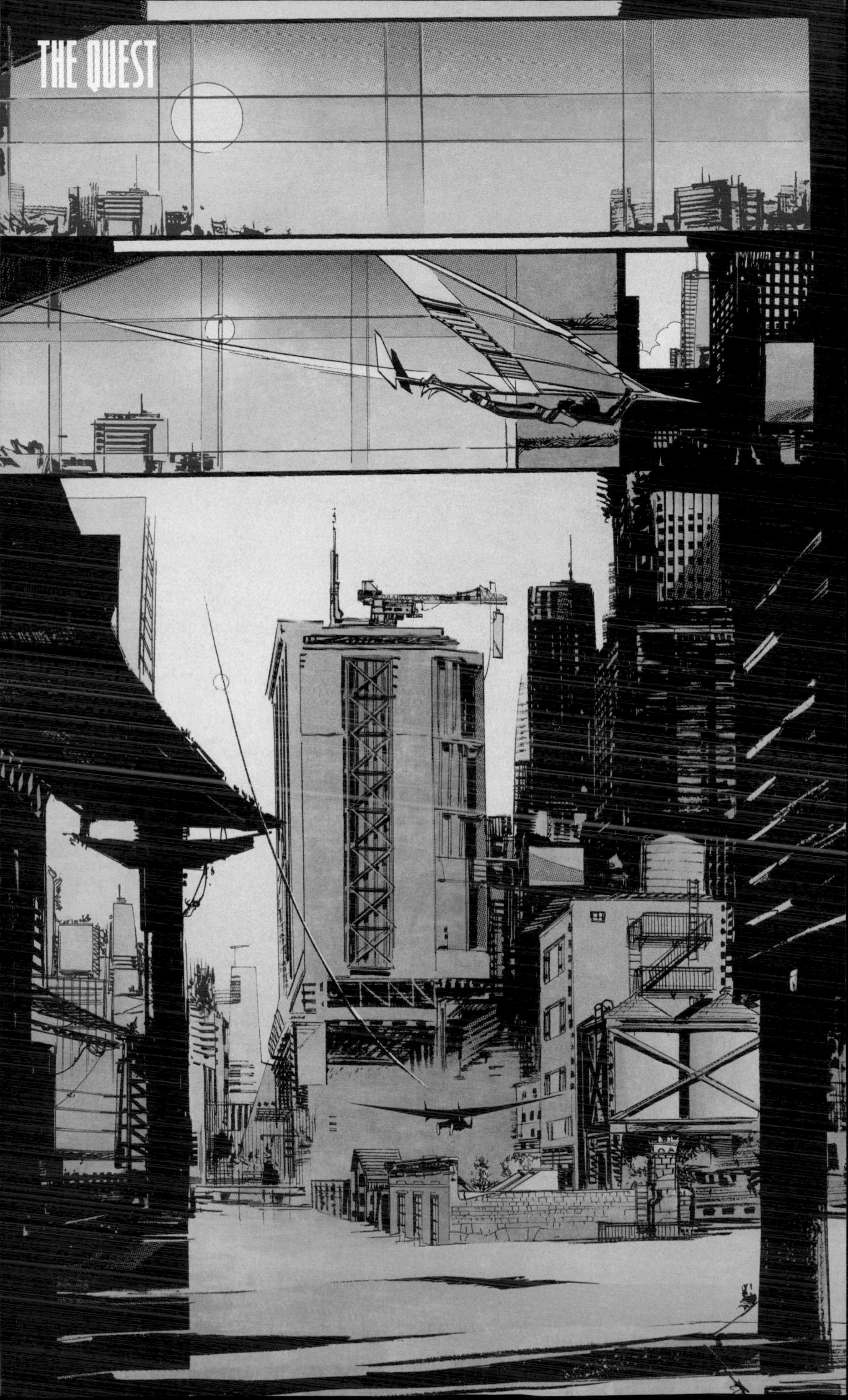
THE QUEST

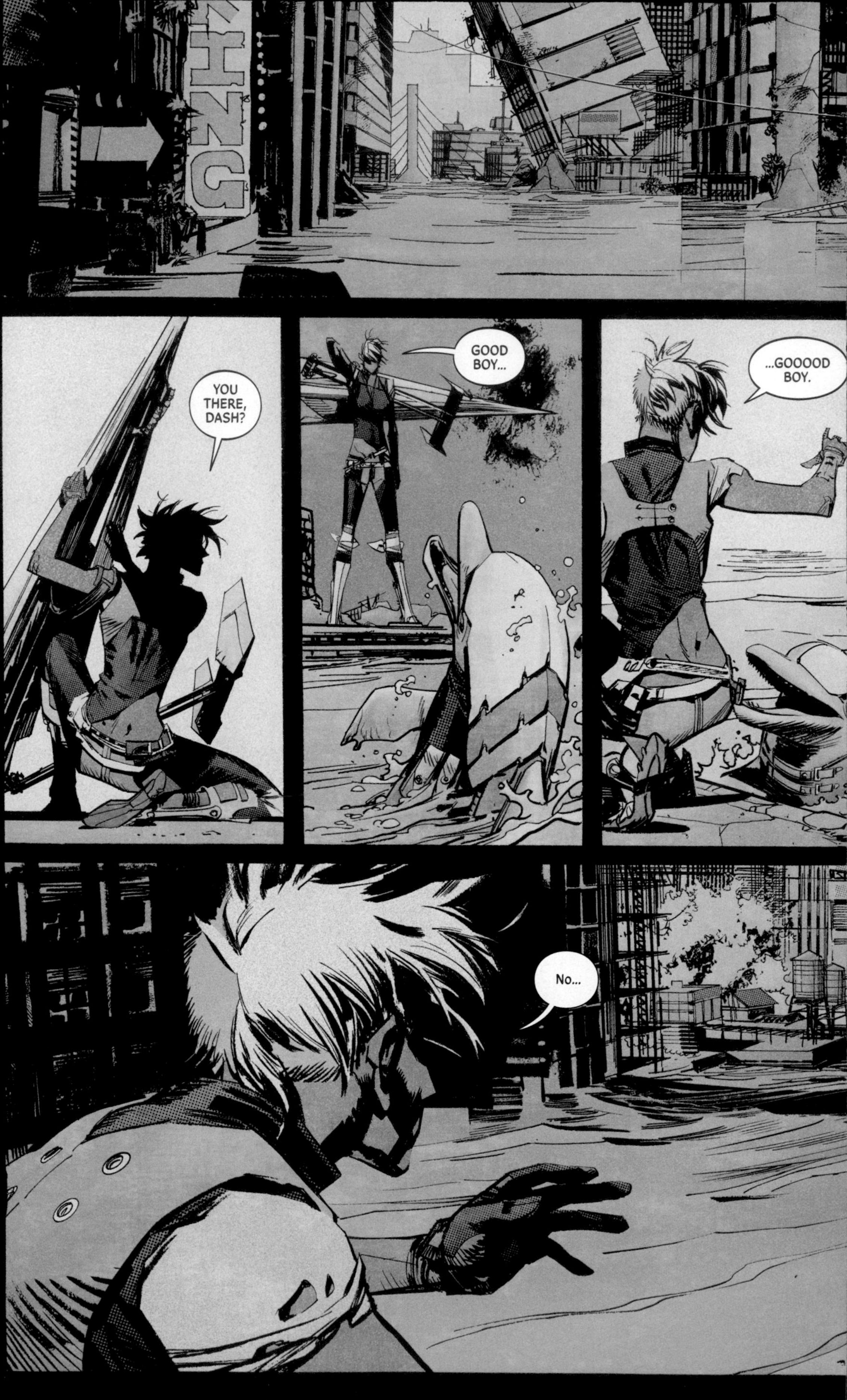
YOU THERE, DASH?
GOOD BOY...
...GOOOOD BOY.
No...

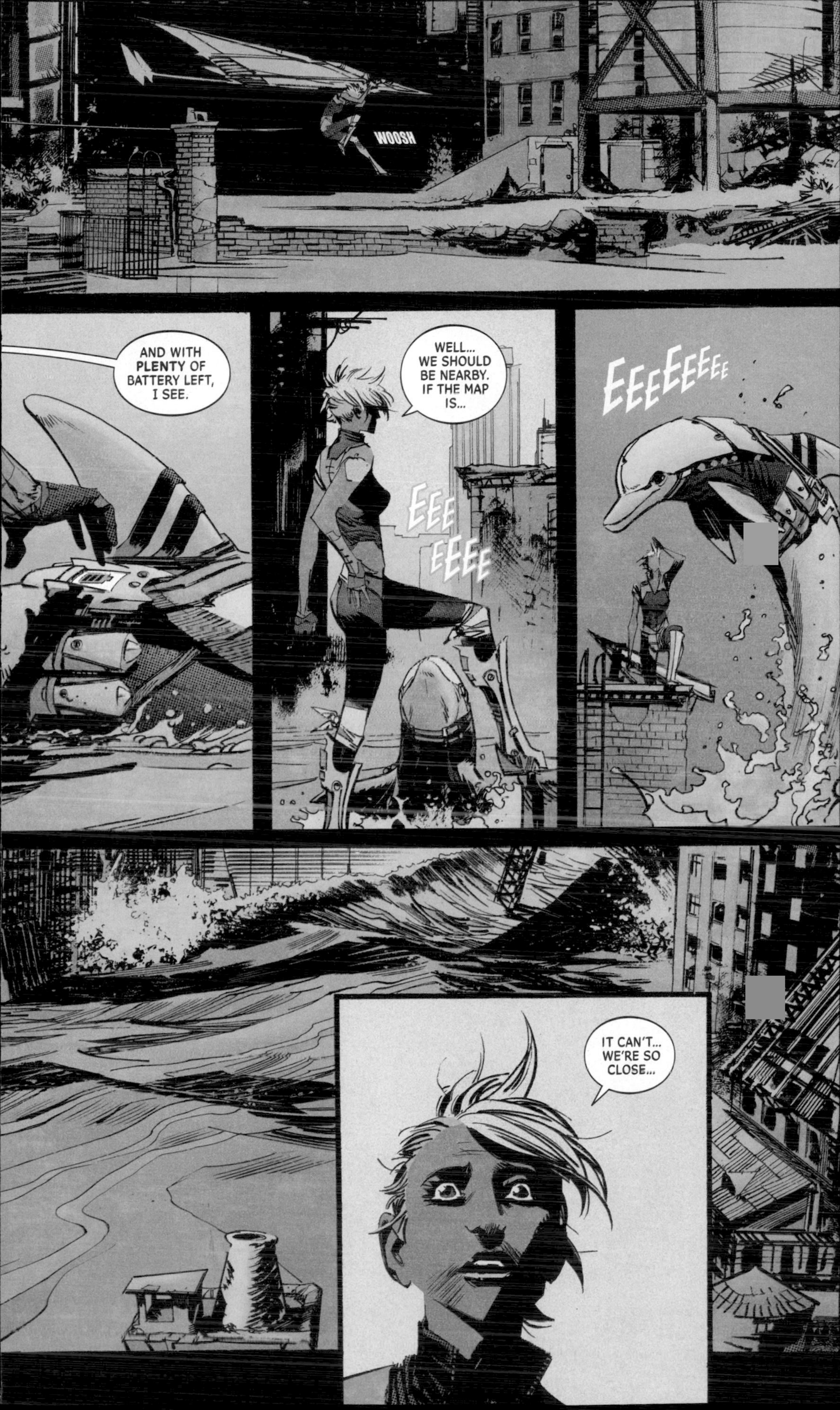
WOOSH
AND WITH PLENTY OF BATTERY LEFT, I SEE.
WELL... WE SHOULD BE NEARBY. IF THE MAP IS...
EEE EEEE
EEEEEEEe
IT CAN'T... WE'RE SO CLOSE...

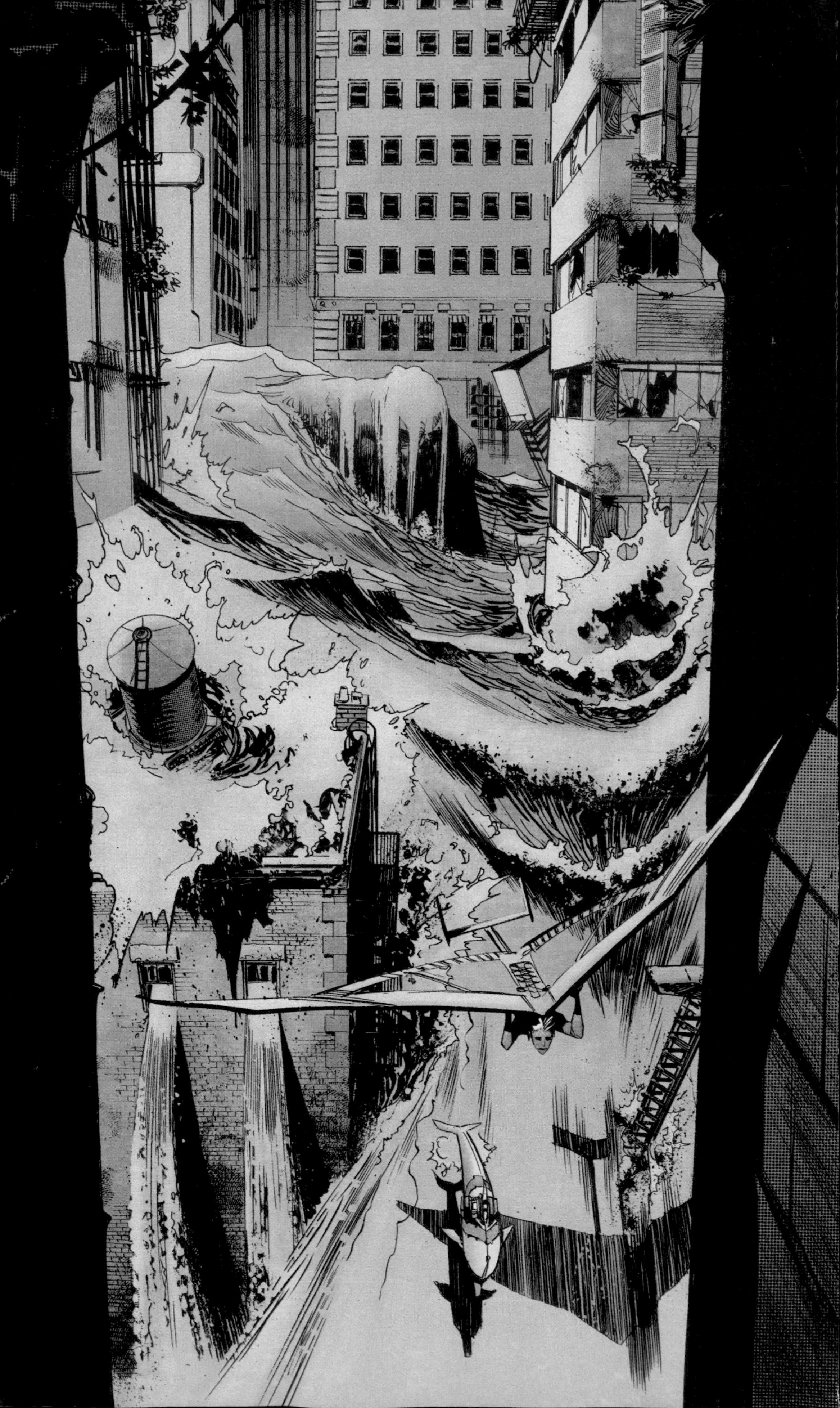

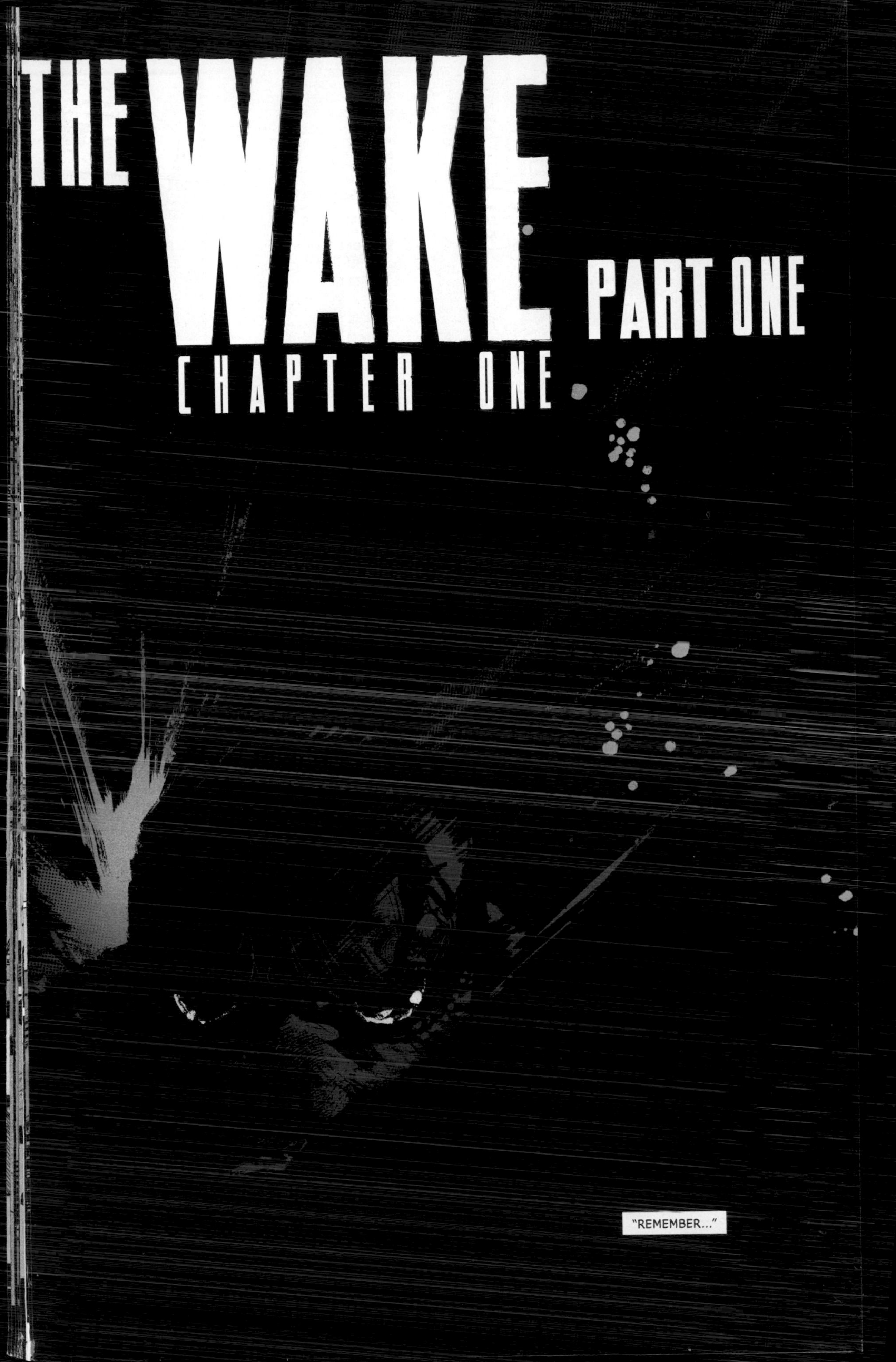
THE WAKE PART ONE
CHAPTER ONE
"REMEMBER..."

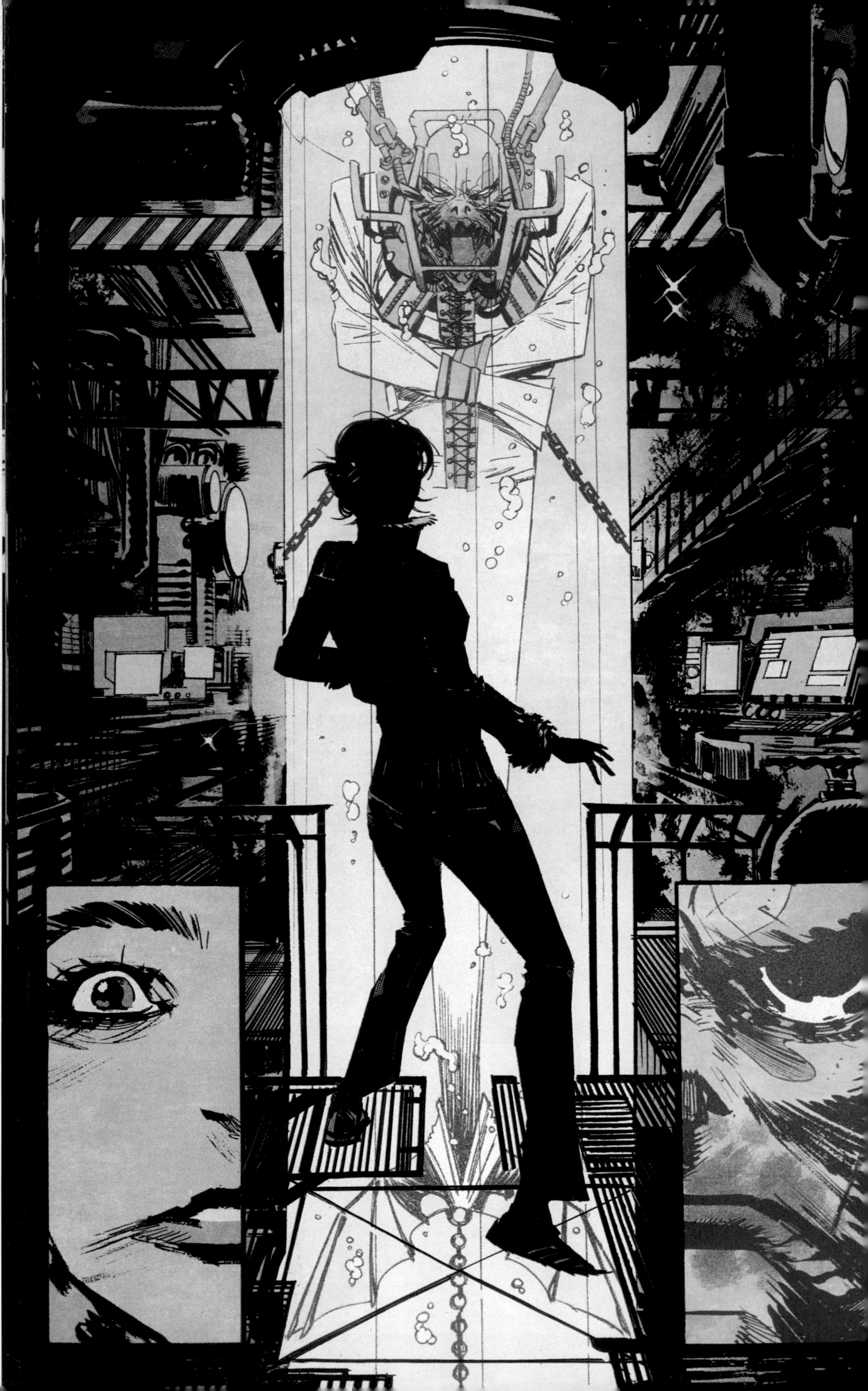

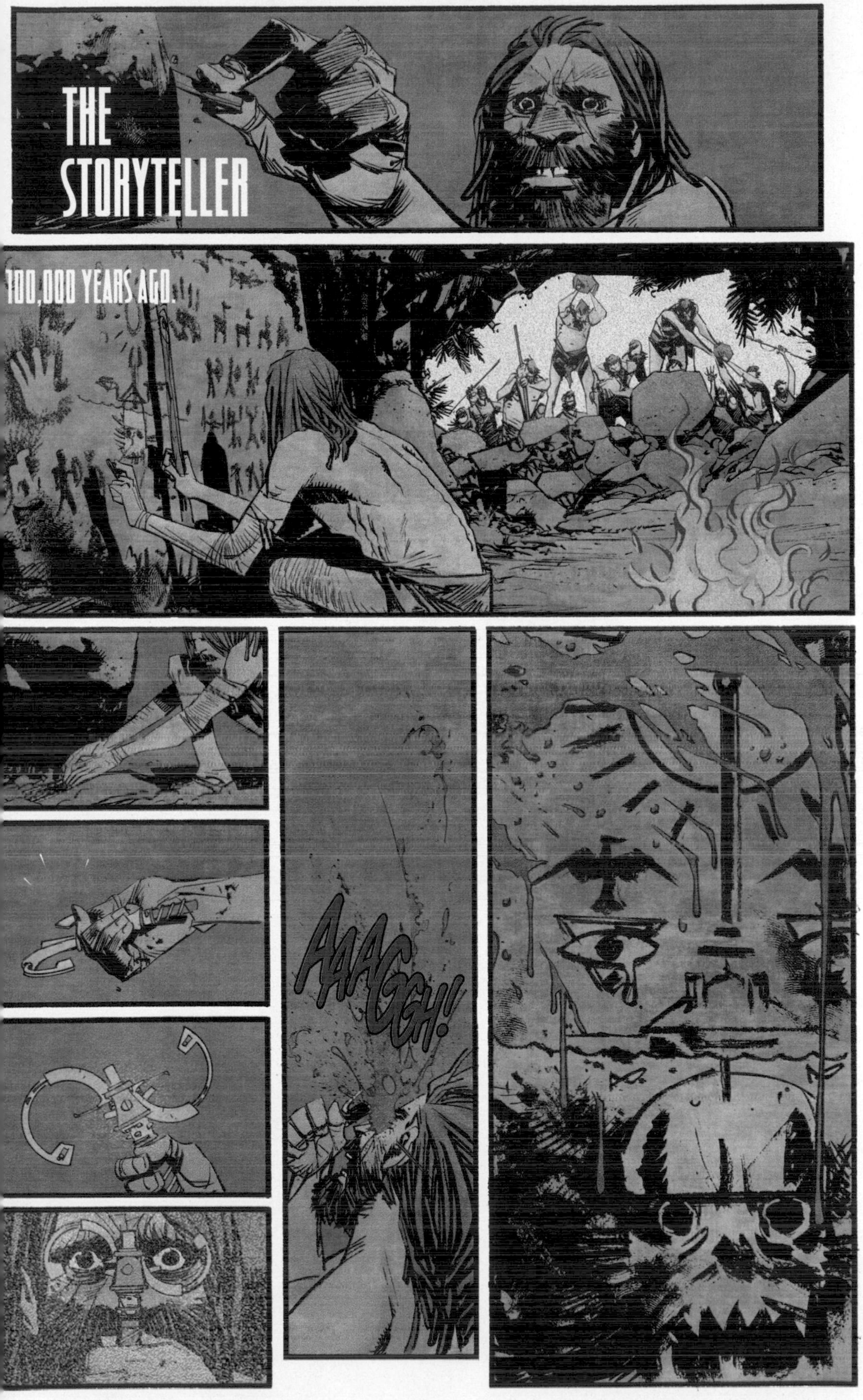
THE STORYTELLER
100,000 YEARS AGO.
AAAGGH!

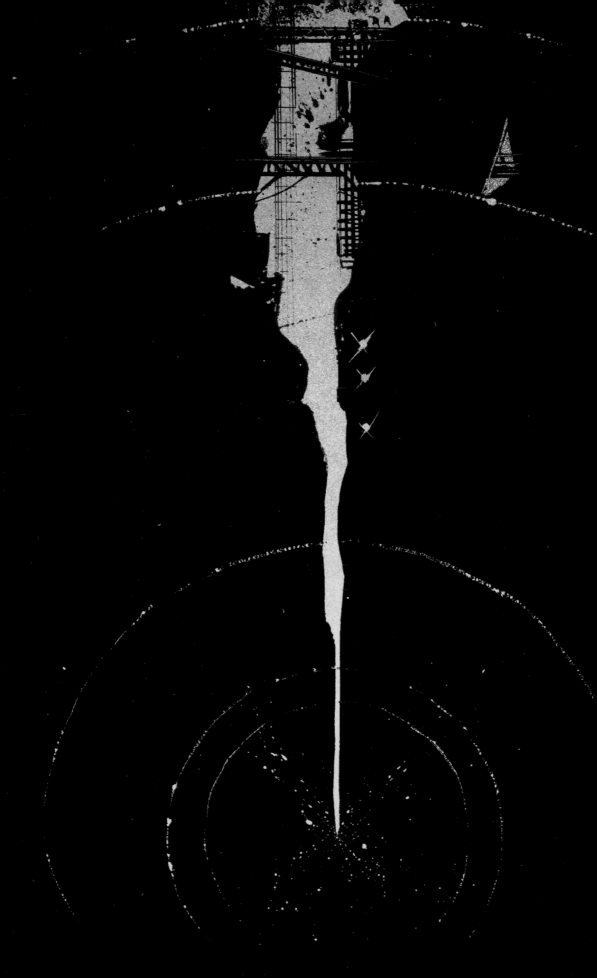

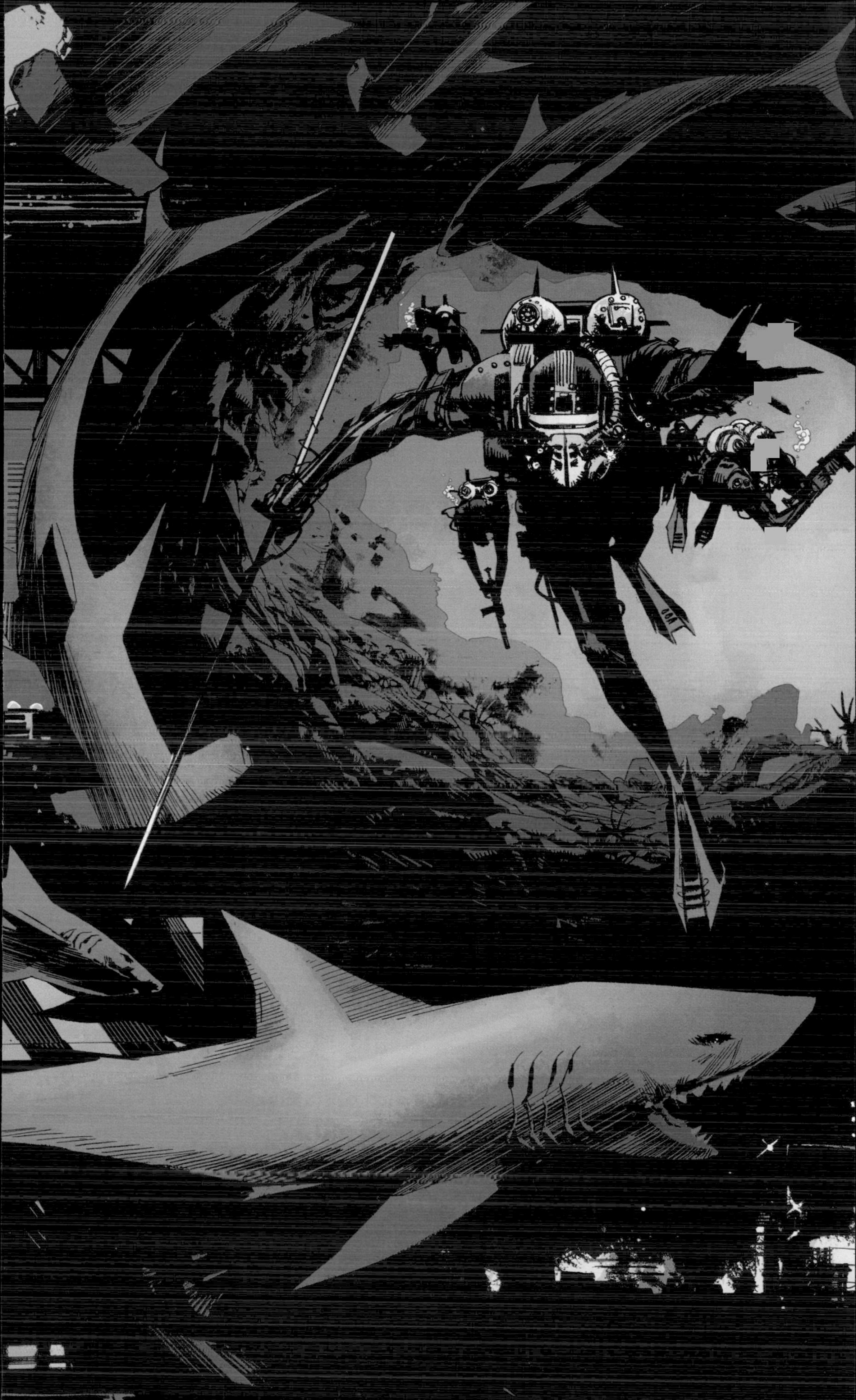

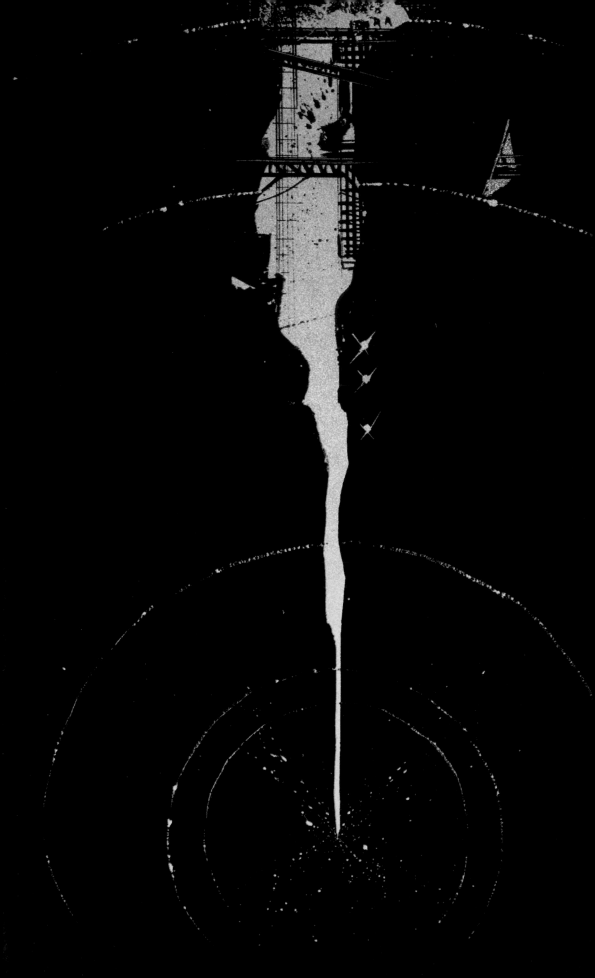

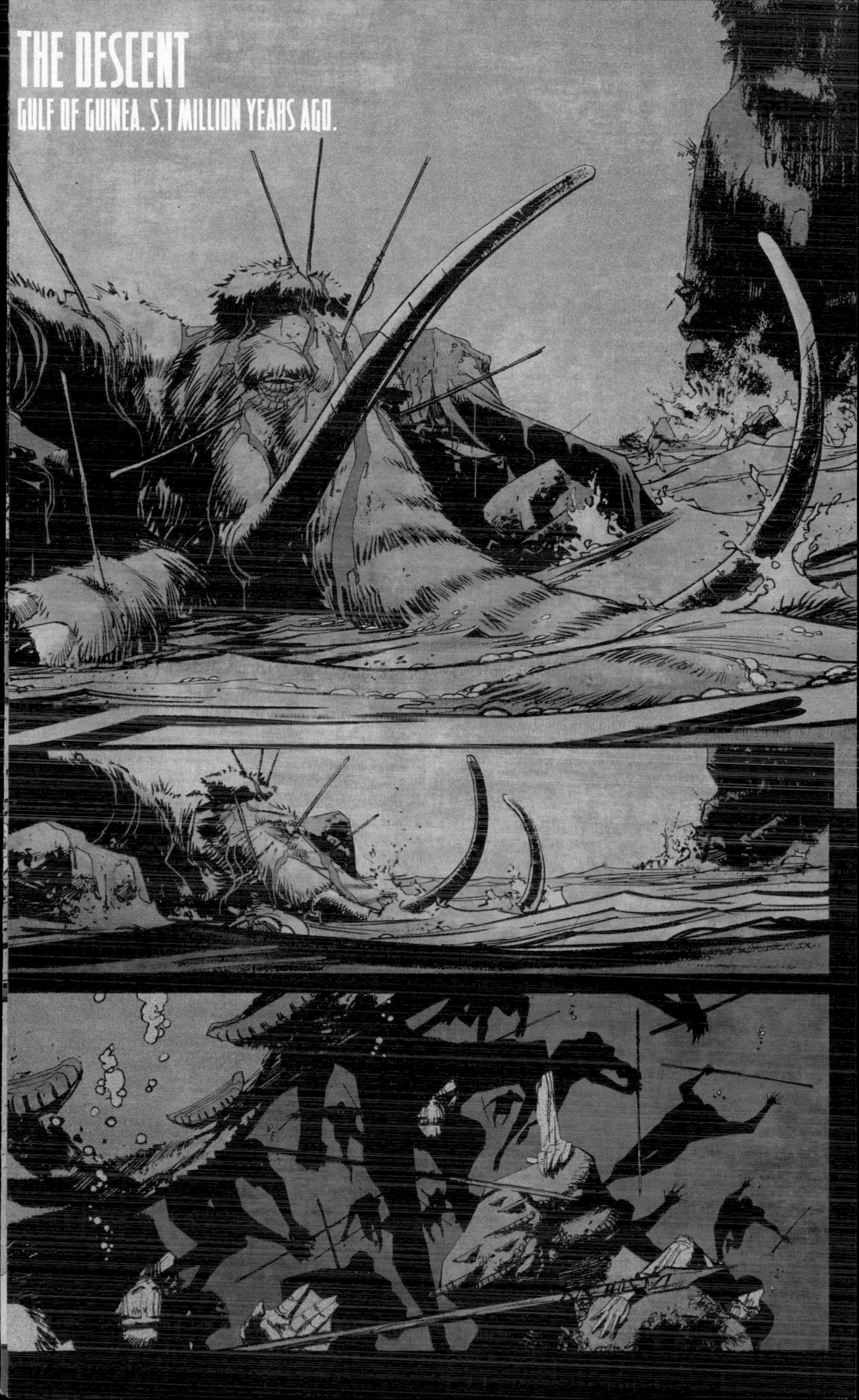
THE DESCENT
GULF OF GUINEA. 5.1 MILLION YEARS AGO.

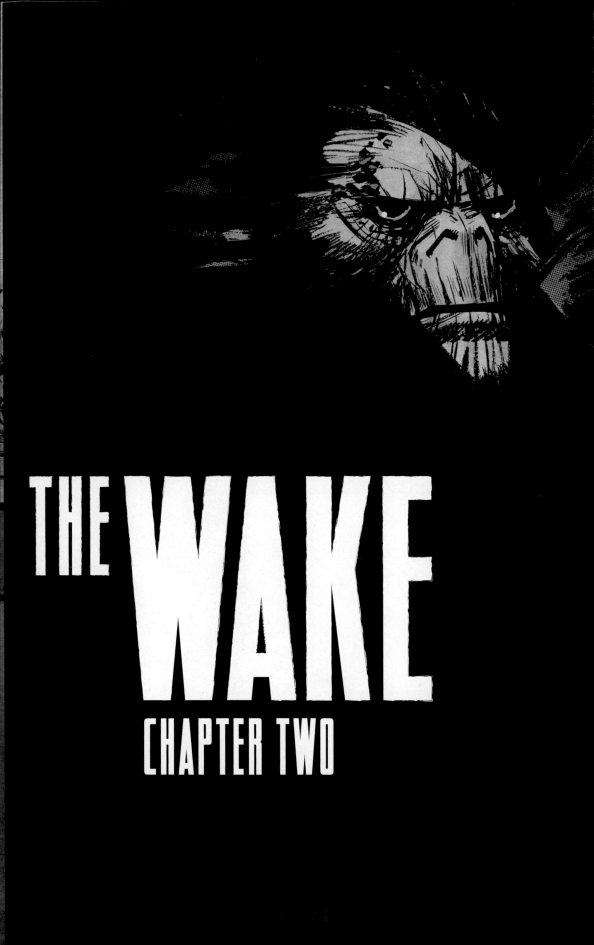

THE WAKE

CHAPTER TWO

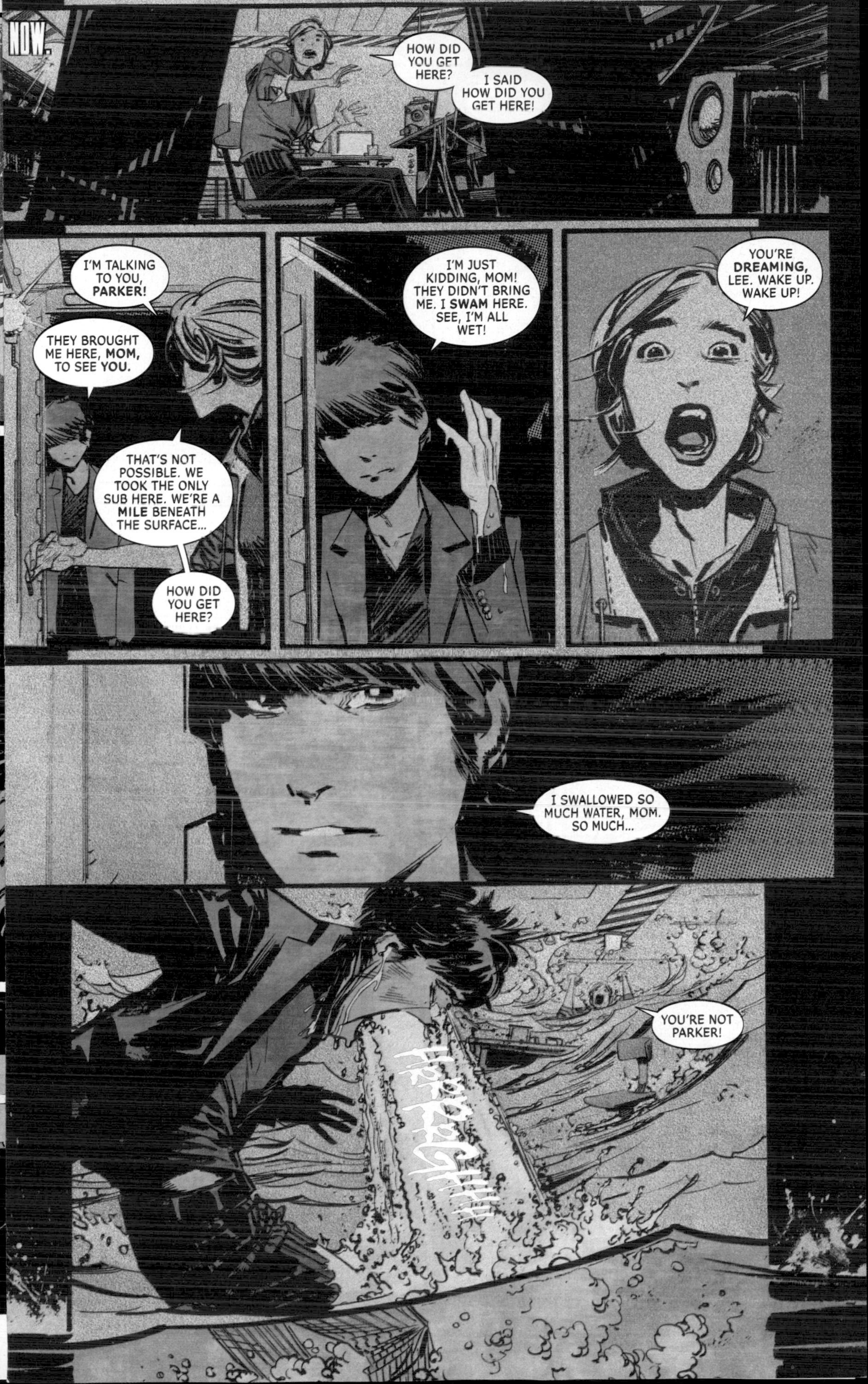
NOW.
HOW DID YOU GET HERE?
I SAID HOW DID YOU GET HERE!
I'M TALKING TO YOU, PARKER!
THEY BROUGHT ME HERE, MOM, TO SEE YOU.
THAT'S NOT POSSIBLE. WE TOOK THE ONLY SUB HERE. WE'RE A MILE BENEATH THE SURFACE...
HOW DID YOU GET HERE?
I'M JUST KIDDING, MOM! THEY DIDN'T BRING ME. I SWAM HERE. SEE, I'M ALL WET!
YOU'RE DREAMING, LEE. WAKE UP. WAKE UP!
I SWALLOWED SO MUCH WATER, MOM. SO MUCH...
YOU'RE NOT PARKER!

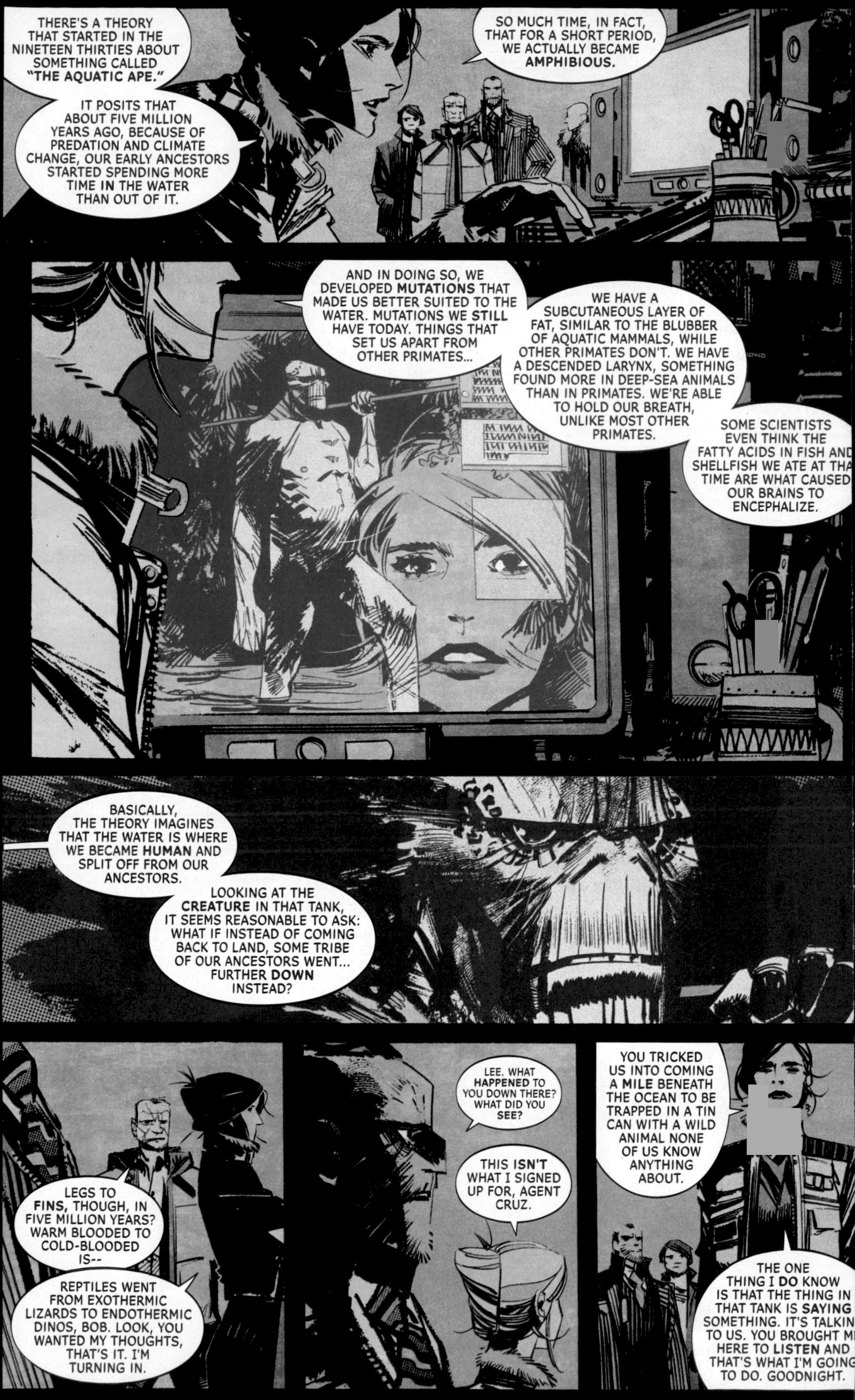
THERE'S A THEORY THAT STARTED IN THE NINETEEN THIRTIES ABOUT SOMETHING CALLED "THE AQUATIC APE."
IT POSITS THAT ABOUT FIVE MILLION YEARS AGO, BECAUSE OF PREDATION AND CLIMATE CHANGE, OUR EARLY ANCESTORS STARTED SPENDING MORE TIME IN THE WATER THAN OUT OF IT.
SO MUCH TIME, IN FACT, THAT FOR A SHORT PERIOD, WE ACTUALLY BECAME AMPHIBIOUS.
AND IN DOING SO, WE DEVELOPED MUTATIONS THAT MADE US BETTER SUITED TO THE WATER. MUTATIONS WE STILL HAVE TODAY. THINGS THAT SET US APART FROM OTHER PRIMATES...
WE HAVE A SUBCUTANEOUS LAYER OF FAT, SIMILAR TO THE BLUBBER OF AQUATIC MAMMALS, WHILE OTHER PRIMATES DON'T. WE HAVE A DESCENDED LARYNX, SOMETHING FOUND MORE IN DEEP-SEA ANIMALS THAN IN PRIMATES. WE'RE ABLE TO HOLD OUR BREATH, UNLIKE MOST OTHER PRIMATES.
SOME SCIENTISTS EVEN THINK THE FATTY ACIDS IN FISH AND SHELLFISH WE ATE AT THA TIME ARE WHAT CAUSED OUR BRAINS TO ENCEPHALIZE.
BASICALLY, THE THEORY IMAGINES THAT THE WATER IS WHERE WE BECAME HUMAN AND SPLIT OFF FROM OUR ANCESTORS.
LOOKING AT THE CREATURE IN THAT TANK, IT SEEMS REASONABLE TO ASK: WHAT IF INSTEAD OF COMING BACK TO LAND, SOME TRIBE OF OUR ANCESTORS WENT... FURTHER DOWN INSTEAD?
LEGS TO FINS, THOUGH, IN FIVE MILLION YEARS? WARM BLOODED TO COLD-BLOODED IS--
REPTILES WENT FROM EXOTHERMIC LIZARDS TO ENDOTHERMIC DINOS, BOB. LOOK, YOU WANTED MY THOUGHTS, THAT'S IT. I'M TURNING IN.
LEE. WHAT HAPPENED TO YOU DOWN THERE? WHAT DID YOU SEE?
THIS ISN'T WHAT I SIGNED UP FOR, AGENT CRUZ.
YOU TRICKED US INTO COMING A MILE BENEATH THE OCEAN TO BE TRAPPED IN A TIN CAN WITH A WILD ANIMAL NONE OF US KNOW ANYTHING ABOUT.
THE ONE THING I DO KNOW IS THAT THE THING IN THAT TANK IS SAYING SOMETHING. IT'S TALKIN TO US. YOU BROUGHT M HERE TO LISTEN AND THAT'S WHAT I'M GOING TO DO. GOODNIGHT.

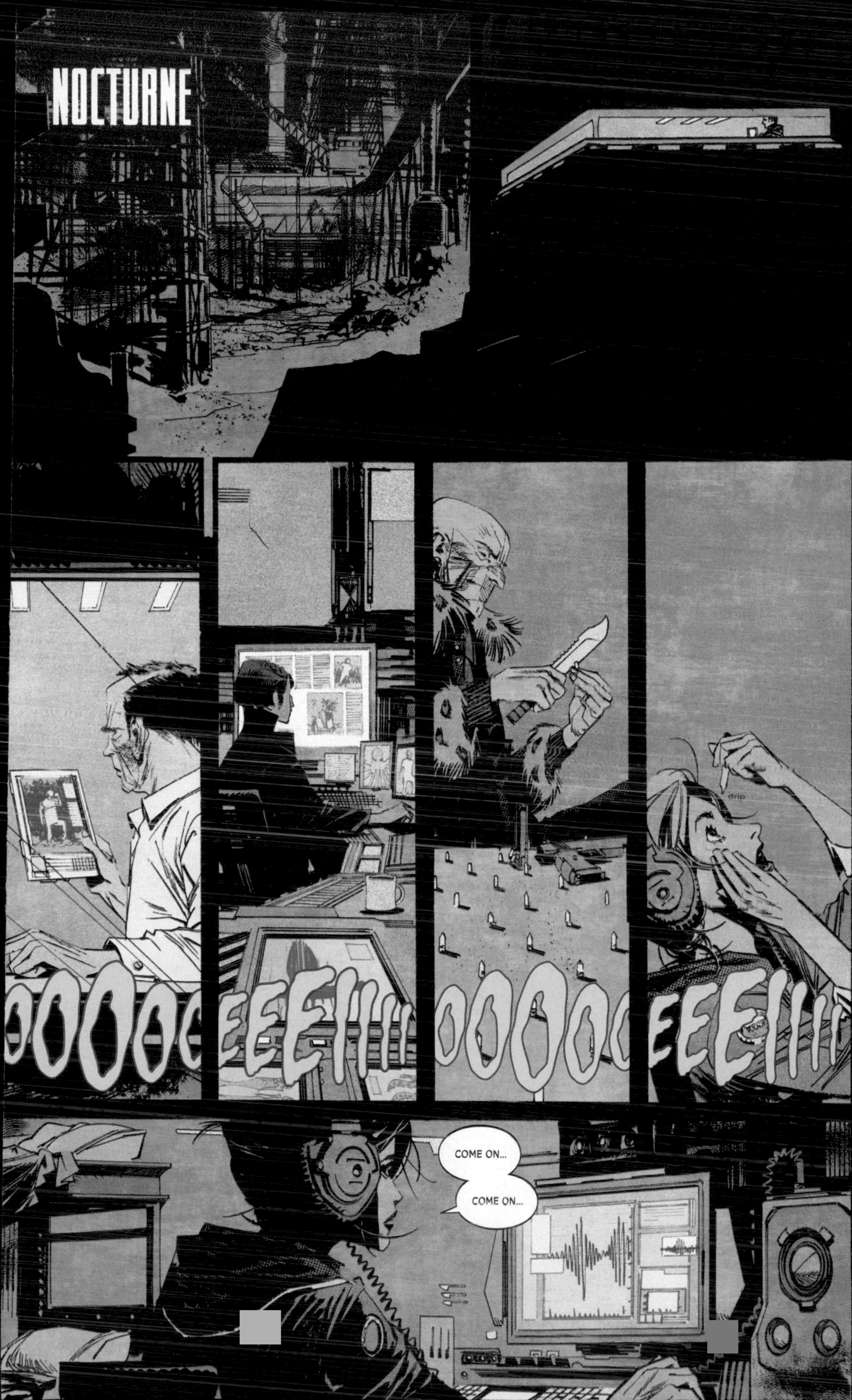
NOCTURNE
drip
OOOOOEEEIIII OOOOOEEEIIII
COME ON...
COME ON...

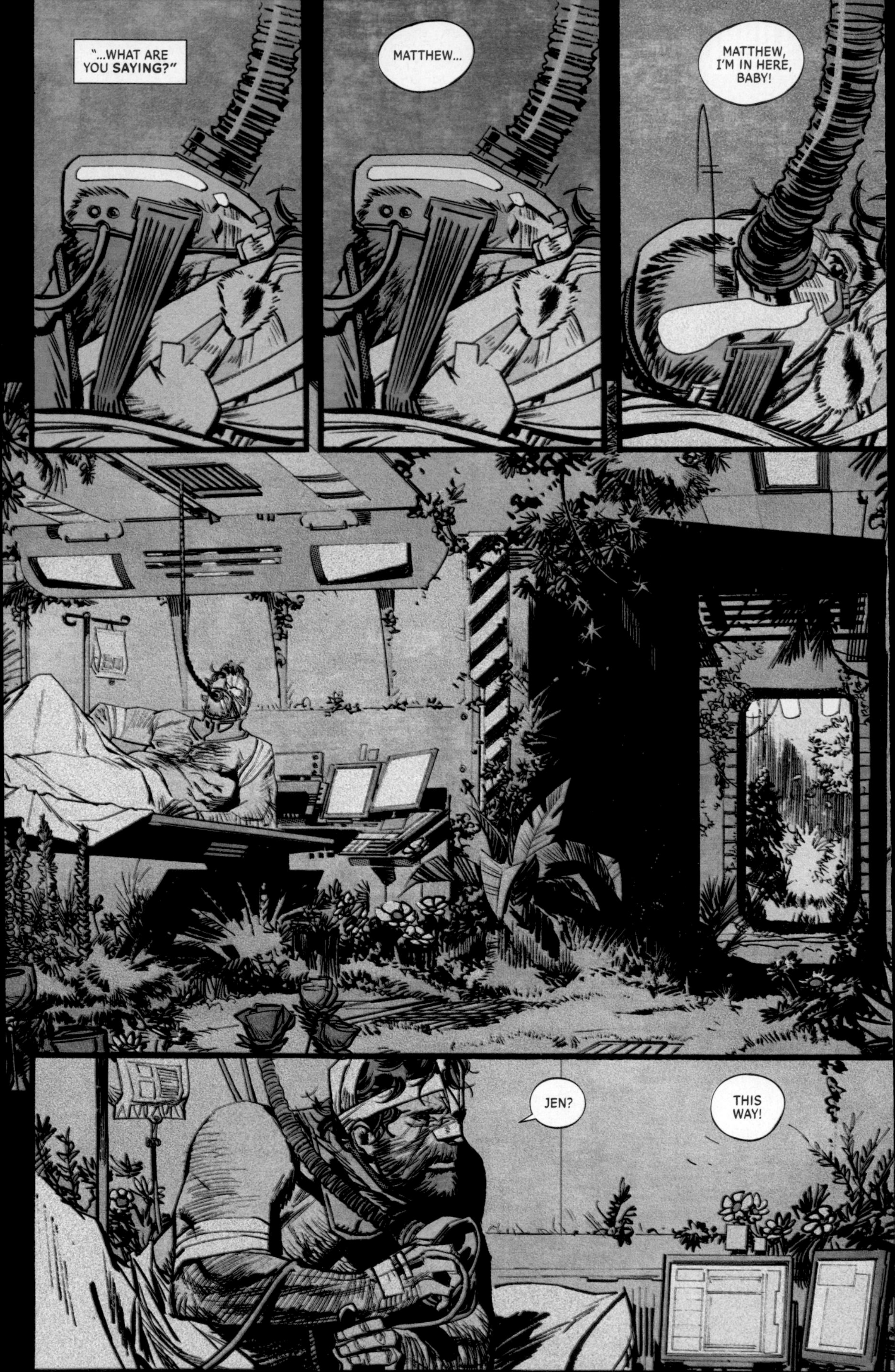
"...WHAT ARE YOU SAYING?"
MATTHEW...
MATTHEW, I'M IN HERE, BABY!
JEN?
THIS WAY!

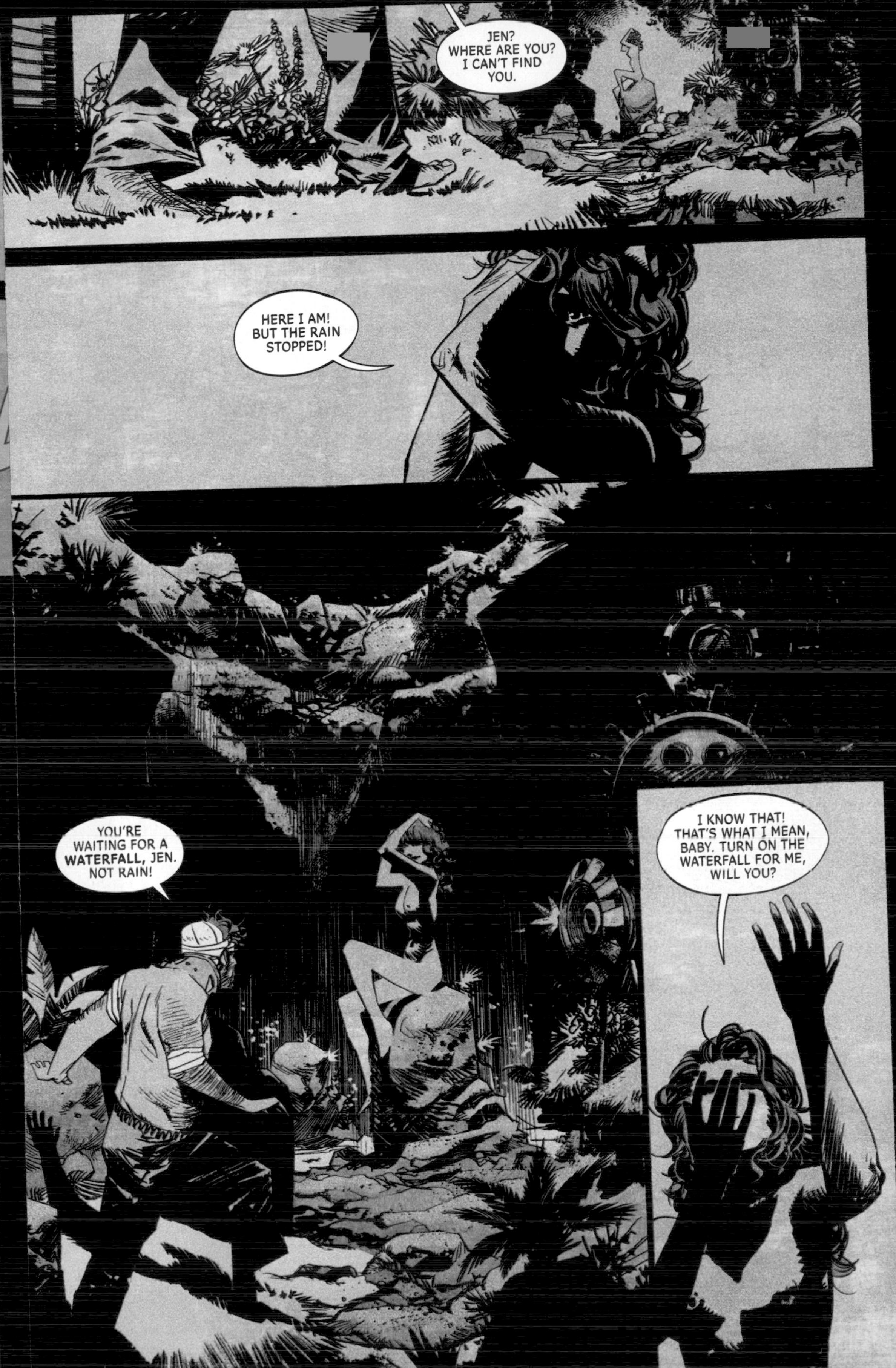
JEN? WHERE ARE YOU? I CAN'T FIND YOU.
HERE I AM! BUT THE RAIN STOPPED!
YOU'RE WAITING FOR A **WATERFALL**, JEN. NOT RAIN!
I KNOW THAT! THAT'S WHAT I MEAN, BABY. TURN ON THE WATERFALL FOR ME, WILL YOU?

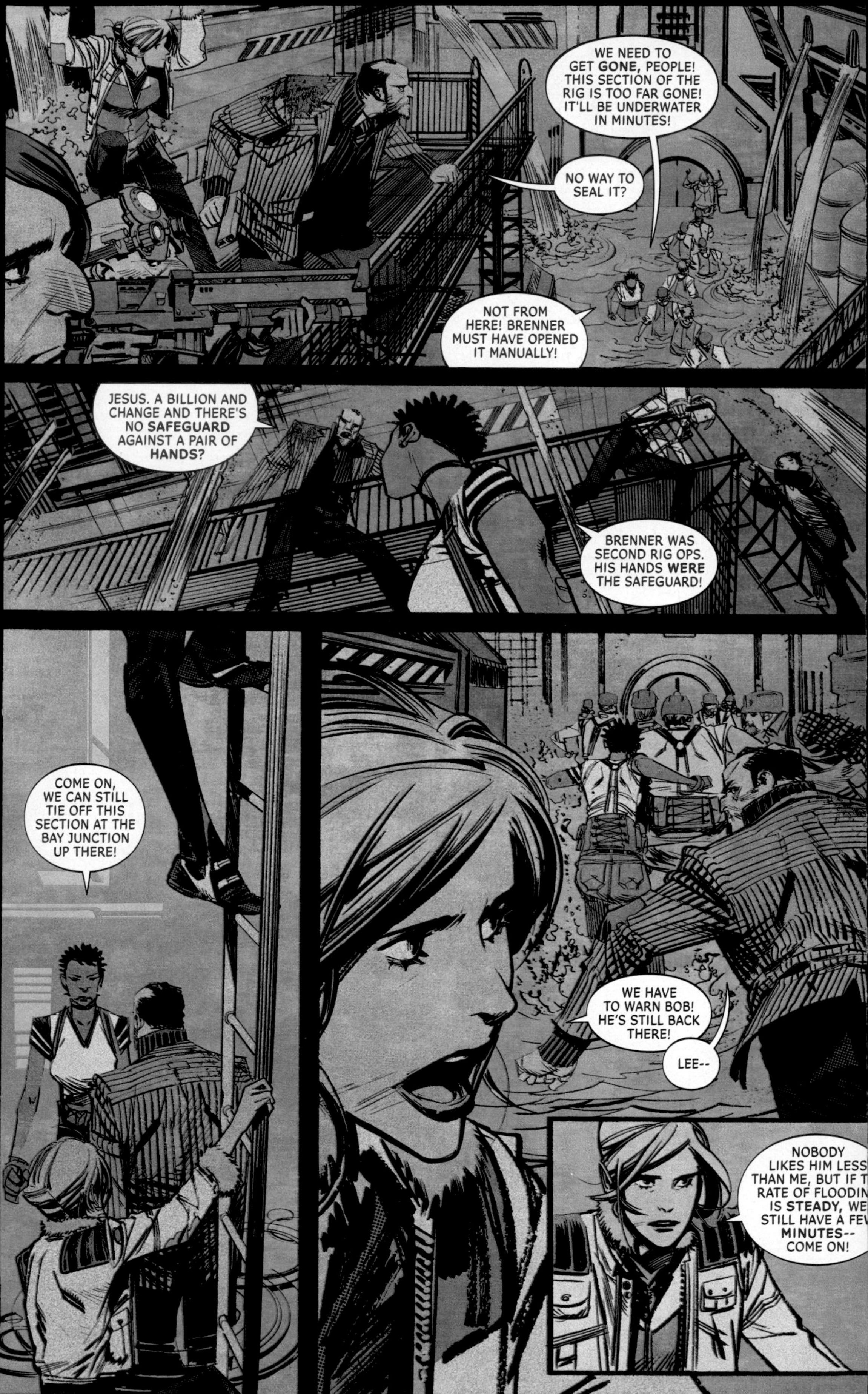
WE NEED TO GET **GONE,** PEOPLE! THIS SECTION OF THE RIG IS TOO FAR GONE! IT'LL BE UNDERWATER IN MINUTES!
NO WAY TO SEAL IT?
NOT FROM HERE! BRENNER MUST HAVE OPENED IT MANUALLY!
JESUS. A BILLION AND CHANGE AND THERE'S NO **SAFEGUARD** AGAINST A PAIR OF **HANDS?**
BRENNER WAS SECOND RIG OPS. HIS HANDS **WERE** THE SAFEGUARD!
COME ON, WE CAN STILL TIE OFF THIS SECTION AT THE BAY JUNCTION UP THERE!
WE HAVE TO WARN BOB! HE'S STILL BACK THERE!
LEE--

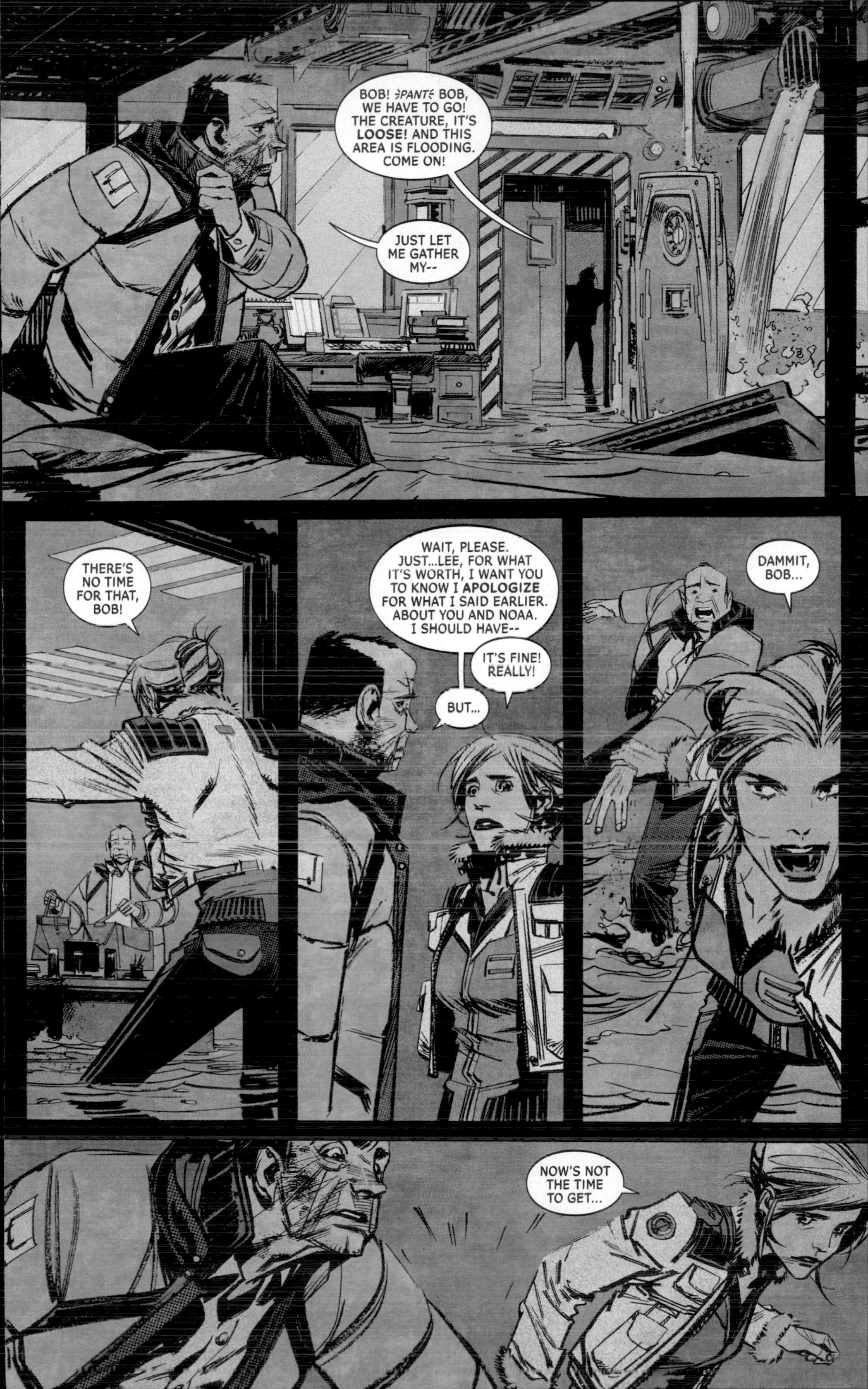
BOB! ⋟PANT⋞ BOB, WE HAVE TO GO! THE CREATURE, IT'S **LOOSE!** AND THIS AREA IS FLOODING. COME ON!
JUST LET ME GATHER MY--
THERE'S NO TIME FOR THAT, BOB!
WAIT, PLEASE. JUST...LEE, FOR WHAT IT'S WORTH, I WANT YOU TO KNOW I **APOLOGIZE** FOR WHAT I SAID EARLIER. ABOUT YOU AND NOAA. I SHOULD HAVE--
IT'S FINE! REALLY!
BUT...
DAMMIT, BOB...
NOW'S NOT THE TIME TO GET...

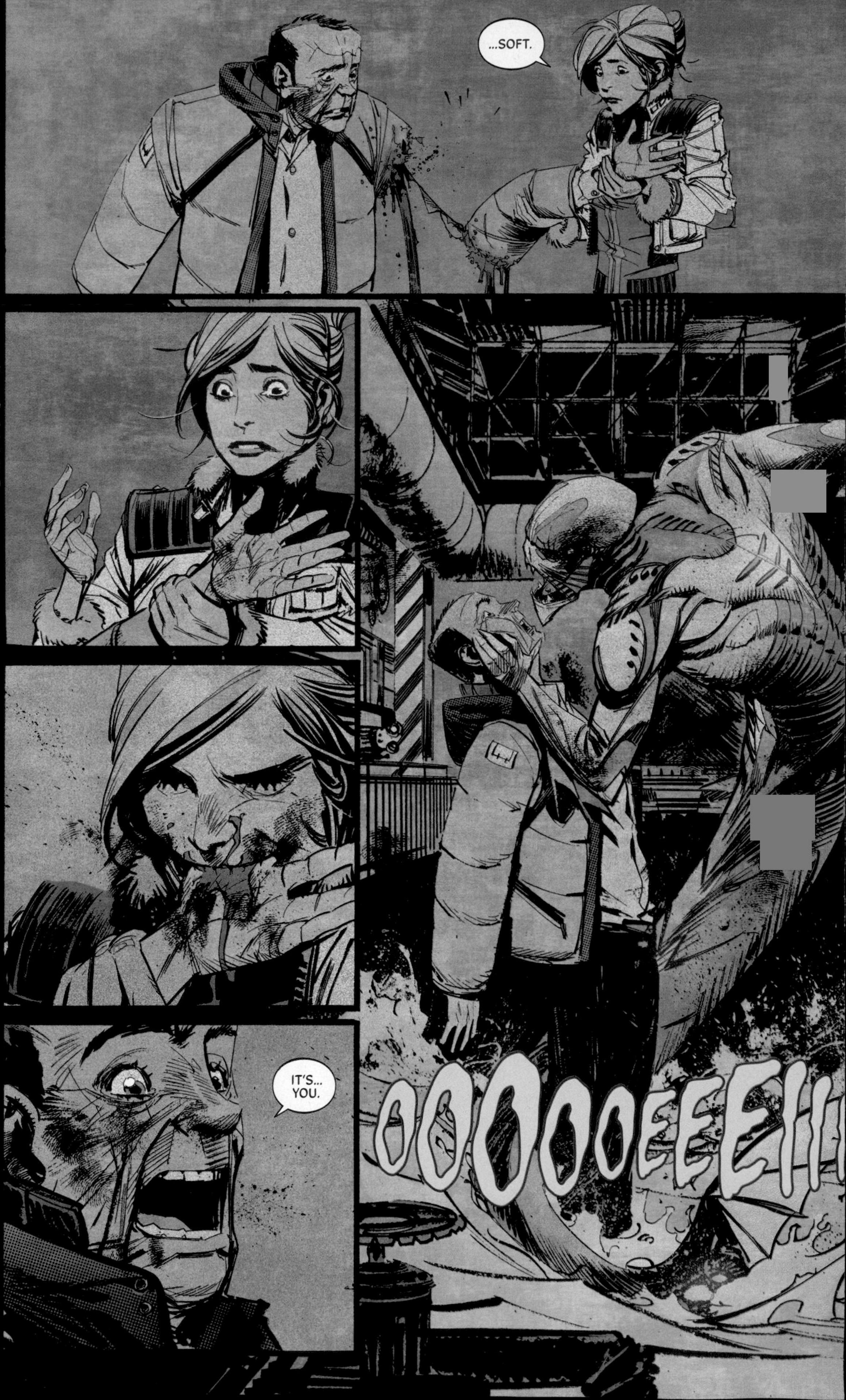
...SOFT.
IT'S... YOU.
OOOOOEEEIII

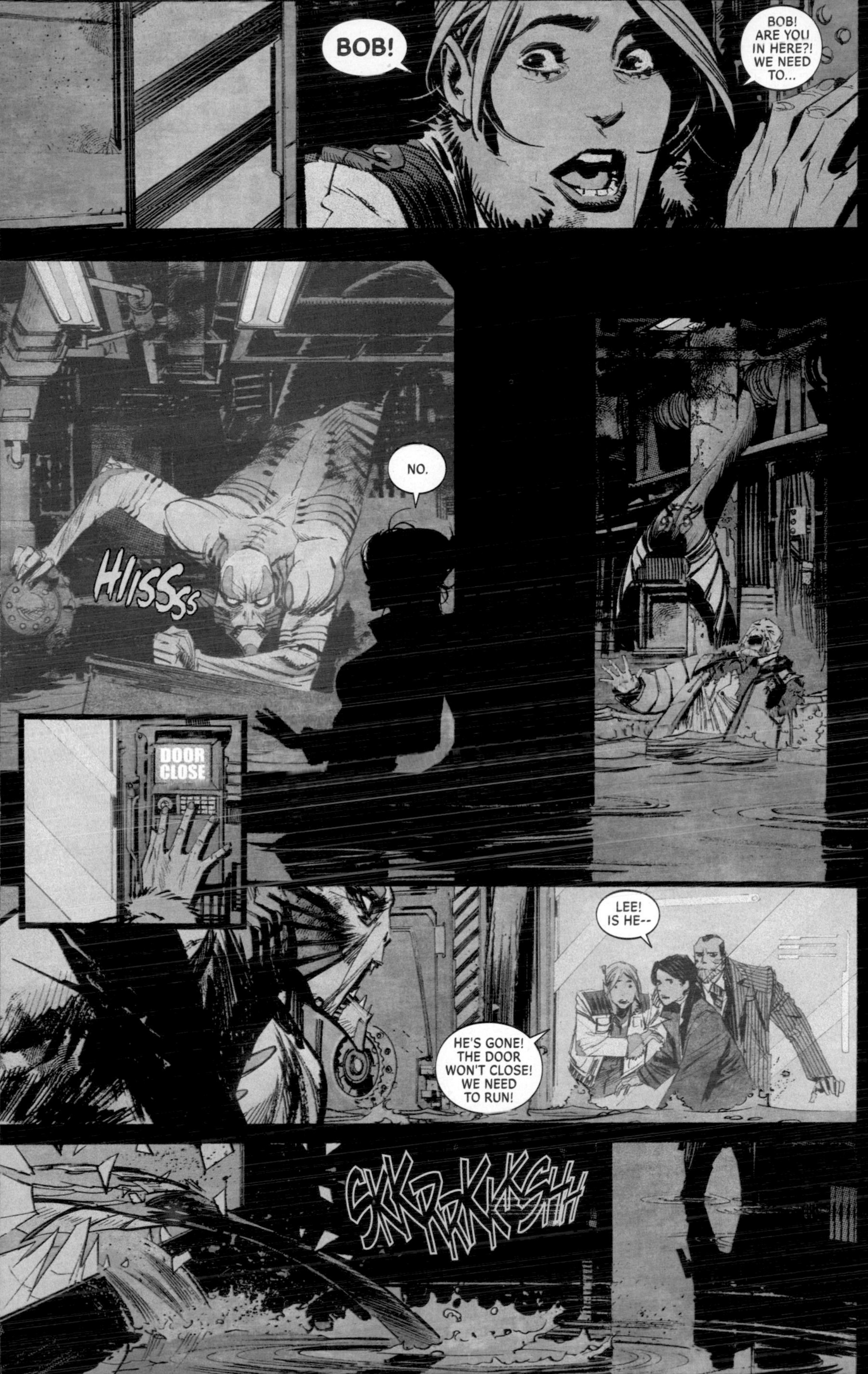
BOB!
BOB! ARE YOU IN HERE?! WE NEED TO...
NO.
HIISSss
DOOR CLOSE
LEE! IS HE--
HE'S GONE! THE DOOR WON'T CLOSE! WE NEED TO RUN!
SKKRKKKSHH

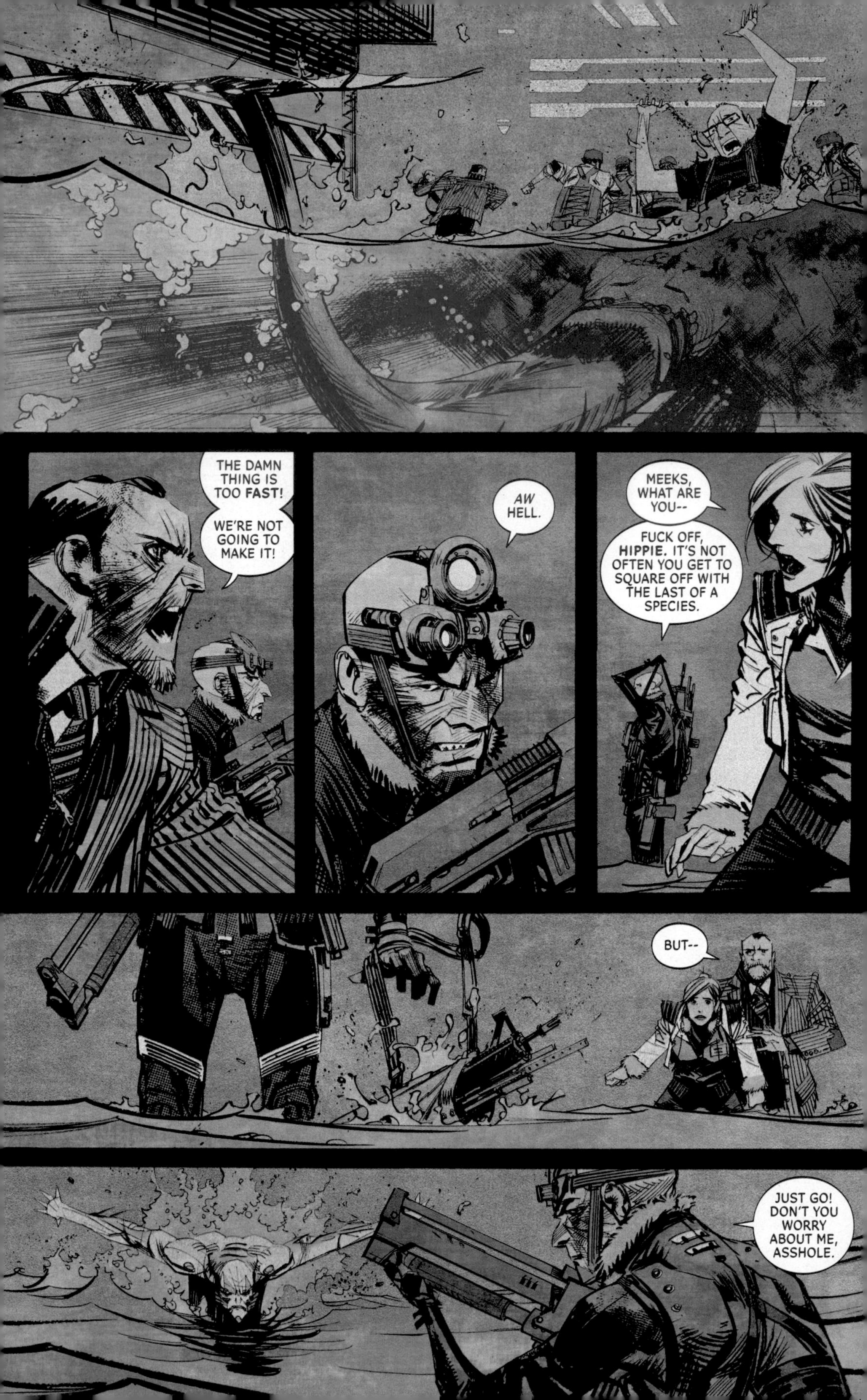
THE DAMN THING IS TOO **FAST**!
WE'RE NOT GOING TO MAKE IT!
AW HELL.
MEEKS, WHAT ARE YOU--
FUCK OFF, **HIPPIE.** IT'S NOT OFTEN YOU GET TO SQUARE OFF WITH THE LAST OF A SPECIES.
BUT--
JUST GO! DON'T YOU WORRY ABOUT ME, ASSHOLE.

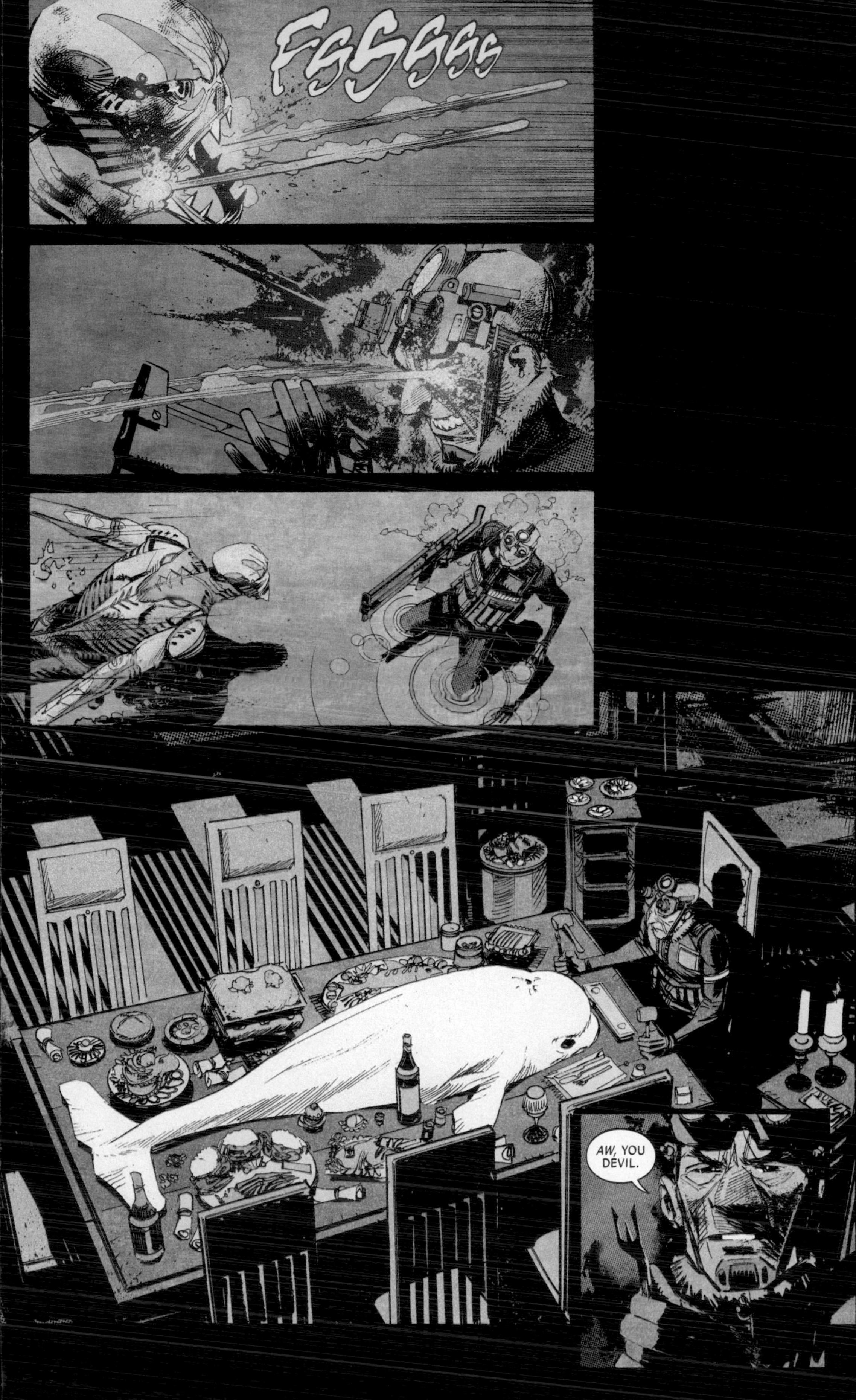
FSSsss
AW, YOU DEVIL.

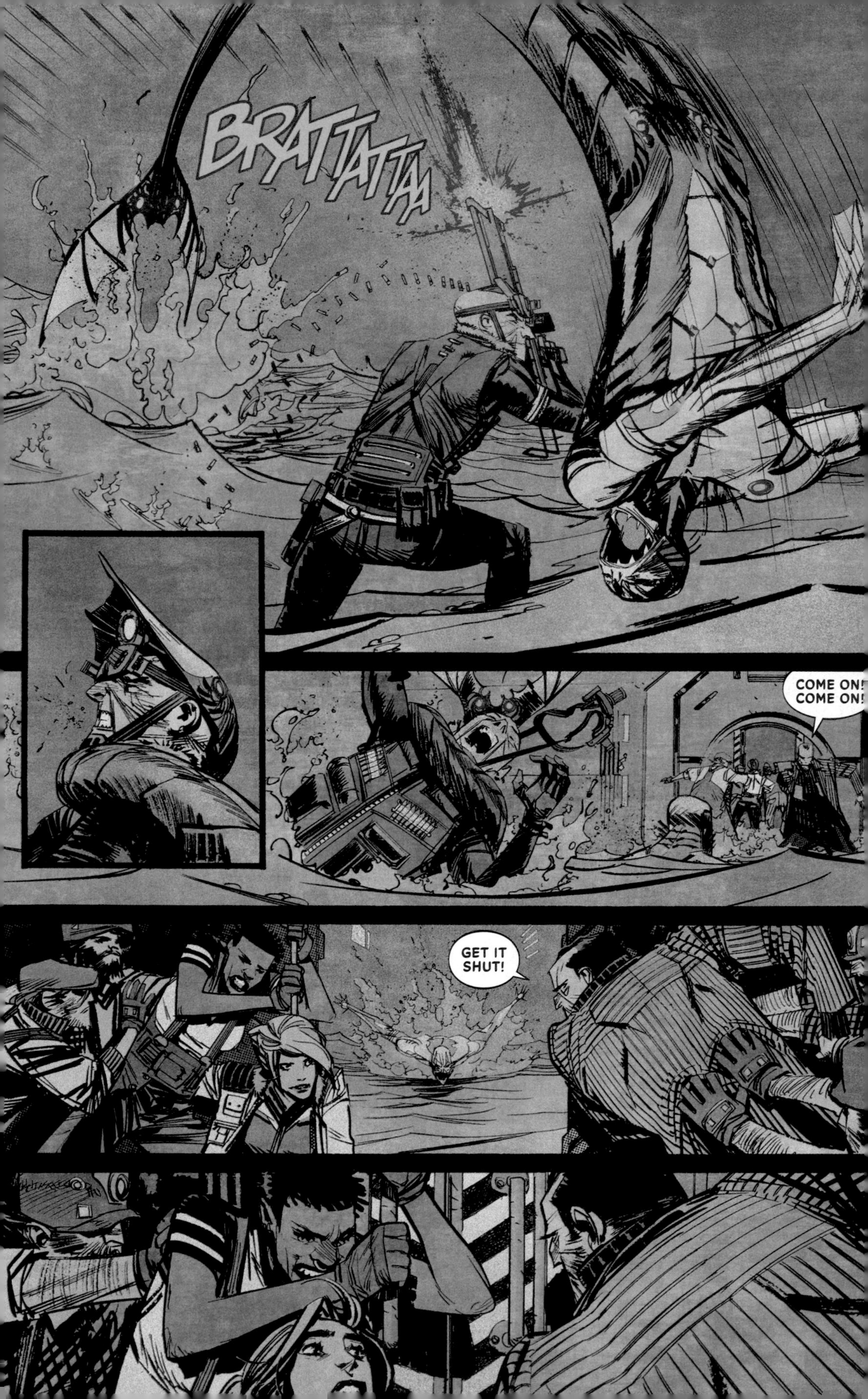
BRATTATTAA
COME ON! COME ON!
GET IT SHUT!

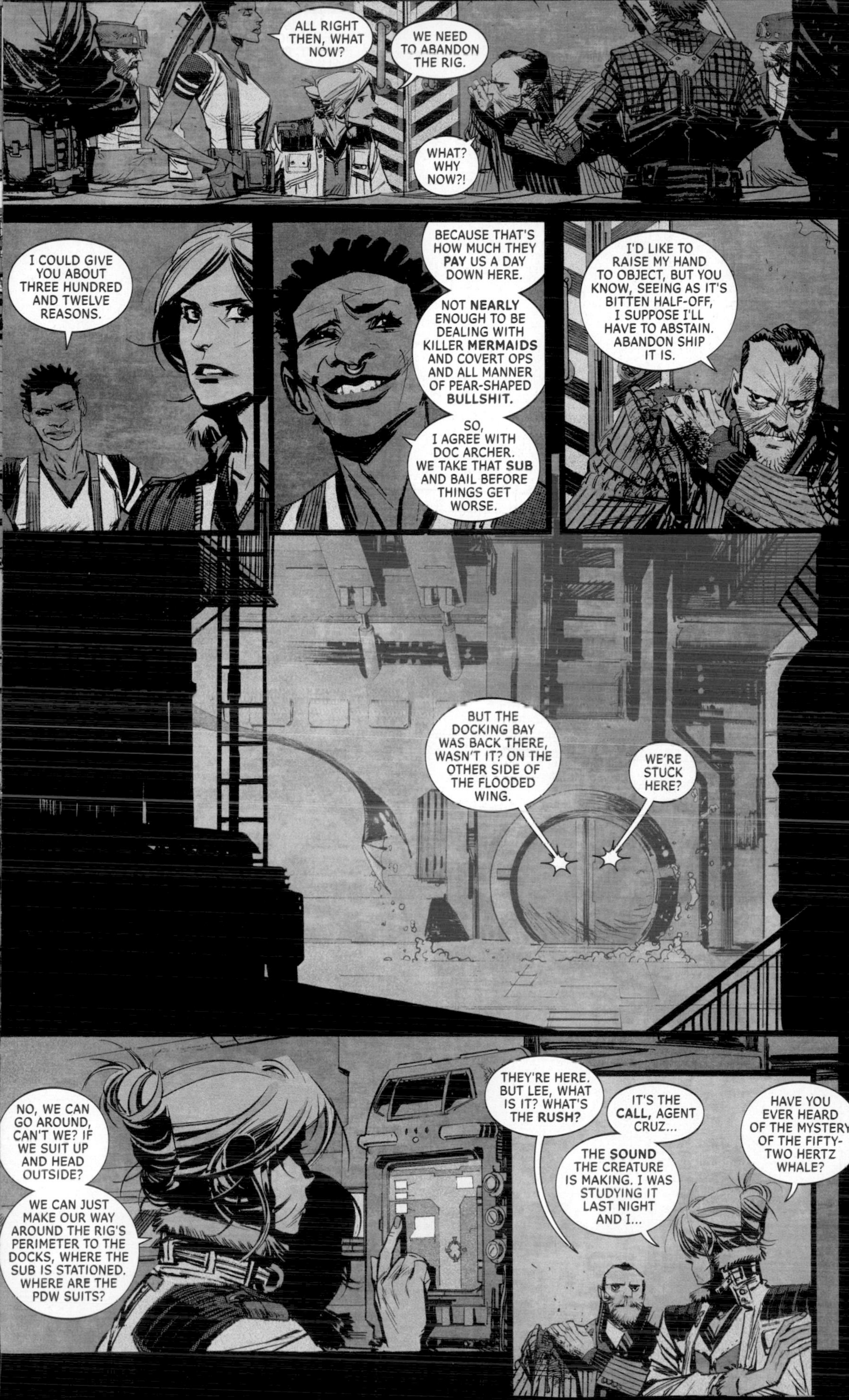
ALL RIGHT THEN, WHAT NOW?
WE NEED TO ABANDON THE RIG.
WHAT? WHY NOW?!
I COULD GIVE YOU ABOUT THREE HUNDRED AND TWELVE REASONS.
BECAUSE THAT'S HOW MUCH THEY PAY US A DAY DOWN HERE.
NOT NEARLY ENOUGH TO BE DEALING WITH KILLER MERMAIDS AND COVERT OPS AND ALL MANNER OF PEAR-SHAPED BULLSHIT.
SO, I AGREE WITH DOC ARCHER. WE TAKE THAT SUB AND BAIL BEFORE THINGS GET WORSE.
I'D LIKE TO RAISE MY HAND TO OBJECT, BUT YOU KNOW, SEEING AS IT'S BITTEN HALF-OFF, I SUPPOSE I'LL HAVE TO ABSTAIN. ABANDON SHIP IT IS.
BUT THE DOCKING BAY WAS BACK THERE, WASN'T IT? ON THE OTHER SIDE OF THE FLOODED WING.
WE'RE STUCK HERE?
NO, WE CAN GO AROUND, CAN'T WE? IF WE SUIT UP AND HEAD OUTSIDE?
WE CAN JUST MAKE OUR WAY AROUND THE RIG'S PERIMETER TO THE DOCKS, WHERE THE SUB IS STATIONED. WHERE ARE THE PDW SUITS?
THEY'RE HERE. BUT LEE, WHAT IS IT? WHAT'S THE RUSH?
IT'S THE CALL, AGENT CRUZ...
THE SOUND THE CREATURE IS MAKING. I WAS STUDYING IT LAST NIGHT AND I...
HAVE YOU EVER HEARD OF THE MYSTERY OF THE FIFTY-TWO HERTZ WHALE?

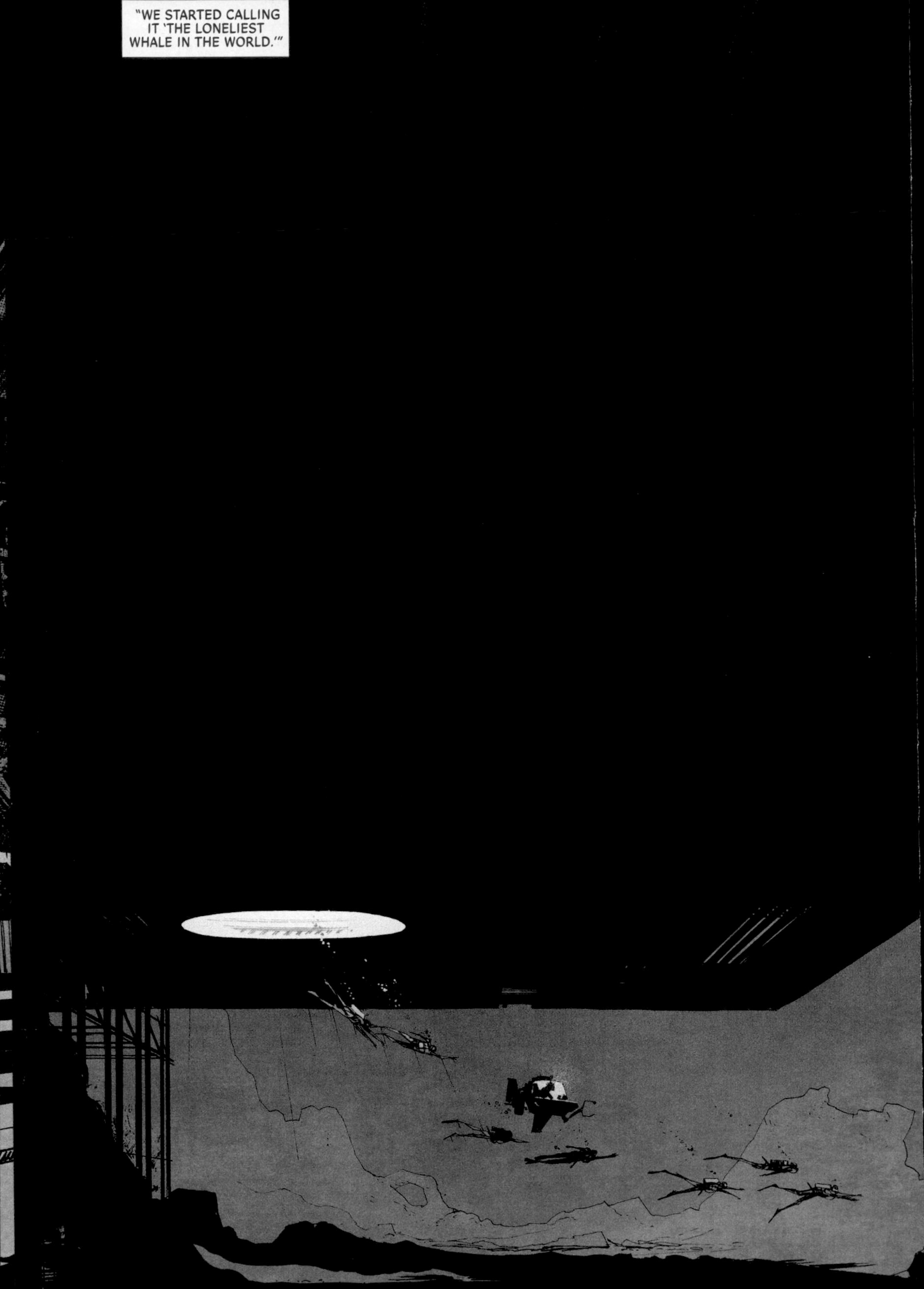
"WE STARTED CALLING IT 'THE LONELIEST WHALE IN THE WORLD.'"

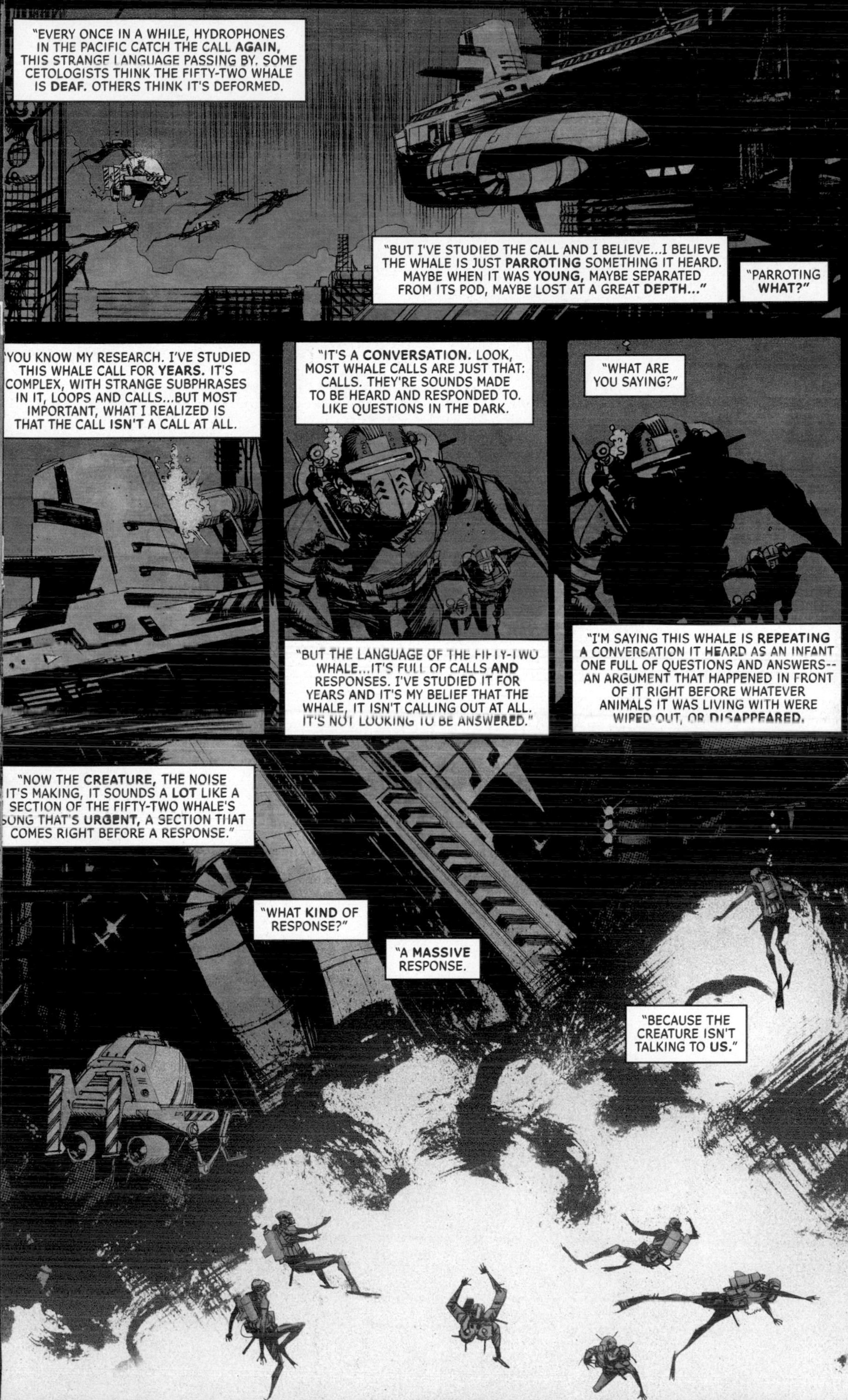
"EVERY ONCE IN A WHILE, HYDROPHONES IN THE PACIFIC CATCH THE CALL AGAIN, THIS STRANGE LANGUAGE PASSING BY. SOME CETOLOGISTS THINK THE FIFTY-TWO WHALE IS DEAF. OTHERS THINK IT'S DEFORMED.
"BUT I'VE STUDIED THE CALL AND I BELIEVE...I BELIEVE THE WHALE IS JUST PARROTING SOMETHING IT HEARD. MAYBE WHEN IT WAS YOUNG, MAYBE SEPARATED FROM ITS POD, MAYBE LOST AT A GREAT DEPTH..."
"PARROTING WHAT?"
"YOU KNOW MY RESEARCH. I'VE STUDIED THIS WHALE CALL FOR YEARS. IT'S COMPLEX, WITH STRANGE SUBPHRASES IN IT, LOOPS AND CALLS...BUT MOST IMPORTANT, WHAT I REALIZED IS THAT THE CALL ISN'T A CALL AT ALL.
"IT'S A CONVERSATION. LOOK, MOST WHALE CALLS ARE JUST THAT: CALLS. THEY'RE SOUNDS MADE TO BE HEARD AND RESPONDED TO. LIKE QUESTIONS IN THE DARK.
"BUT THE LANGUAGE OF THE FIFTY-TWO WHALE...IT'S FULL OF CALLS AND RESPONSES. I'VE STUDIED IT FOR YEARS AND IT'S MY BELIEF THAT THE WHALE, IT ISN'T CALLING OUT AT ALL. IT'S NOT LOOKING TO BE ANSWERED."
"WHAT ARE YOU SAYING?"
"I'M SAYING THIS WHALE IS REPEATING A CONVERSATION IT HEARD AS AN INFANT ONE FULL OF QUESTIONS AND ANSWERS-- AN ARGUMENT THAT HAPPENED IN FRONT OF IT RIGHT BEFORE WHATEVER ANIMALS IT WAS LIVING WITH WERE WIPED OUT, OR DISAPPEARED.
"NOW THE CREATURE, THE NOISE IT'S MAKING, IT SOUNDS A LOT LIKE A SECTION OF THE FIFTY-TWO WHALE'S SONG THAT'S URGENT, A SECTION THAT COMES RIGHT BEFORE A RESPONSE."
"WHAT KIND OF RESPONSE?"
"A MASSIVE RESPONSE.
"BECAUSE THE CREATURE ISN'T TALKING TO US."

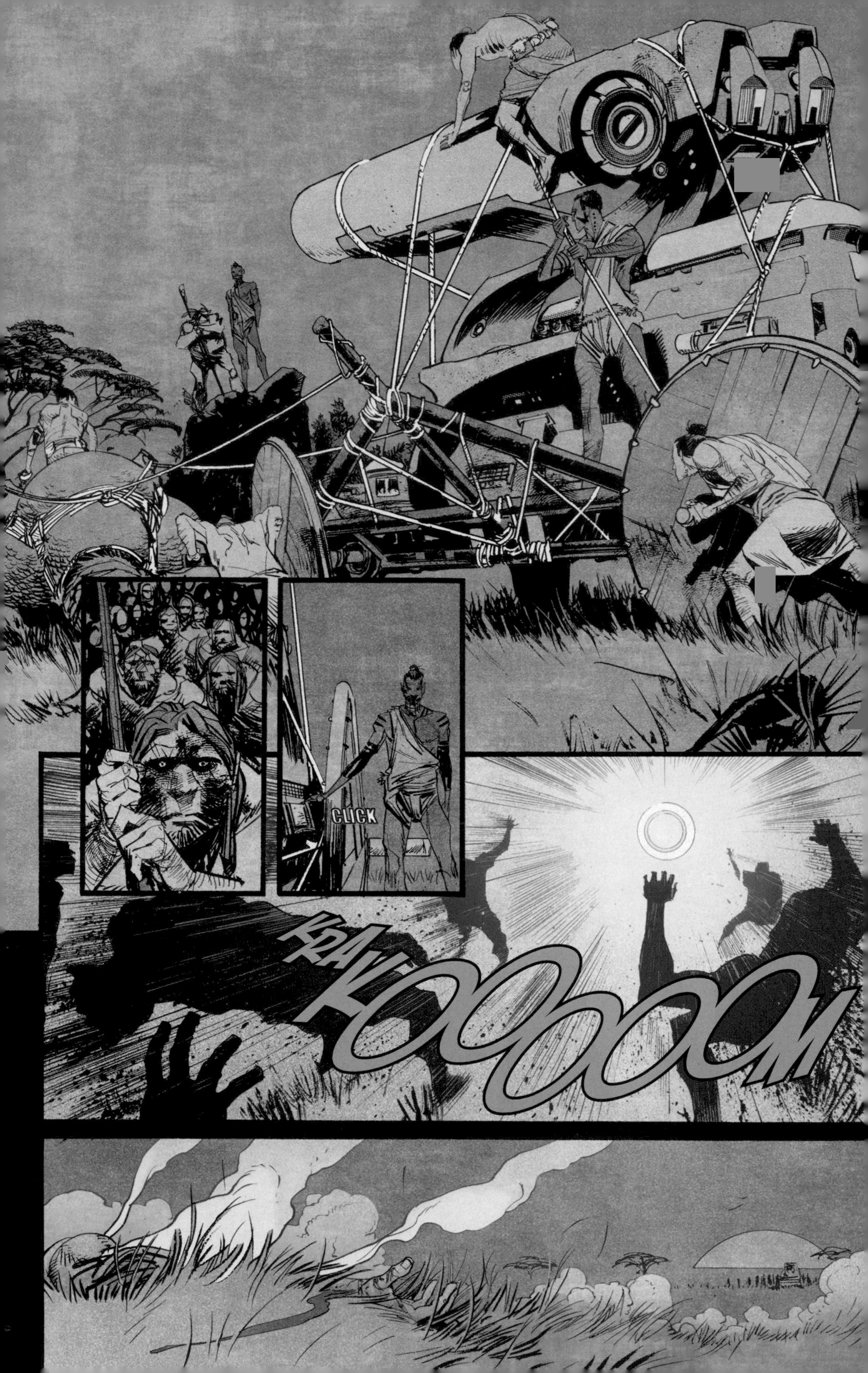
CLICK
KRAKOOOOM

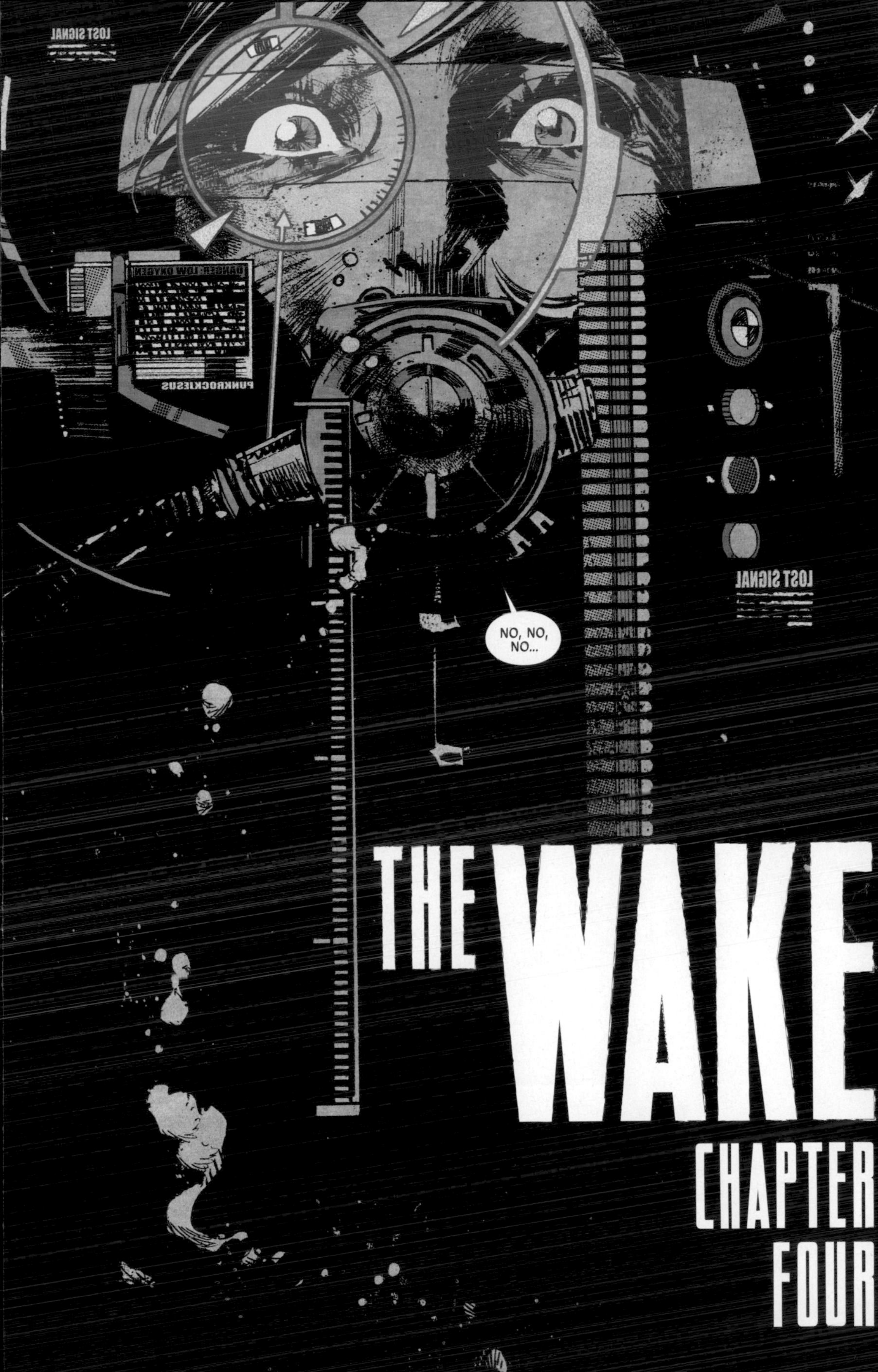
NO, NO, NO...
THE WAKE
CHAPTER FOUR

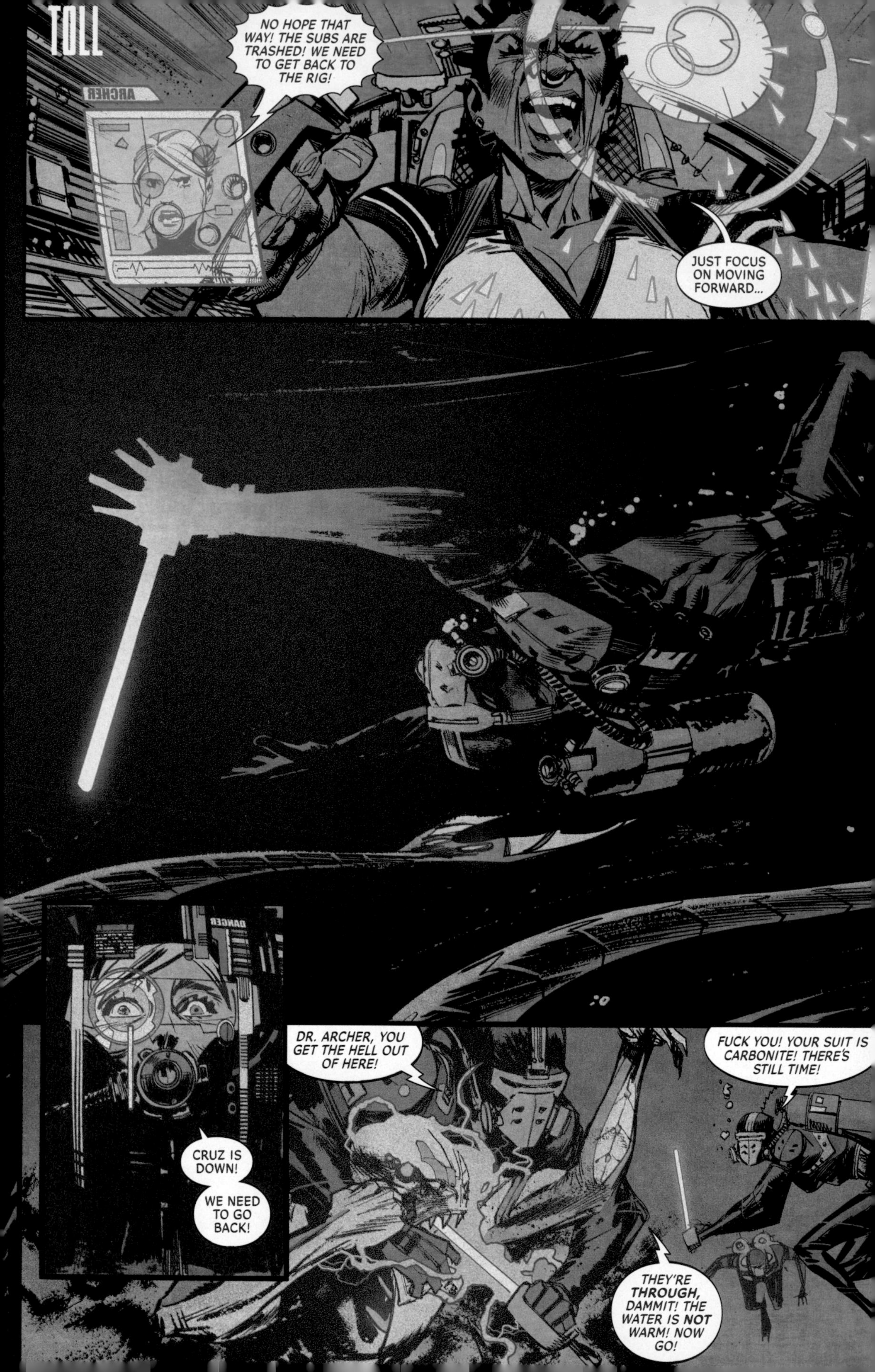
TOLL
NO HOPE THAT WAY! THE SUBS ARE TRASHED! WE NEED TO GET BACK TO THE RIG!
ARCHER
JUST FOCUS ON MOVING FORWARD...
DANGER
CRUZ IS DOWN!
WE NEED TO GO BACK!
DR. ARCHER, YOU GET THE HELL OUT OF HERE!
FUCK YOU! YOUR SUIT IS CARBONITE! THERE'S STILL TIME!
THEY'RE THROUGH, DAMMIT! THE WATER IS NOT WARM! NOW GO!

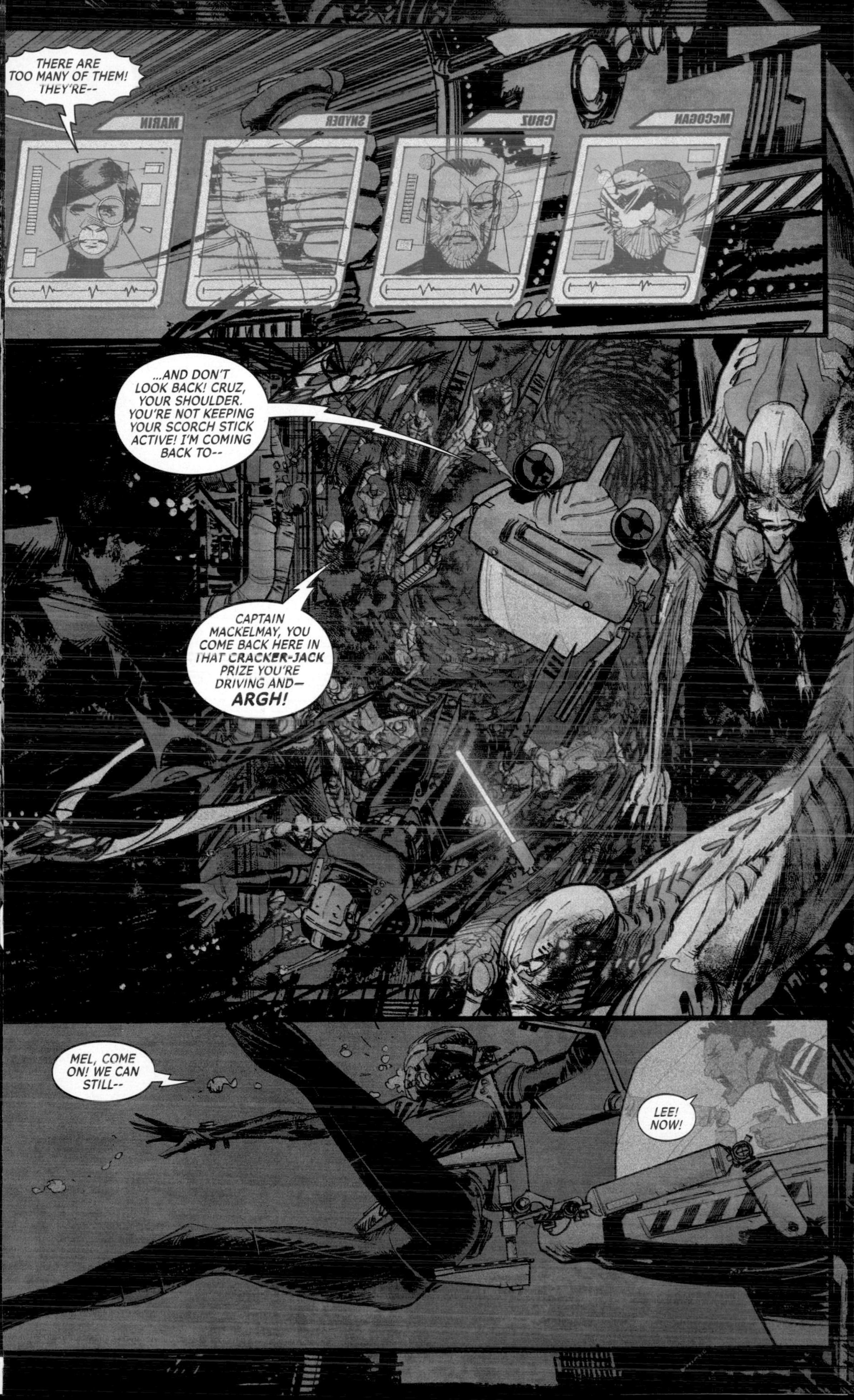
THERE ARE TOO MANY OF THEM! THEY'RE--
MARIN
SNYDER
CRUZ
McCOGAN
...AND DON'T LOOK BACK! CRUZ, YOUR SHOULDER. YOU'RE NOT KEEPING YOUR SCORCH STICK ACTIVE! I'M COMING BACK TO--
CAPTAIN MACKELMAY, YOU COME BACK HERE IN THAT CRACKER-JACK PRIZE YOU'RE DRIVING AND— ARGH!
MEL, COME ON! WE CAN STILL--
LEE! NOW!

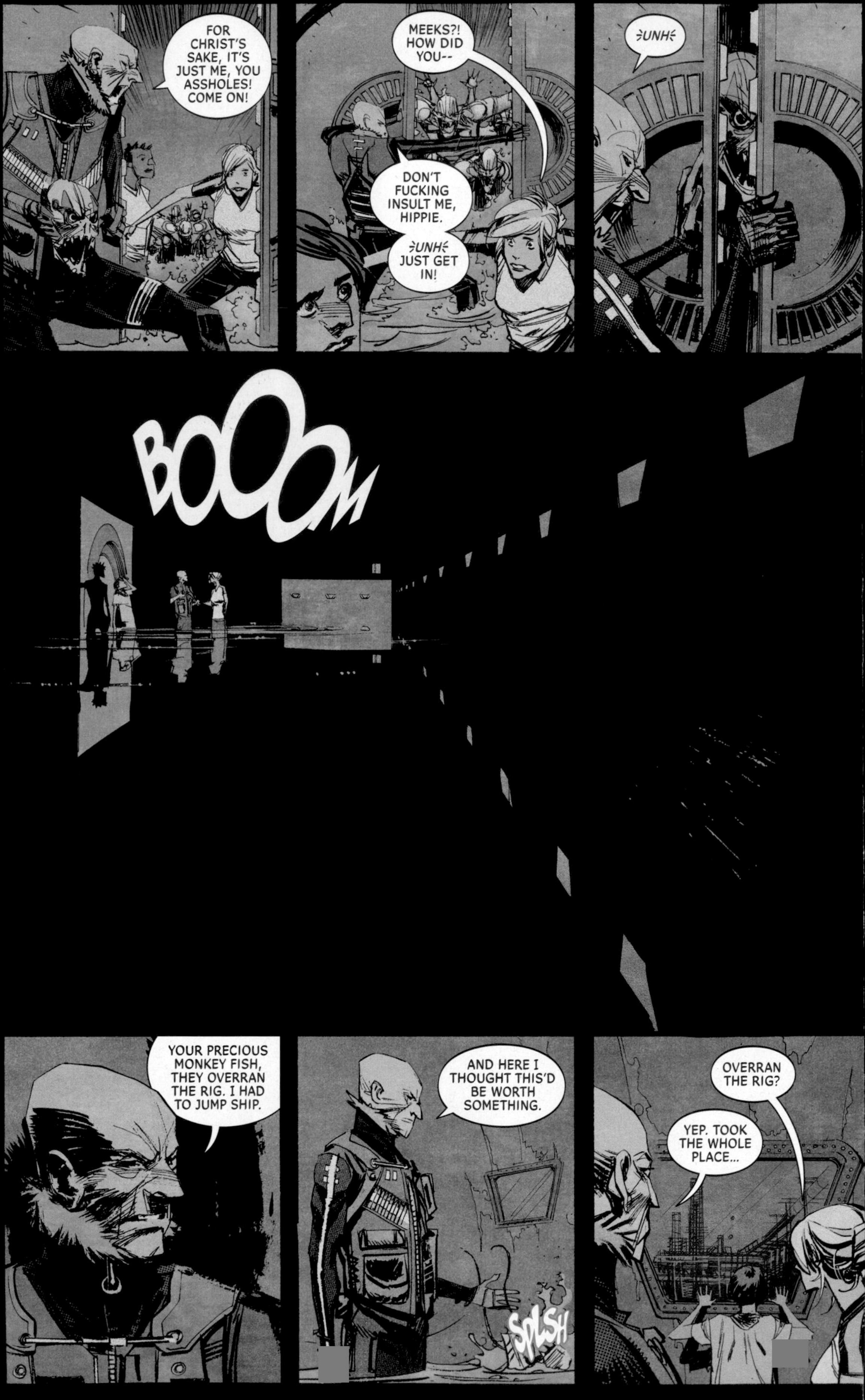
FOR CHRIST'S SAKE, IT'S JUST ME, YOU ASSHOLES! COME ON!
MEEKS?! HOW DID YOU--
DON'T FUCKING INSULT ME, HIPPIE.
UNH JUST GET IN!
UNH
BOOOM
YOUR PRECIOUS MONKEY FISH, THEY OVERRAN THE RIG. I HAD TO JUMP SHIP.
AND HERE I THOUGHT THIS'D BE WORTH SOMETHING.
SPLSH
OVERRAN THE RIG?
YEP. TOOK THE WHOLE PLACE...

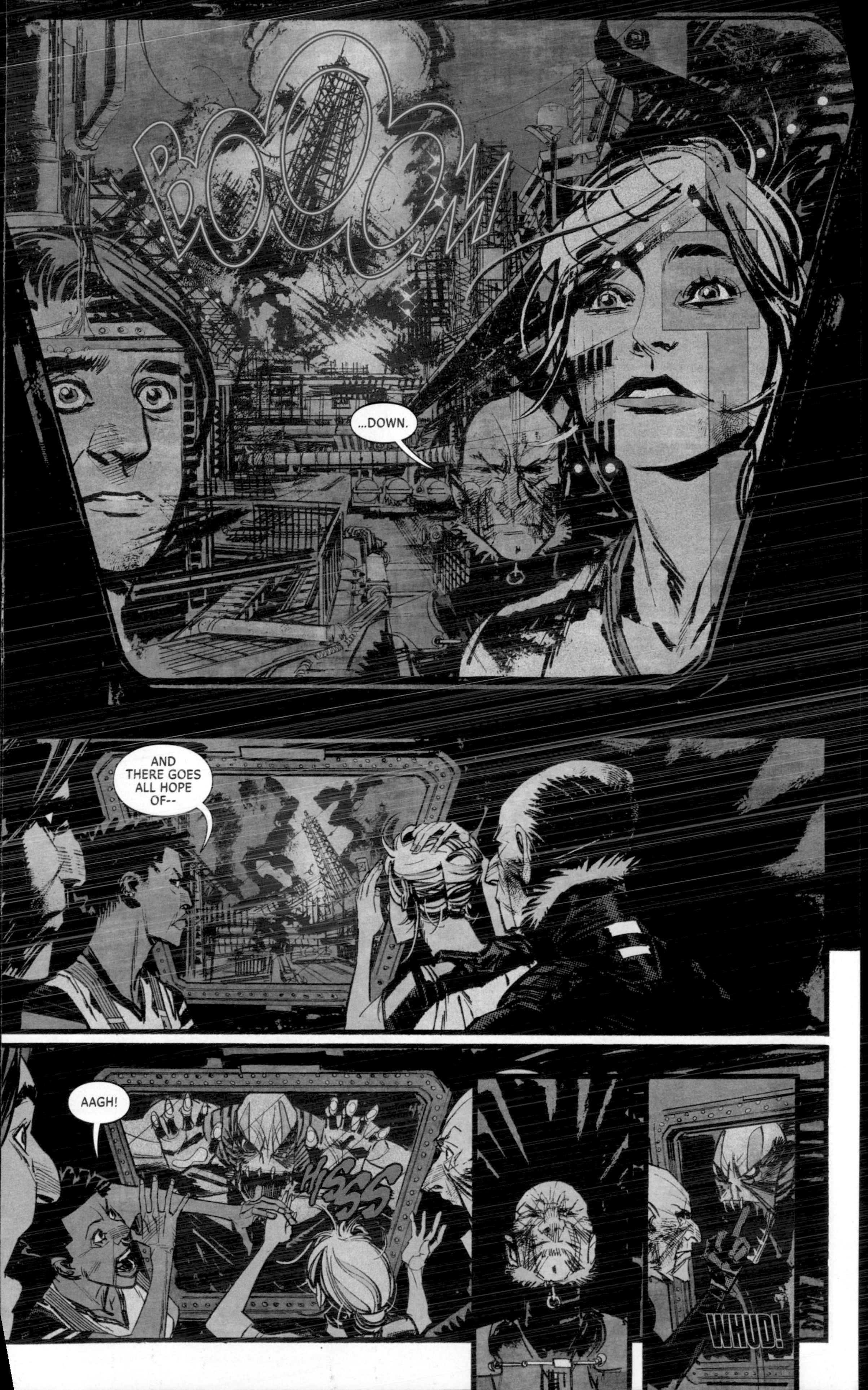
BOOOOM
...DOWN.
AND THERE GOES ALL HOPE OF--
AAGH!
HISSS
WHUD!

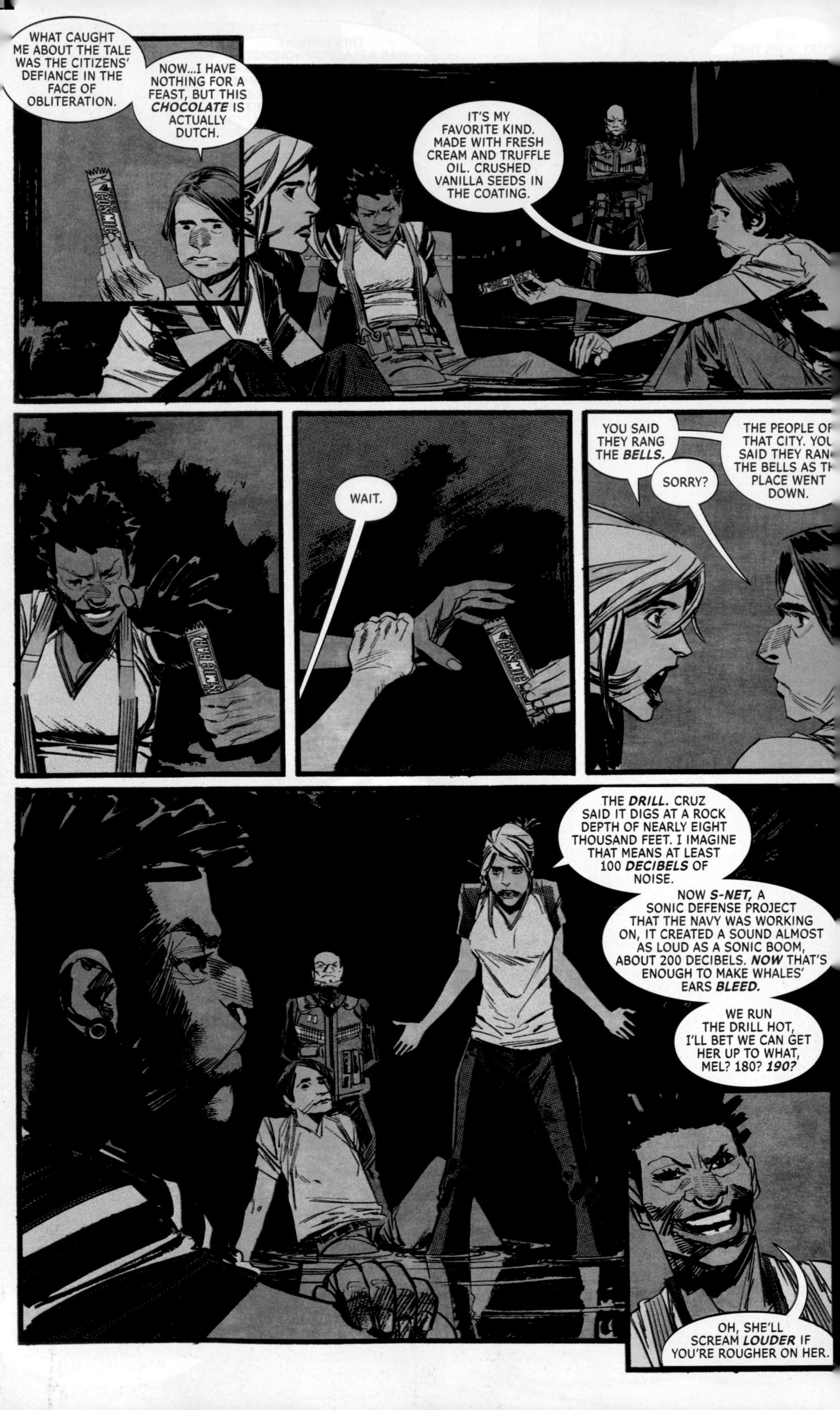
WHAT CAUGHT ME ABOUT THE TALE WAS THE CITIZENS' DEFIANCE IN THE FACE OF OBLITERATION.
NOW...I HAVE NOTHING FOR A FEAST, BUT THIS *CHOCOLATE* IS ACTUALLY DUTCH.
COSMIC
IT'S MY FAVORITE KIND. MADE WITH FRESH CREAM AND TRUFFLE OIL. CRUSHED VANILLA SEEDS IN THE COATING.
COSMIC
WAIT.
COSMIC
YOU SAID THEY RANG THE *BELLS.*
SORRY?
THE PEOPLE OF THAT CITY. YOU SAID THEY RANG THE BELLS AS TH PLACE WENT DOWN.
THE *DRILL.* CRUZ SAID IT DIGS AT A ROCK DEPTH OF NEARLY EIGHT THOUSAND FEET. I IMAGINE THAT MEANS AT LEAST 100 *DECIBELS* OF NOISE.
NOW *S-NET,* A SONIC DEFENSE PROJECT THAT THE NAVY WAS WORKING ON, IT CREATED A SOUND ALMOST AS LOUD AS A SONIC BOOM, ABOUT 200 DECIBELS. *NOW* THAT'S ENOUGH TO MAKE WHALES' EARS *BLEED.*
WE RUN THE DRILL HOT, I'LL BET WE CAN GET HER UP TO WHAT, MEL? 180? *190?*
OH, SHE'LL SCREAM *LOUDER* IF YOU'RE ROUGHER ON HER.

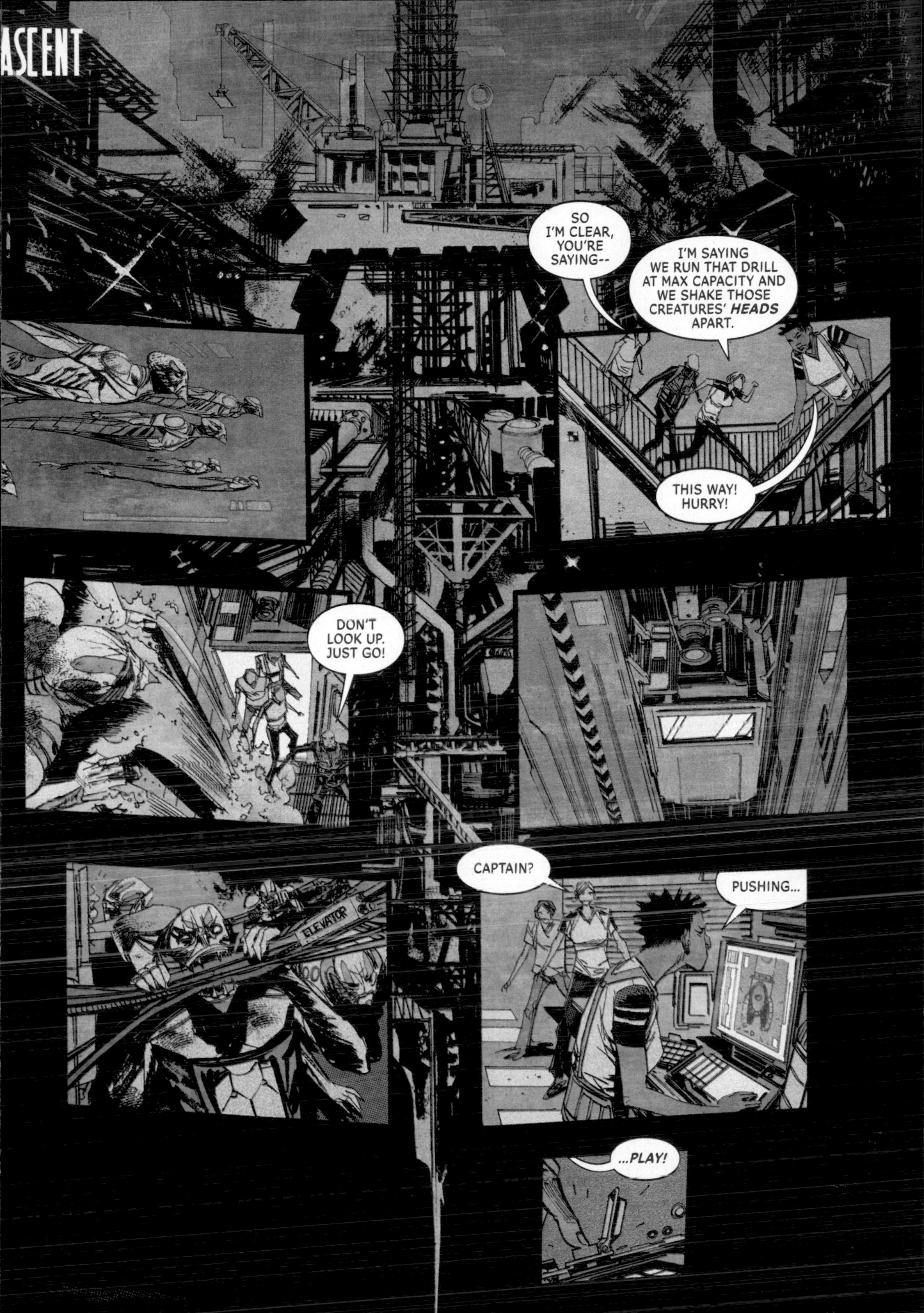
ASCENT
SO I'M CLEAR, YOU'RE SAYING--
I'M SAYING WE RUN THAT DRILL AT MAX CAPACITY AND WE SHAKE THOSE CREATURES' ***HEADS*** APART.
THIS WAY! HURRY!
DON'T LOOK UP. JUST GO!
ELEVATOR
CAPTAIN?
PUSHING...
...PLAY!

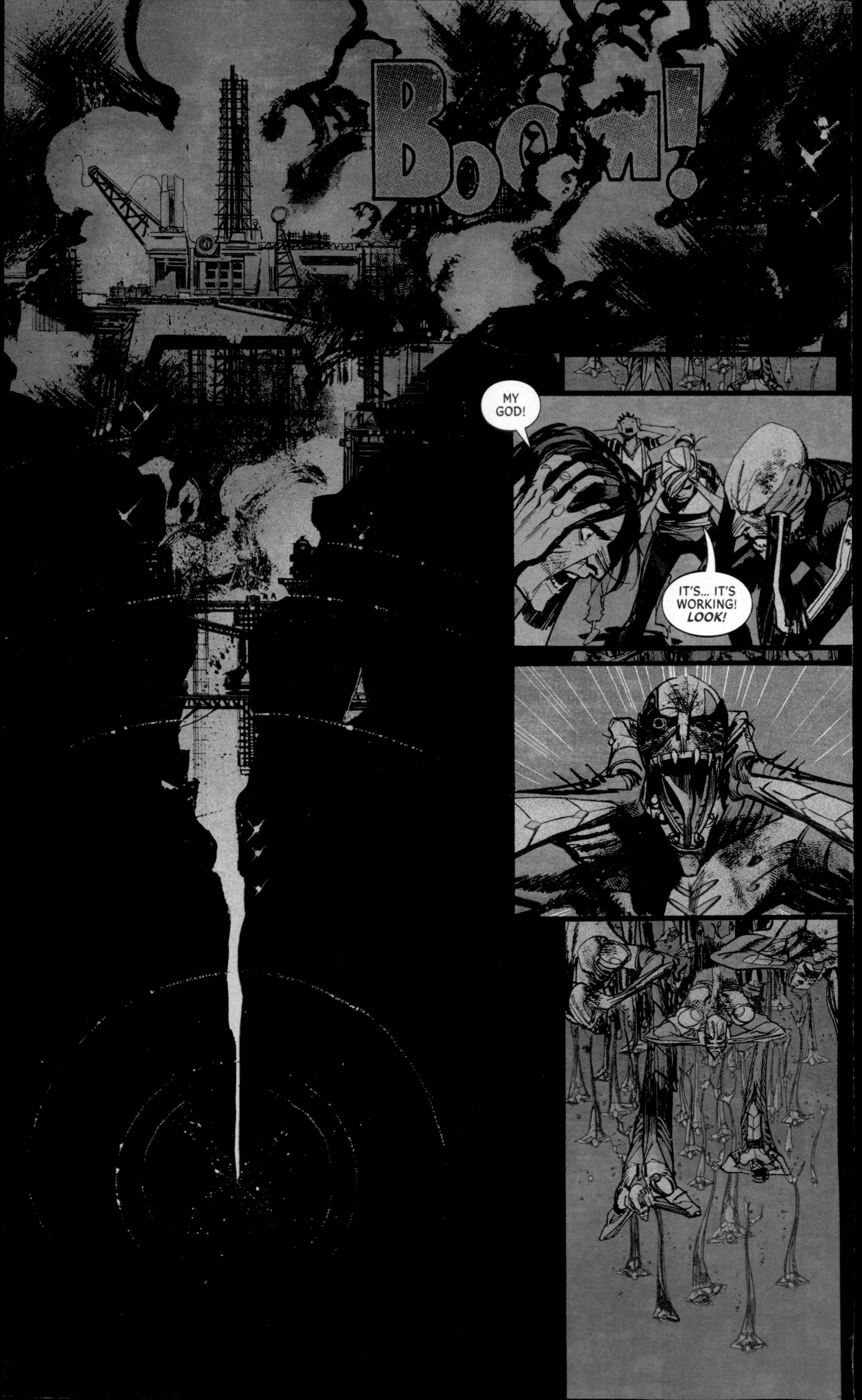
BOOM!
MY GOD!
IT'S... IT'S WORKING! LOOK!

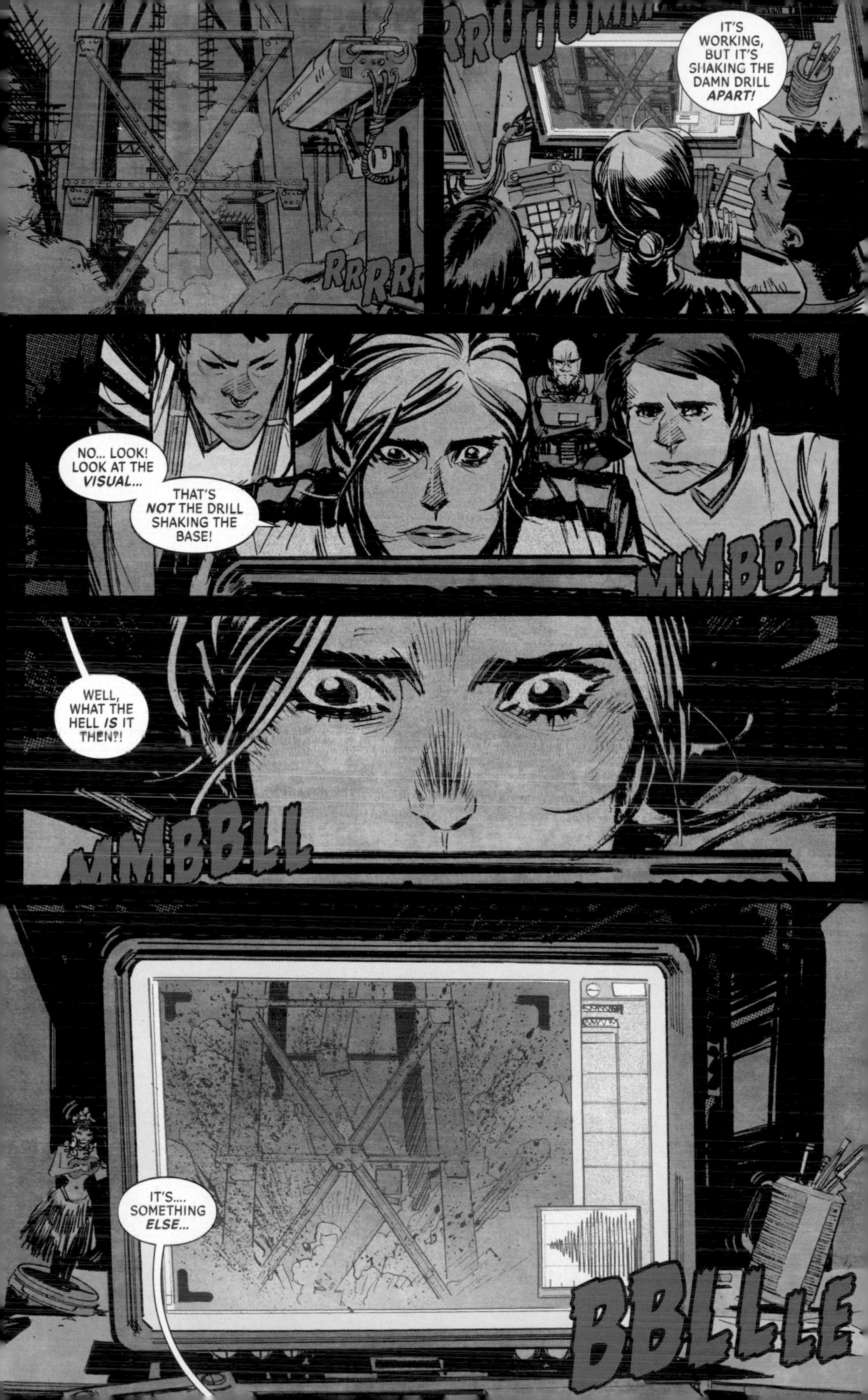
RRUUUMM
IT'S WORKING, BUT IT'S SHAKING THE DAMN DRILL APART!
RRRRR
NO... LOOK! LOOK AT THE VISUAL...
THAT'S NOT THE DRILL SHAKING THE BASE!
MMBBLL
WELL, WHAT THE HELL IS IT THEN?!
MMBBLL
IT'S.... SOMETHING ELSE...
BBLLLE

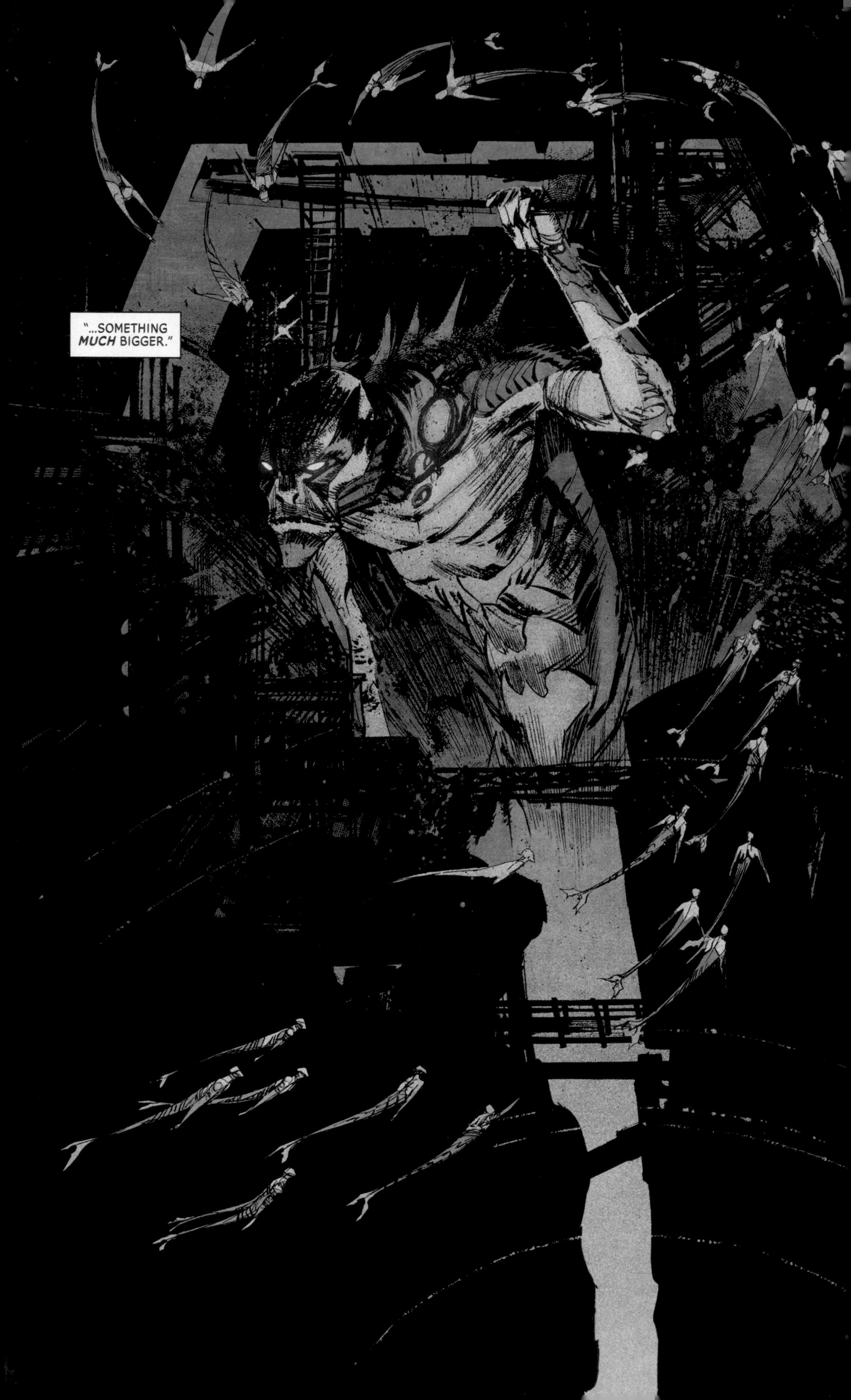
"...SOMETHING *MUCH* BIGGER."

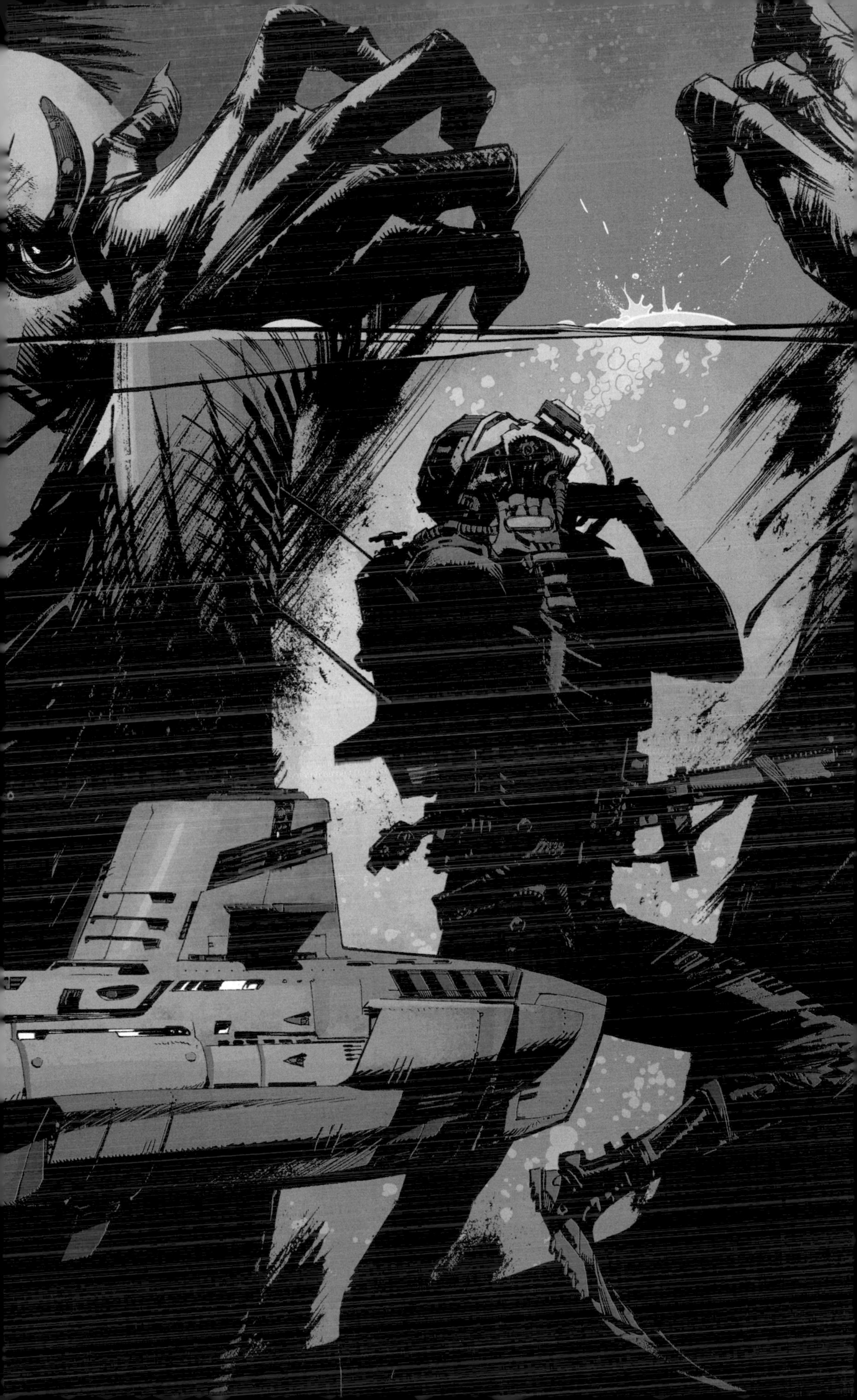

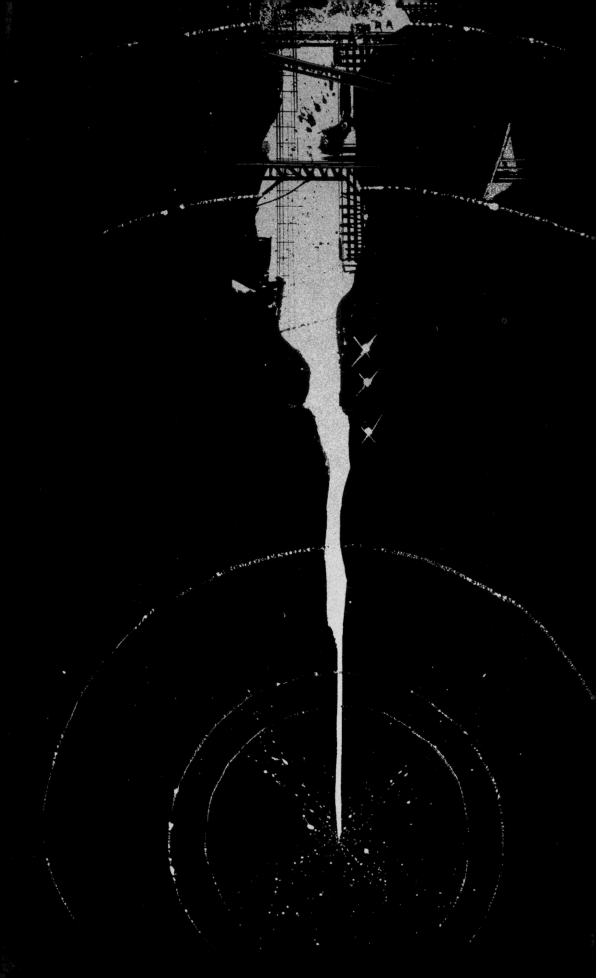

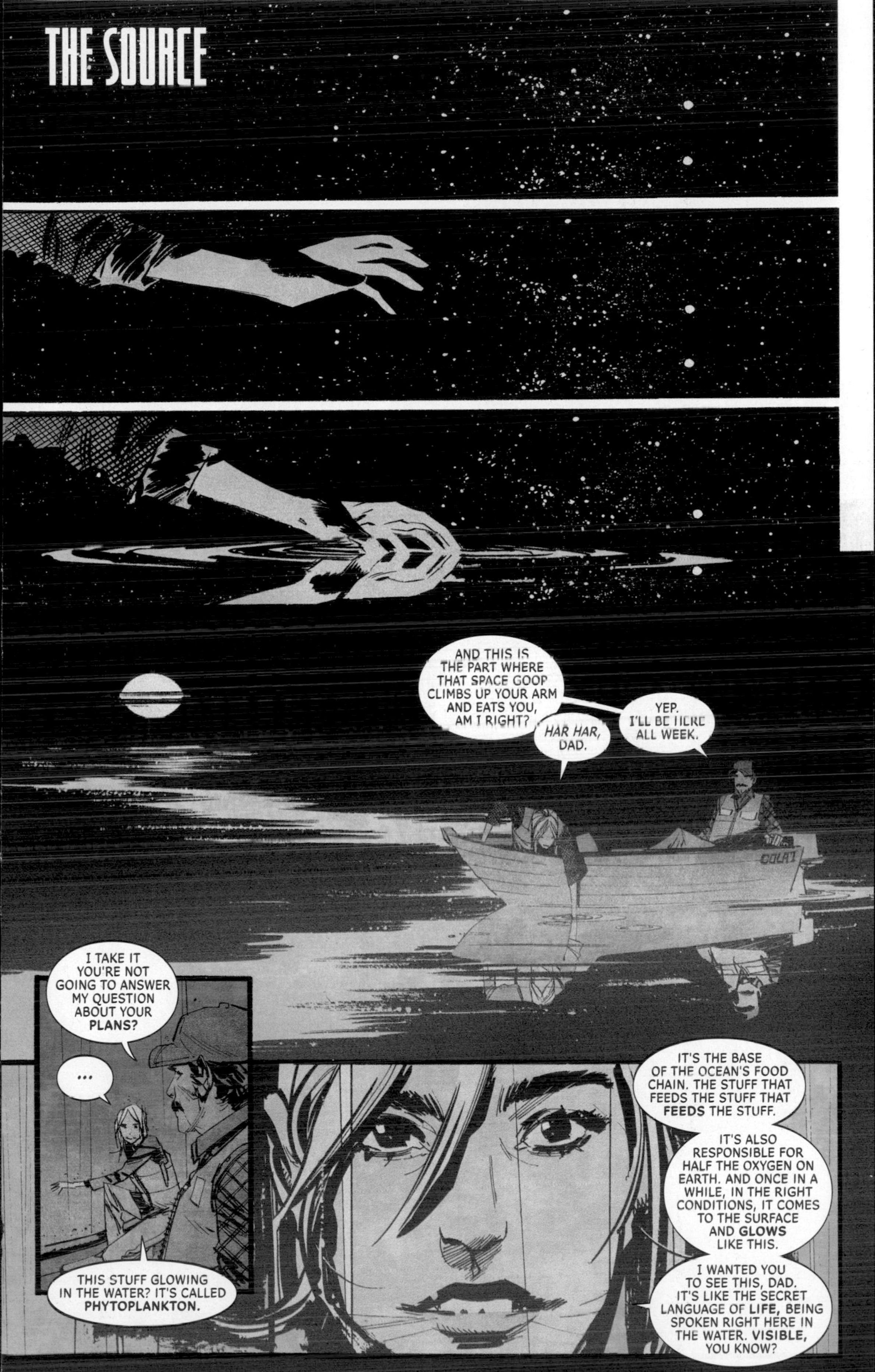
THE SOURCE
AND THIS IS THE PART WHERE THAT SPACE GOOP CLIMBS UP YOUR ARM AND EATS YOU, AM I RIGHT?
HAR HAR, DAD.
YEP. I'LL BE HERE ALL WEEK.
I TAKE IT YOU'RE NOT GOING TO ANSWER MY QUESTION ABOUT YOUR PLANS?
...
THIS STUFF GLOWING IN THE WATER? IT'S CALLED PHYTOPLANKTON.
IT'S THE BASE OF THE OCEAN'S FOOD CHAIN. THE STUFF THAT FEEDS THE STUFF THAT FEEDS THE STUFF.
IT'S ALSO RESPONSIBLE FOR HALF THE OXYGEN ON EARTH. AND ONCE IN A WHILE, IN THE RIGHT CONDITIONS, IT COMES TO THE SURFACE AND GLOWS LIKE THIS.
I WANTED YOU TO SEE THIS, DAD. IT'S LIKE THE SECRET LANGUAGE OF LIFE, BEING SPOKEN RIGHT HERE IN THE WATER. VISIBLE, YOU KNOW?

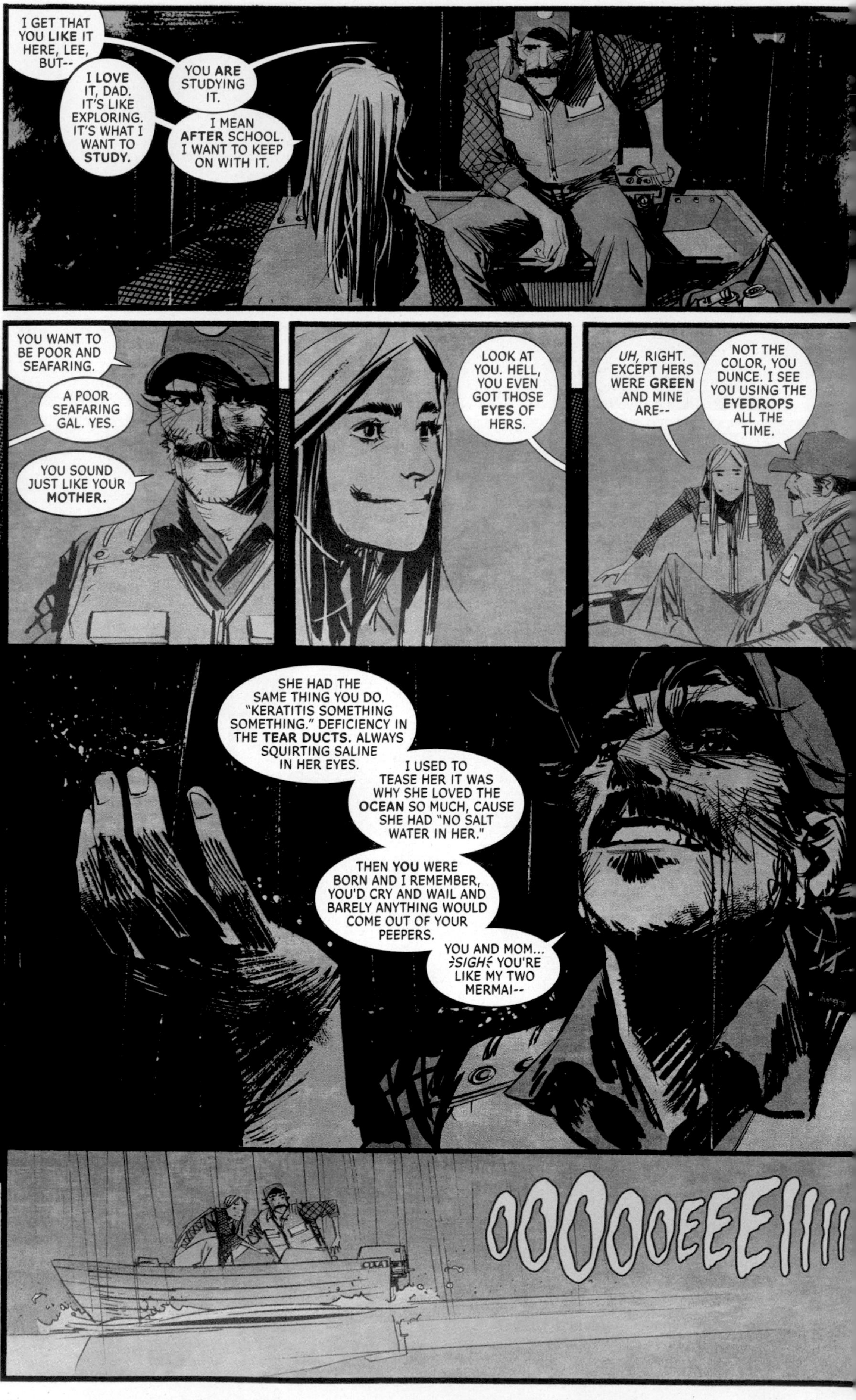
I GET THAT YOU LIKE IT HERE, LEE, BUT--
I LOVE IT, DAD. IT'S LIKE EXPLORING. IT'S WHAT I WANT TO STUDY.
YOU ARE STUDYING IT.
I MEAN AFTER SCHOOL. I WANT TO KEEP ON WITH IT.
YOU WANT TO BE POOR AND SEAFARING.
A POOR SEAFARING GAL. YES.
YOU SOUND JUST LIKE YOUR MOTHER.
LOOK AT YOU. HELL, YOU EVEN GOT THOSE EYES OF HERS.
UH, RIGHT. EXCEPT HERS WERE GREEN AND MINE ARE--
NOT THE COLOR, YOU DUNCE. I SEE YOU USING THE EYEDROPS ALL THE TIME.
SHE HAD THE SAME THING YOU DO. "KERATITIS SOMETHING SOMETHING." DEFICIENCY IN THE TEAR DUCTS. ALWAYS SQUIRTING SALINE IN HER EYES.
I USED TO TEASE HER IT WAS WHY SHE LOVED THE OCEAN SO MUCH, CAUSE SHE HAD "NO SALT WATER IN HER."
THEN YOU WERE BORN AND I REMEMBER, YOU'D CRY AND WAIL AND BARELY ANYTHING WOULD COME OUT OF YOUR PEEPERS.
YOU AND MOM... SIGH YOU'RE LIKE MY TWO MERMAI--
OOOOOEEEIIII

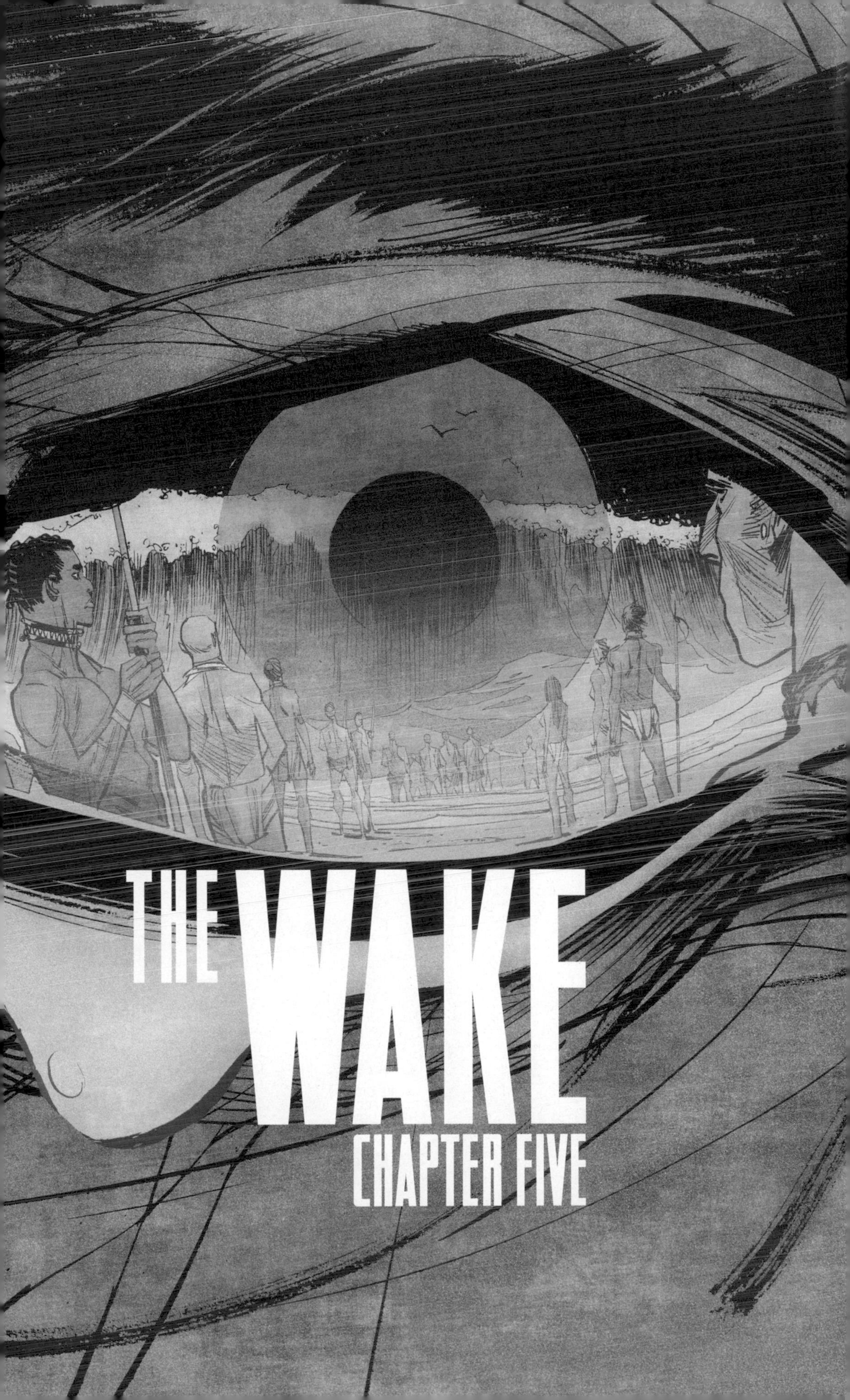
THE WAKE
CHAPTER FIVE

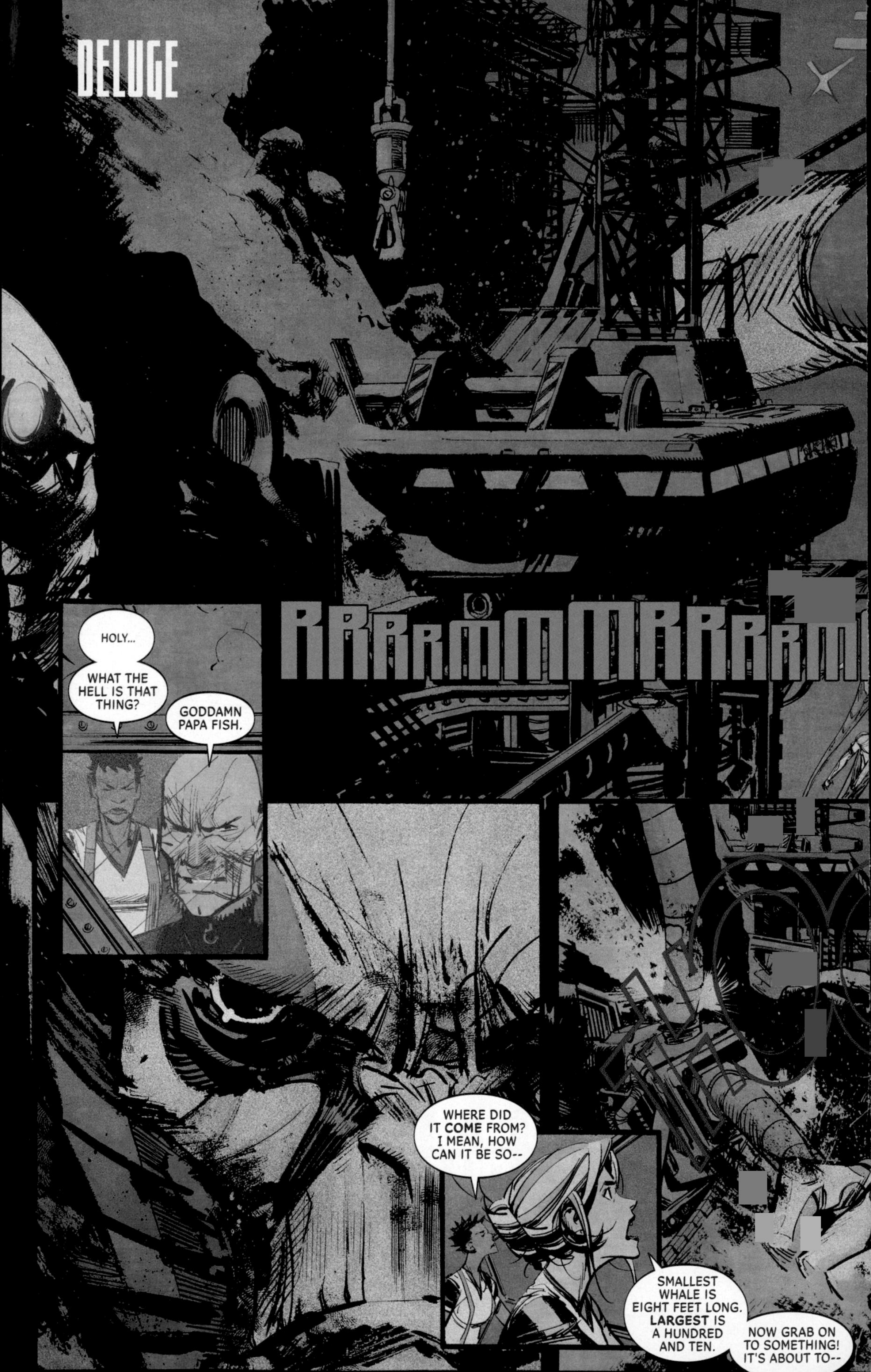
DELUGE
HOLY...
WHAT THE HELL IS THAT THING?
GODDAMN PAPA FISH.
RRRRMMMMRRRRRM
WHERE DID IT COME FROM? I MEAN, HOW CAN IT BE SO--
SMALLEST WHALE IS EIGHT FEET LONG. LARGEST IS A HUNDRED AND TEN.
NOW GRAB ON TO SOMETHING! IT'S ABOUT TO--

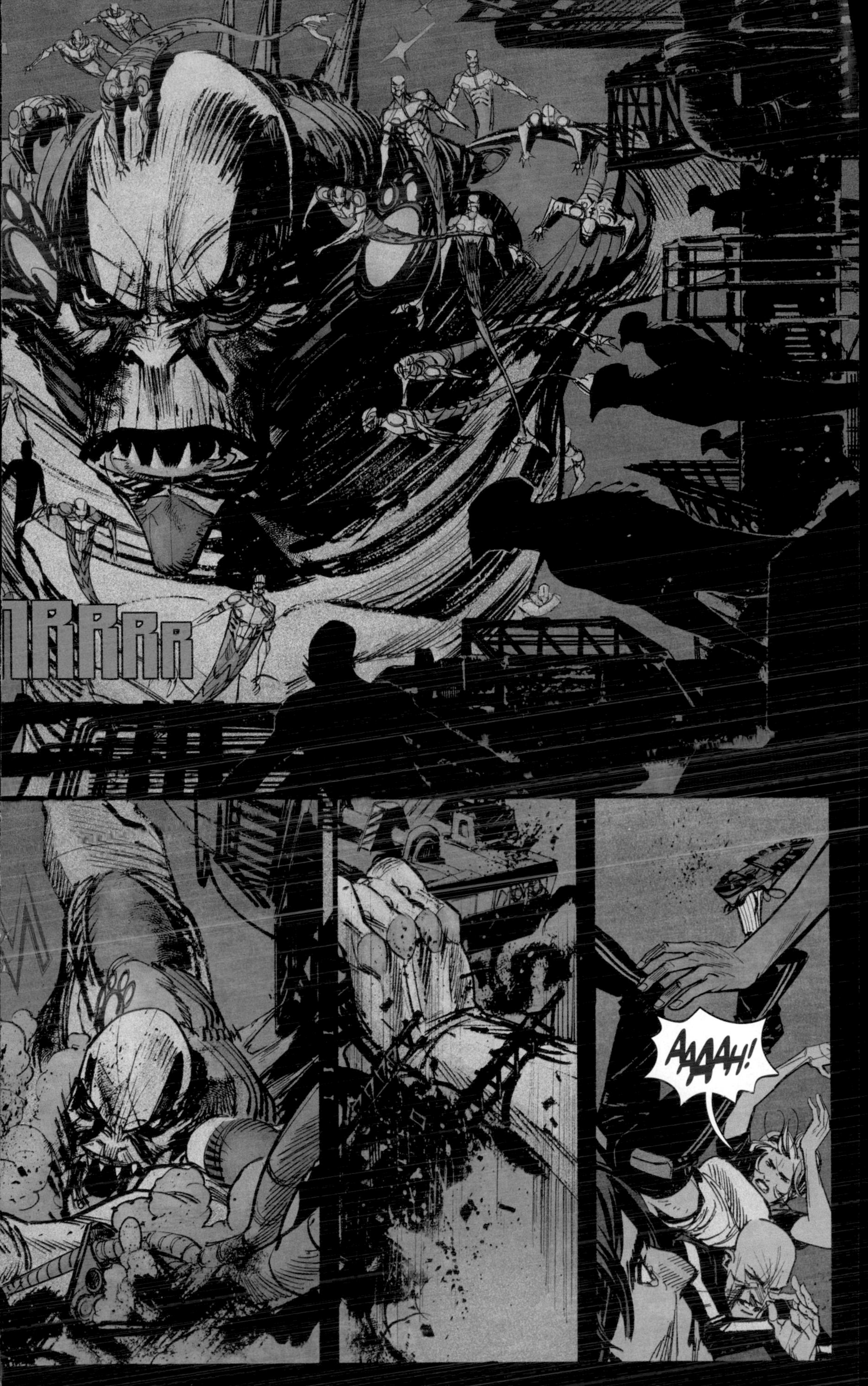
RRRR
AAAAH!

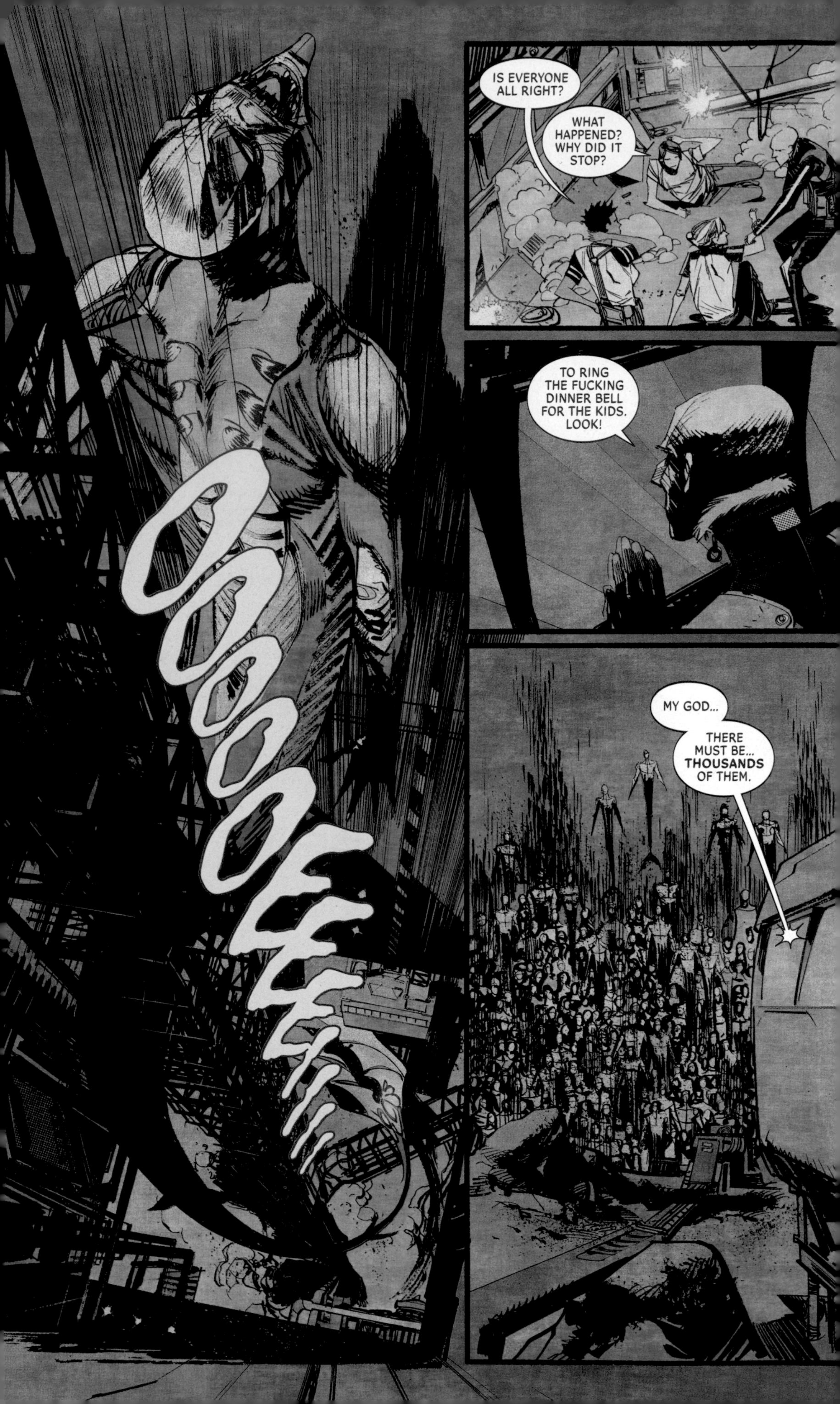
OOOOOOHHH!!!
IS EVERYONE ALL RIGHT?
WHAT HAPPENED? WHY DID IT STOP?
TO RING THE FUCKING DINNER BELL FOR THE KIDS. LOOK!
MY GOD...
THERE MUST BE... **THOUSANDS** OF THEM.

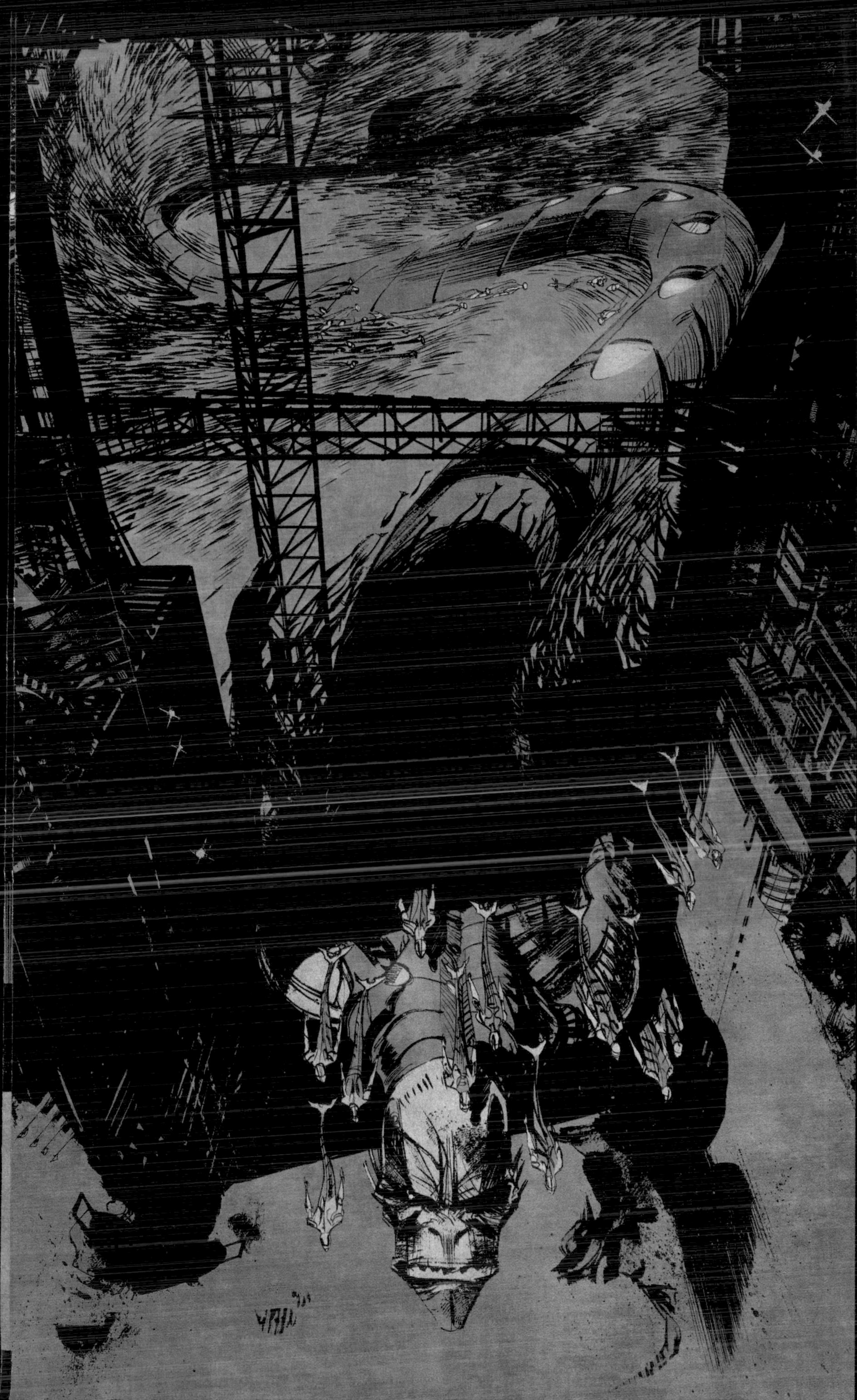

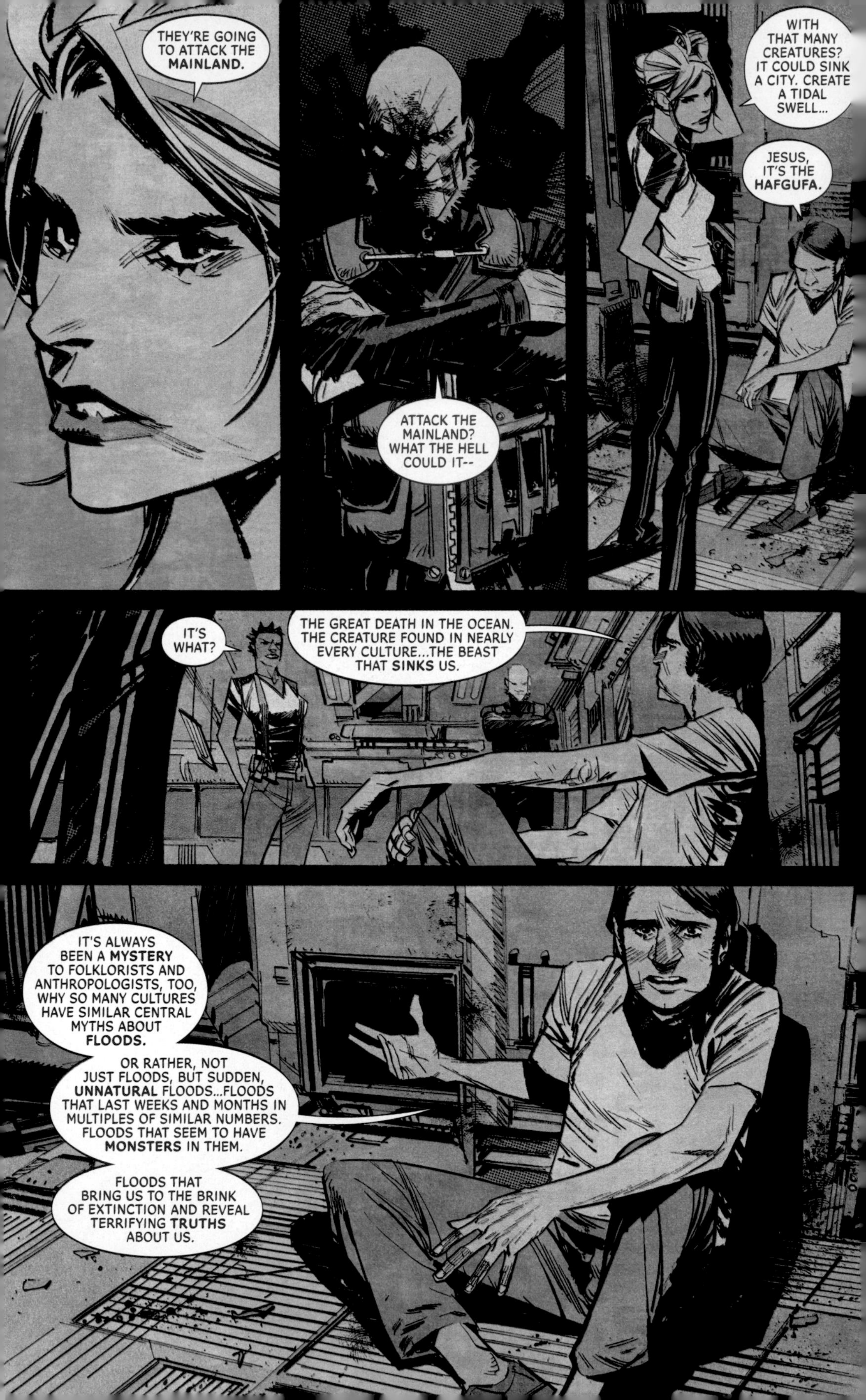
THEY'RE GOING TO ATTACK THE MAINLAND.
ATTACK THE MAINLAND? WHAT THE HELL COULD IT--
WITH THAT MANY CREATURES? IT COULD SINK A CITY. CREATE A TIDAL SWELL...
JESUS, IT'S THE HAFGUFA.
IT'S WHAT?
THE GREAT DEATH IN THE OCEAN. THE CREATURE FOUND IN NEARLY EVERY CULTURE...THE BEAST THAT SINKS US.
IT'S ALWAYS BEEN A MYSTERY TO FOLKLORISTS AND ANTHROPOLOGISTS, TOO, WHY SO MANY CULTURES HAVE SIMILAR CENTRAL MYTHS ABOUT FLOODS.
OR RATHER, NOT JUST FLOODS, BUT SUDDEN, UNNATURAL FLOODS...FLOODS THAT LAST WEEKS AND MONTHS IN MULTIPLES OF SIMILAR NUMBERS. FLOODS THAT SEEM TO HAVE MONSTERS IN THEM.
FLOODS THAT BRING US TO THE BRINK OF EXTINCTION AND REVEAL TERRIFYING TRUTHS ABOUT US.

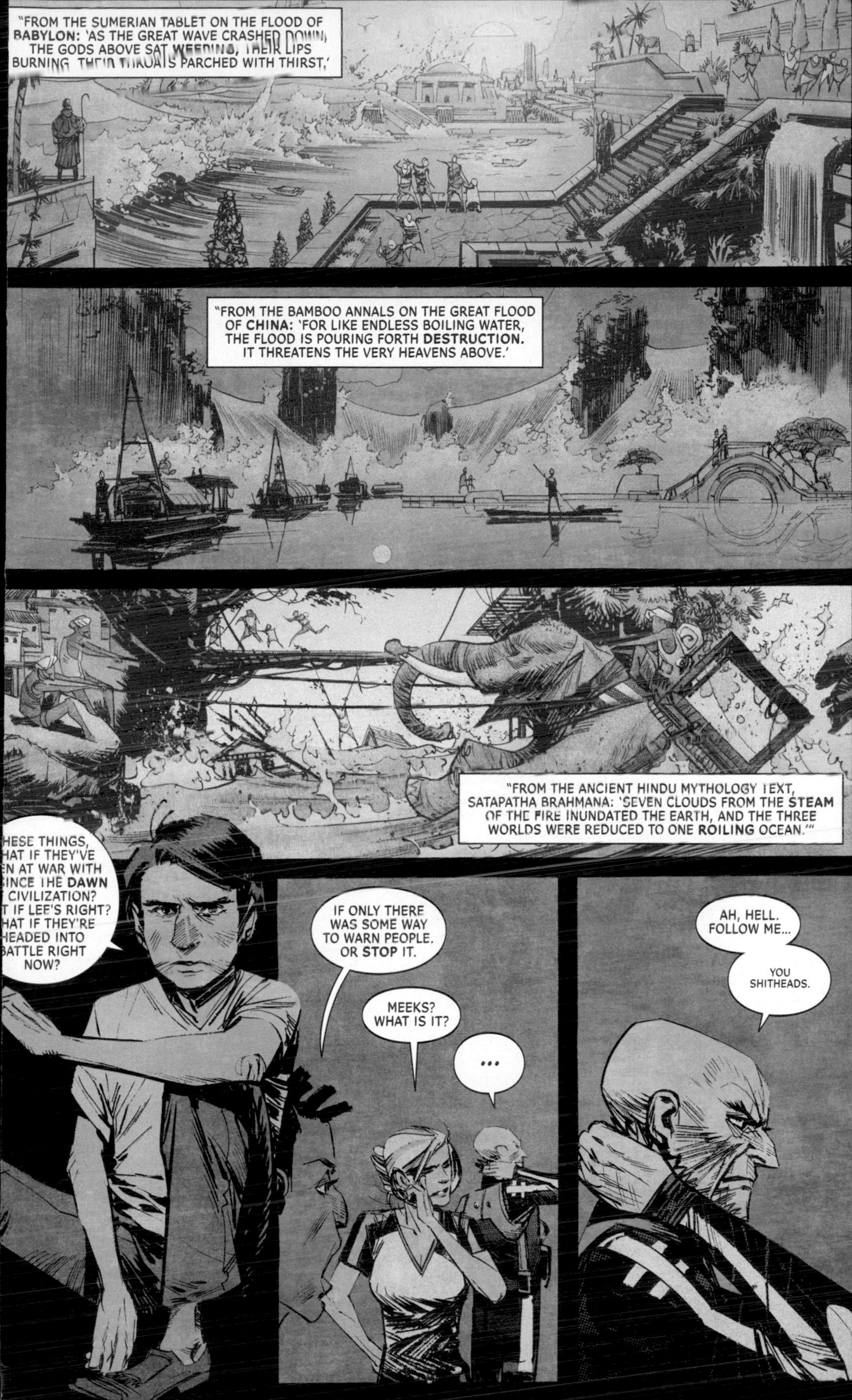
"FROM THE SUMERIAN TABLET ON THE FLOOD OF BABYLON: 'AS THE GREAT WAVE CRASHED DOWN, THE GODS ABOVE SAT WEEPING, THEIR LIPS BURNING, THEIR THROATS PARCHED WITH THIRST.'
"FROM THE BAMBOO ANNALS ON THE GREAT FLOOD OF CHINA: 'FOR LIKE ENDLESS BOILING WATER, THE FLOOD IS POURING FORTH DESTRUCTION. IT THREATENS THE VERY HEAVENS ABOVE.'
"FROM THE ANCIENT HINDU MYTHOLOGY TEXT, SATAPATHA BRAHMANA: 'SEVEN CLOUDS FROM THE STEAM OF THE FIRE INUNDATED THE EARTH, AND THE THREE WORLDS WERE REDUCED TO ONE ROILING OCEAN.'"
HESE THINGS, HAT IF THEY'VE EN AT WAR WITH INCE THE DAWN CIVILIZATION? T IF LEE'S RIGHT? HAT IF THEY'RE HEADED INTO BATTLE RIGHT NOW?
IF ONLY THERE WAS SOME WAY TO WARN PEOPLE. OR STOP IT.
MEEKS? WHAT IS IT?
...
AH, HELL. FOLLOW ME...
YOU SHITHEADS.

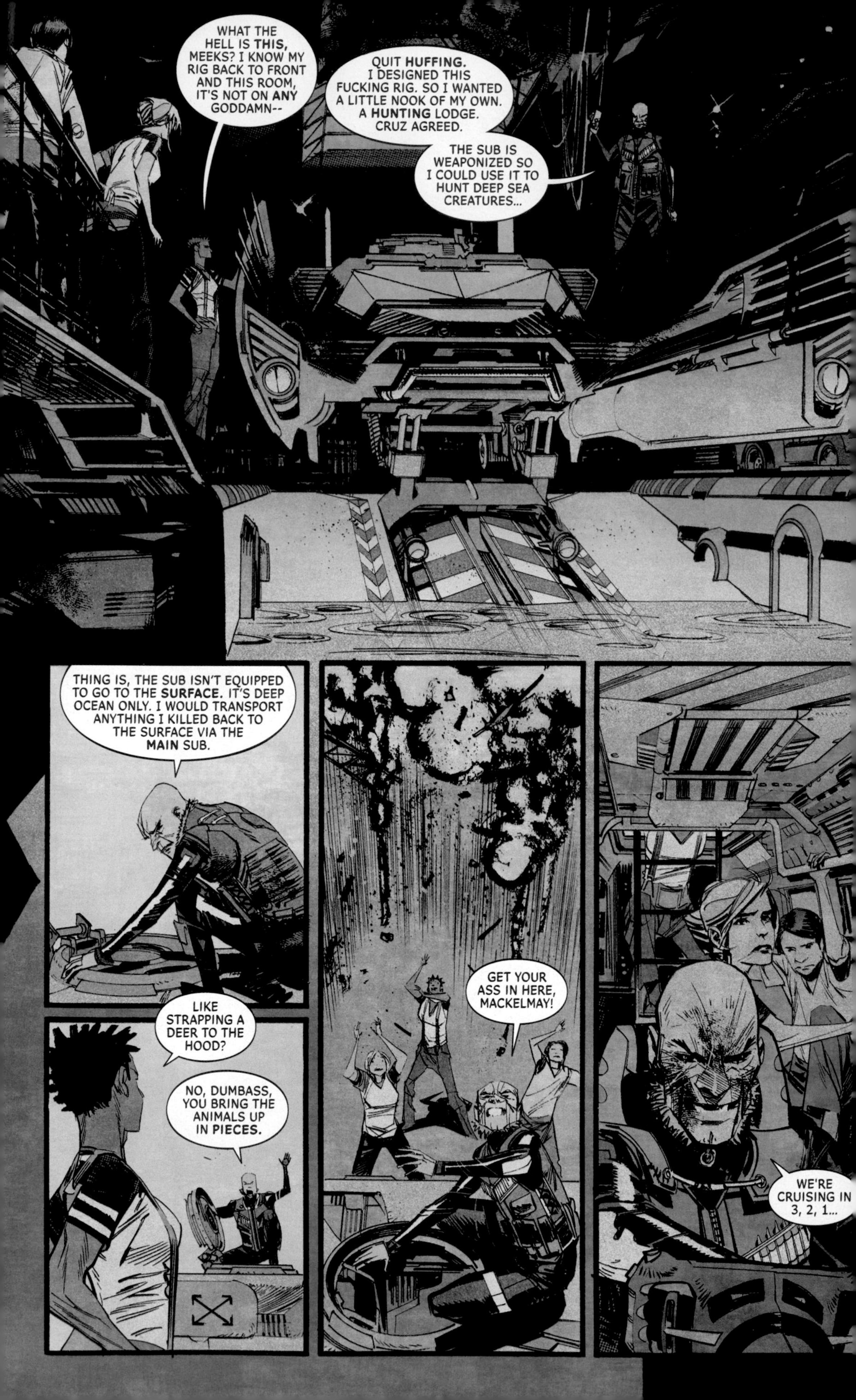
WHAT THE HELL IS THIS, MEEKS? I KNOW MY RIG BACK TO FRONT AND THIS ROOM, IT'S NOT ON ANY GODDAMN--
QUIT HUFFING. I DESIGNED THIS FUCKING RIG. SO I WANTED A LITTLE NOOK OF MY OWN. A HUNTING LODGE. CRUZ AGREED.
THE SUB IS WEAPONIZED SO I COULD USE IT TO HUNT DEEP SEA CREATURES...
THING IS, THE SUB ISN'T EQUIPPED TO GO TO THE SURFACE. IT'S DEEP OCEAN ONLY. I WOULD TRANSPORT ANYTHING I KILLED BACK TO THE SURFACE VIA THE MAIN SUB.
LIKE STRAPPING A DEER TO THE HOOD?
NO, DUMBASS, YOU BRING THE ANIMALS UP IN PIECES.
GET YOUR ASS IN HERE, MACKELMAY!
WE'RE CRUISING IN 3, 2, 1...

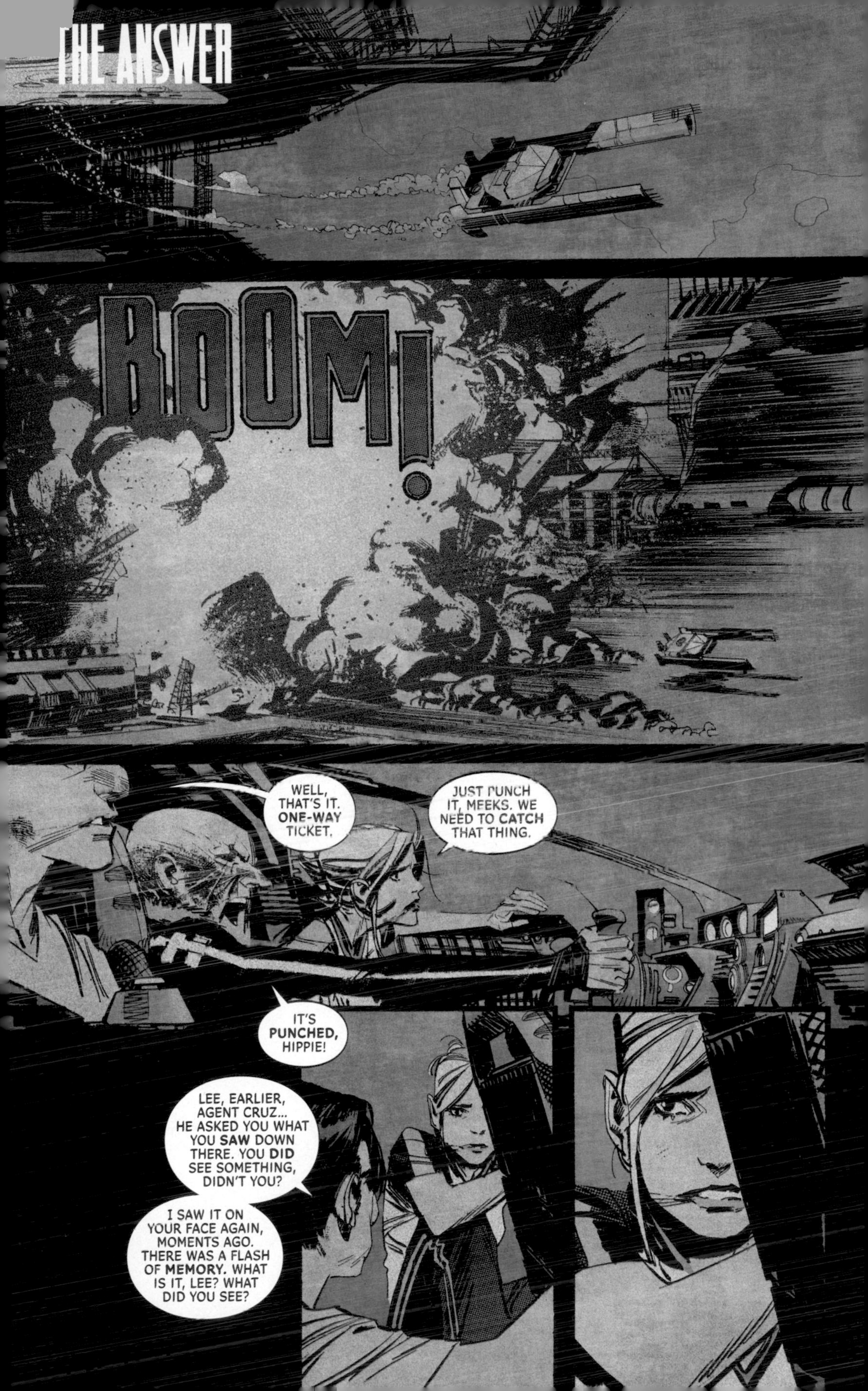
THE ANSWER
BOOM!
WELL, THAT'S IT. ONE-WAY TICKET.
JUST PUNCH IT, MEEKS. WE NEED TO CATCH THAT THING.
IT'S PUNCHED, HIPPIE!
LEE, EARLIER, AGENT CRUZ... HE ASKED YOU WHAT YOU SAW DOWN THERE. YOU DID SEE SOMETHING, DIDN'T YOU?
I SAW IT ON YOUR FACE AGAIN, MOMENTS AGO. THERE WAS A FLASH OF MEMORY. WHAT IS IT, LEE? WHAT DID YOU SEE?

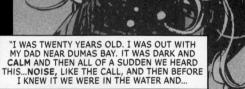

"...AND THEN I COULD FEEL SOMETHING PULLING ME **DOWN**. DRAGGING ME. BUT I KNEW THAT WAS IMPOSSIBLE, AND THAT NOISE WAS IN MY EARS AND I THOUGHT TO MYSELF, 'LEE, YOU BANGED YOUR HEAD. YOU'RE UNCONSCIOUS. YOU'RE **DROWNING**.'"

"I WAS TWENTY YEARS OLD. I WAS OUT WITH MY DAD NEAR DUMAS BAY. IT WAS DARK AND **CALM** AND THEN ALL OF A SUDDEN WE HEARD THIS...**NOISE**, LIKE THE CALL, AND THEN BEFORE I KNEW IT WE WERE IN THE WATER AND..."

"BUT THEN I SAW..."

"YOU SAW WHAT? **WHAT**, LEE?"

"I SAW **PEOPLE** DOWN THERE.

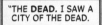

"THE **DEAD**. I SAW A CITY OF THE DEAD.

"IT WAS **BEAUTIFUL**, GUYS. I MEAN IT. SPIRITS AT THE BOTTOM OF THE OCEAN AND THEY WERE TRYING TO **TALK** TO ME..

"THEY WERE REACHING OUT..."

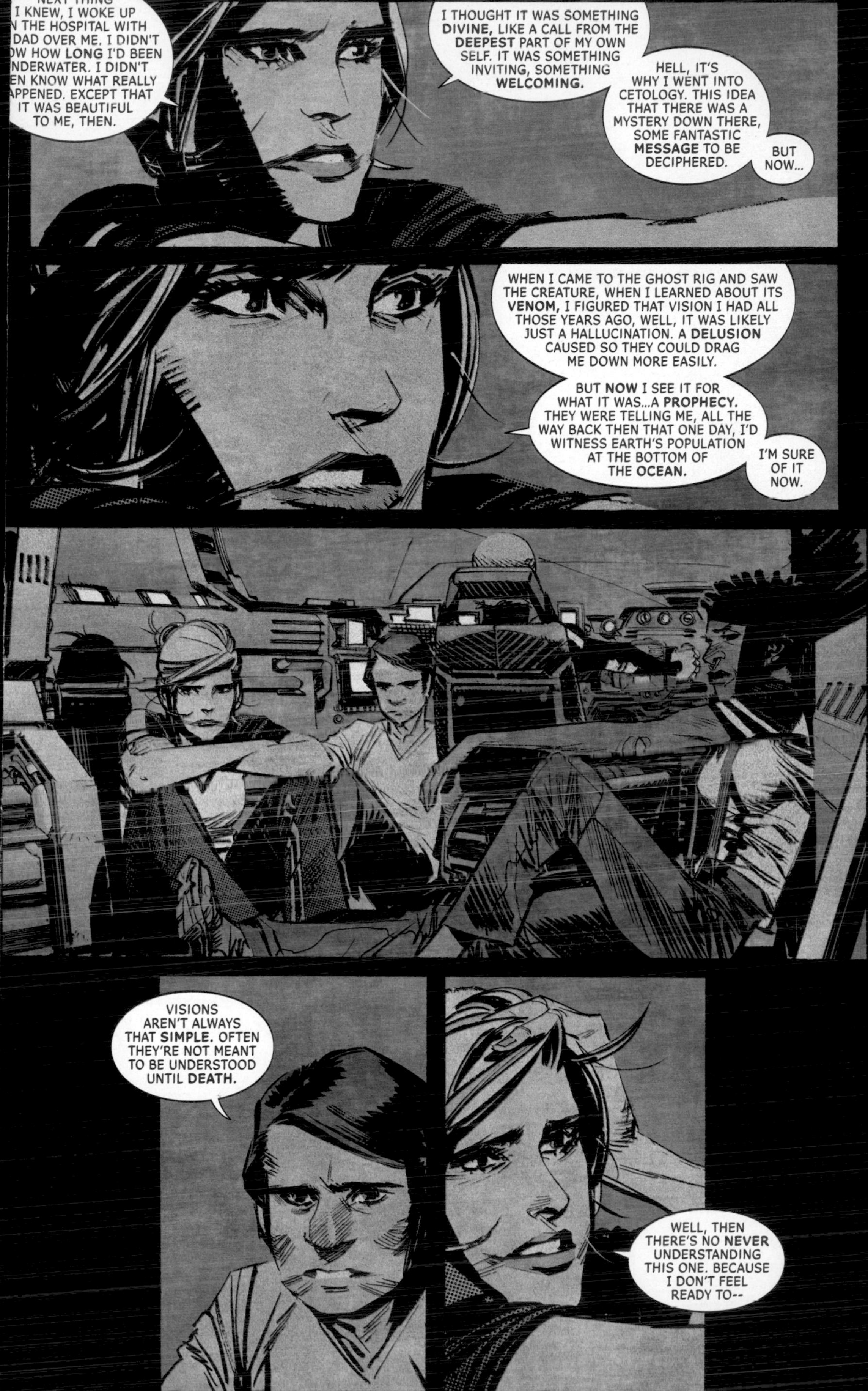
NEXT THING I KNEW, I WOKE UP IN THE HOSPITAL WITH DAD OVER ME. I DIDN'T KNOW HOW LONG I'D BEEN UNDERWATER. I DIDN'T EVEN KNOW WHAT REALLY HAPPENED. EXCEPT THAT IT WAS BEAUTIFUL TO ME, THEN.
I THOUGHT IT WAS SOMETHING DIVINE, LIKE A CALL FROM THE DEEPEST PART OF MY OWN SELF. IT WAS SOMETHING INVITING, SOMETHING WELCOMING.
HELL, IT'S WHY I WENT INTO CETOLOGY. THIS IDEA THAT THERE WAS A MYSTERY DOWN THERE, SOME FANTASTIC MESSAGE TO BE DECIPHERED.
BUT NOW...
WHEN I CAME TO THE GHOST RIG AND SAW THE CREATURE, WHEN I LEARNED ABOUT ITS VENOM, I FIGURED THAT VISION I HAD ALL THOSE YEARS AGO, WELL, IT WAS LIKELY JUST A HALLUCINATION. A DELUSION CAUSED SO THEY COULD DRAG ME DOWN MORE EASILY.
BUT NOW I SEE IT FOR WHAT IT WAS...A PROPHECY. THEY WERE TELLING ME, ALL THE WAY BACK THEN THAT ONE DAY, I'D WITNESS EARTH'S POPULATION AT THE BOTTOM OF THE OCEAN.
I'M SURE OF IT NOW.
VISIONS AREN'T ALWAYS THAT SIMPLE. OFTEN THEY'RE NOT MEANT TO BE UNDERSTOOD UNTIL DEATH.
WELL, THEN THERE'S NO NEVER UNDERSTANDING THIS ONE. BECAUSE I DON'T FEEL READY TO--

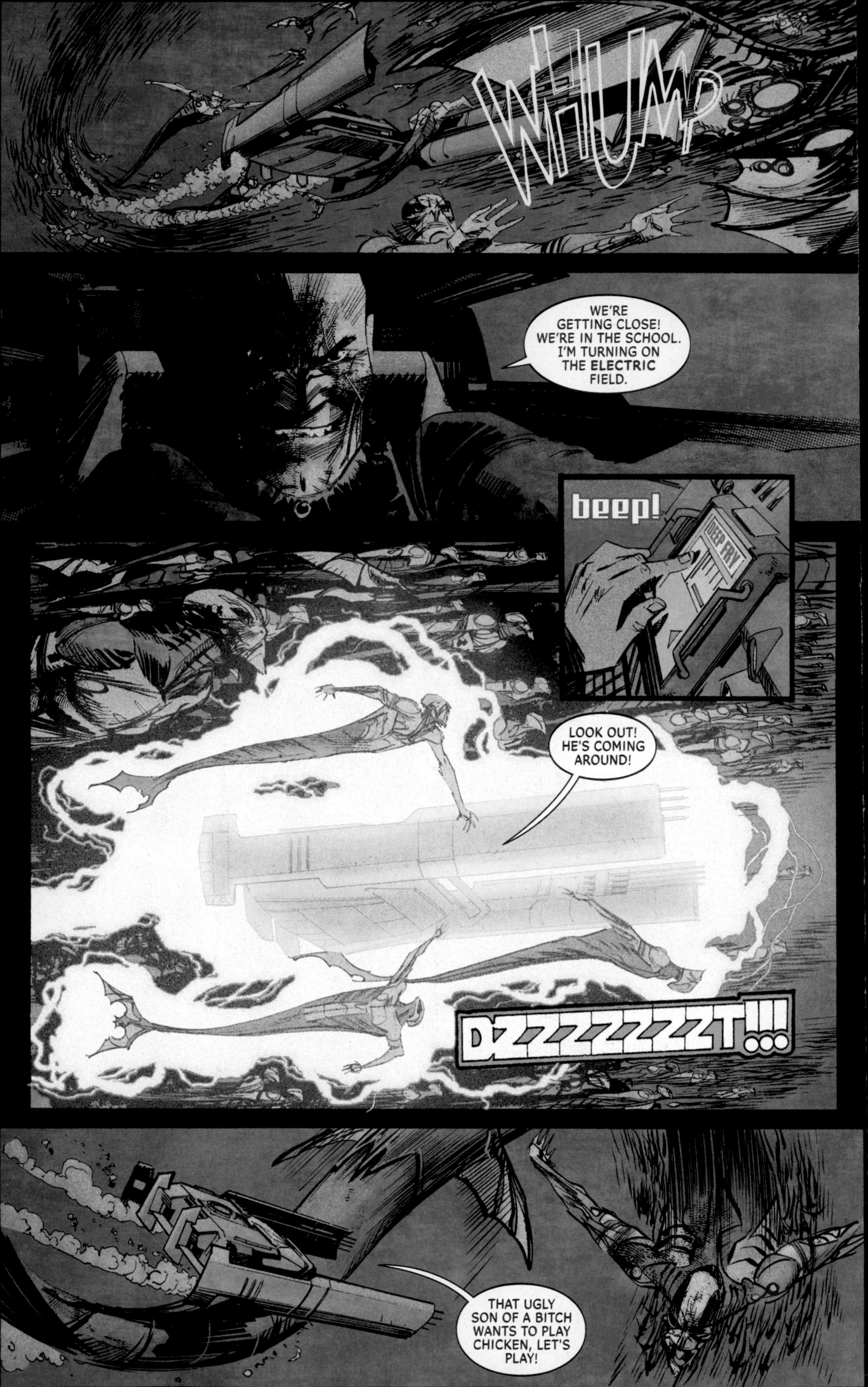
WHUMP
WE'RE GETTING CLOSE! WE'RE IN THE SCHOOL. I'M TURNING ON THE ELECTRIC FIELD.
beep!
DEEP FRY
LOOK OUT! HE'S COMING AROUND!
DZZZZZZZZT!!!
THAT UGLY SON OF A BITCH WANTS TO PLAY CHICKEN, LET'S PLAY!

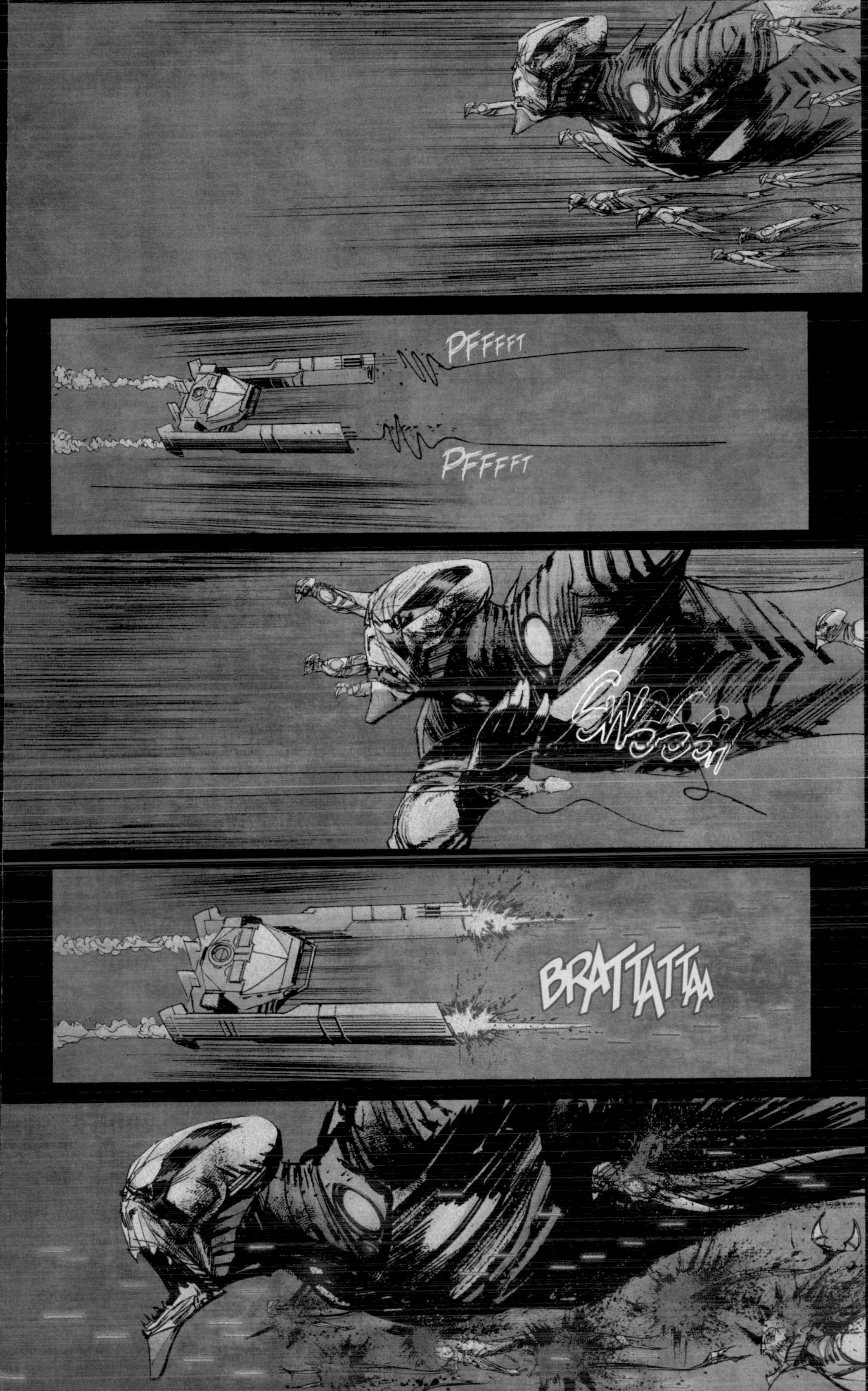
PFFFFT
PFFFFT
BRATTATTAA

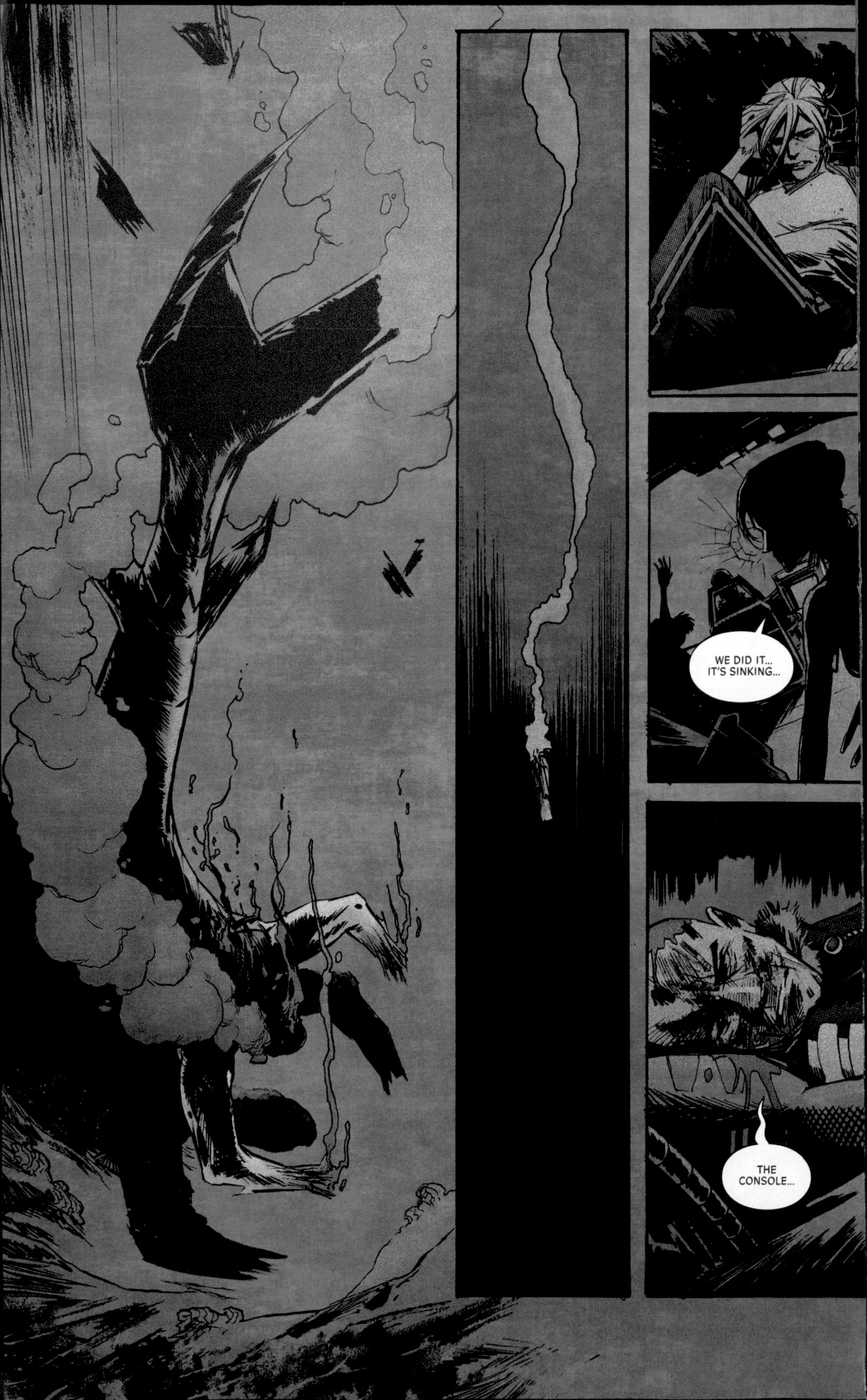
WE DID IT...
IT'S SINKING...
THE
CONSOLE...

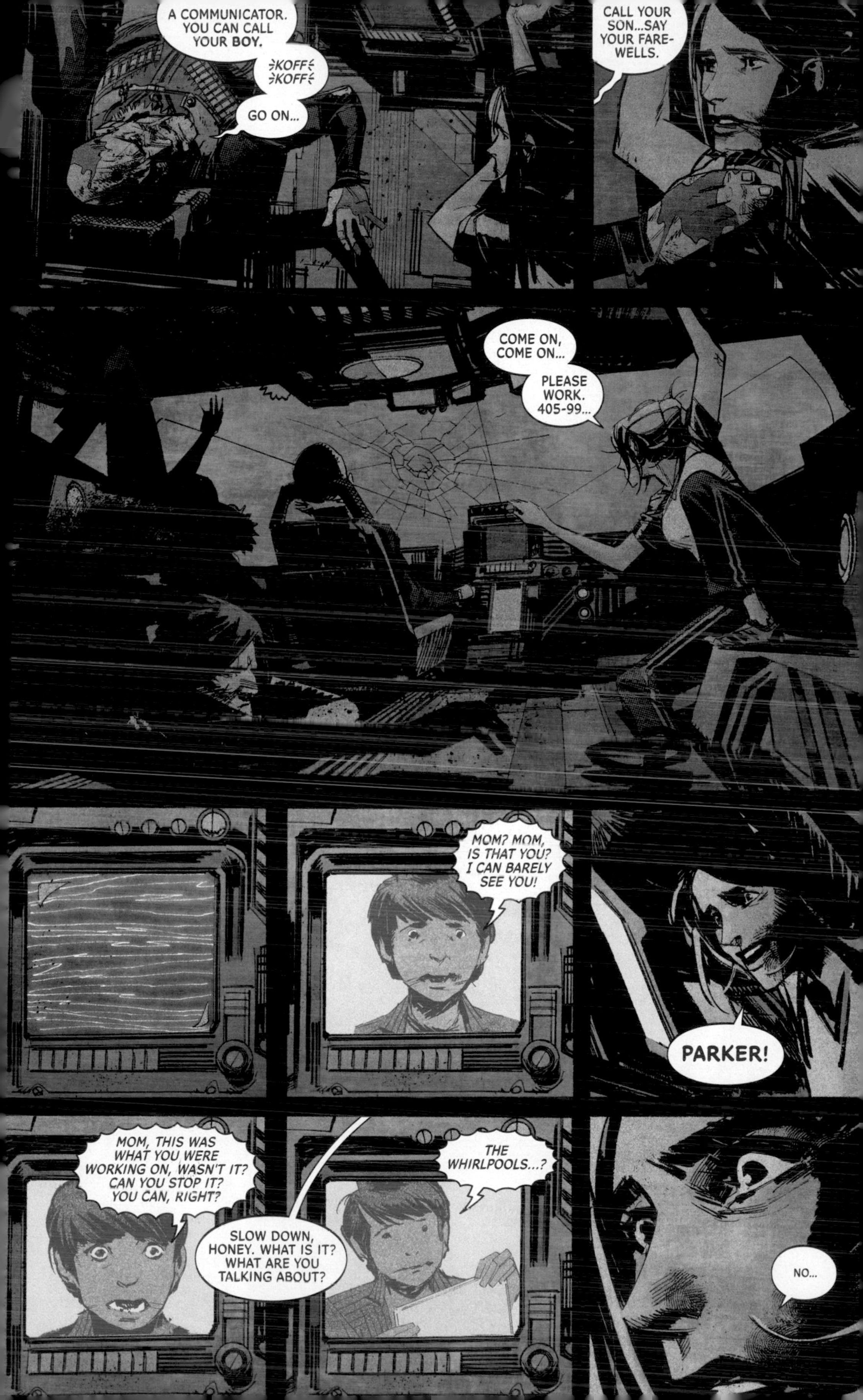
A COMMUNICATOR. YOU CAN CALL YOUR BOY.
KOFF *KOFF*
GO ON...
CALL YOUR SON...SAY YOUR FARE-WELLS.
COME ON, COME ON...
PLEASE WORK. 405-99...
MOM? MOM, IS THAT YOU? I CAN BARELY SEE YOU!
PARKER!
MOM, THIS WAS WHAT YOU WERE WORKING ON, WASN'T IT? CAN YOU STOP IT? YOU CAN, RIGHT?
SLOW DOWN, HONEY. WHAT IS IT? WHAT ARE YOU TALKING ABOUT?
THE WHIRLPOOLS...?
NO...

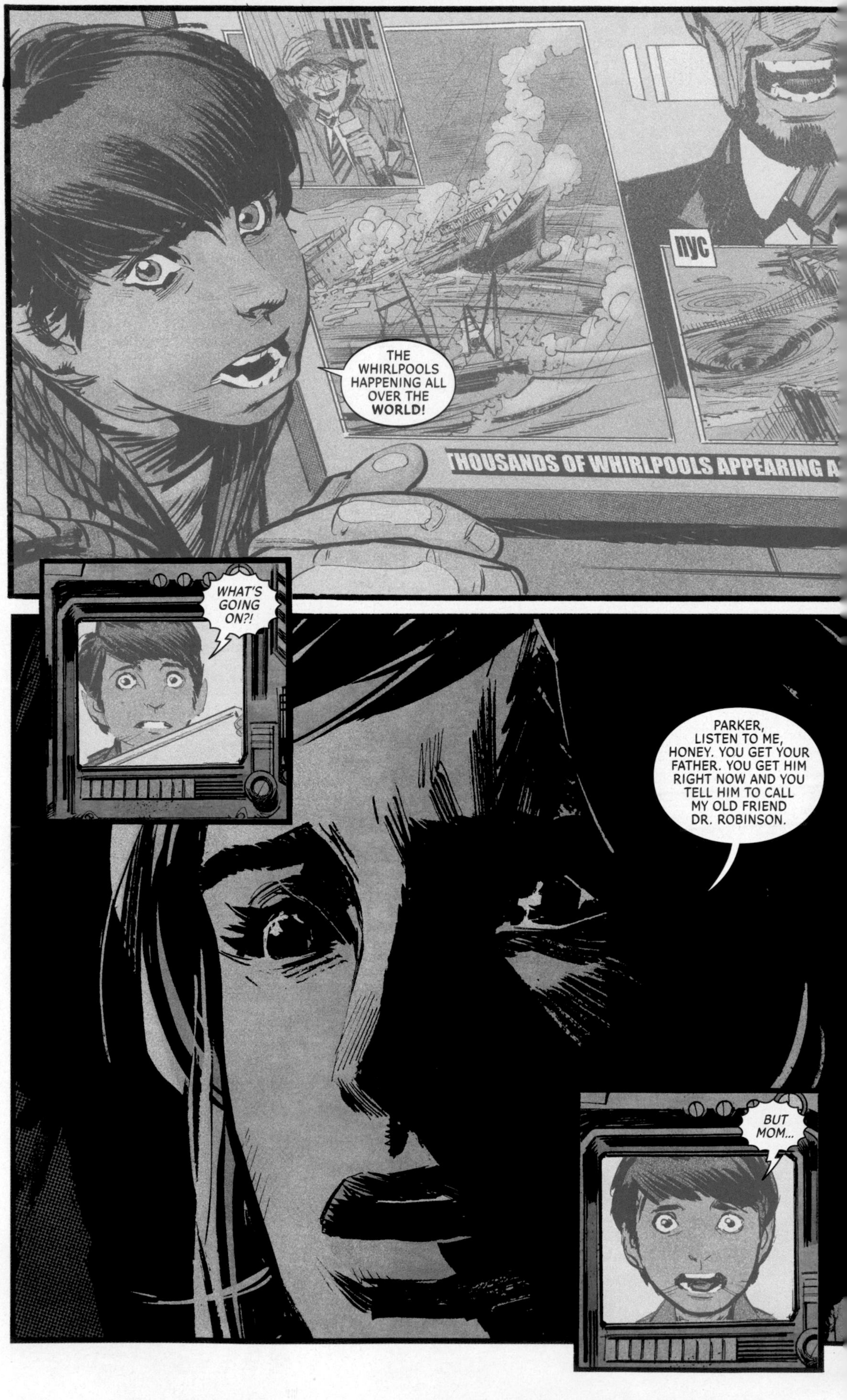
LIVE
NYC
THOUSANDS OF WHIRLPOOLS APPEARING A
THE WHIRLPOOLS HAPPENING ALL OVER THE WORLD!
WHAT'S GOING ON?!
PARKER, LISTEN TO ME, HONEY. YOU GET YOUR FATHER. YOU GET HIM RIGHT NOW AND YOU TELL HIM TO CALL MY OLD FRIEND DR. ROBINSON.
BUT MOM...

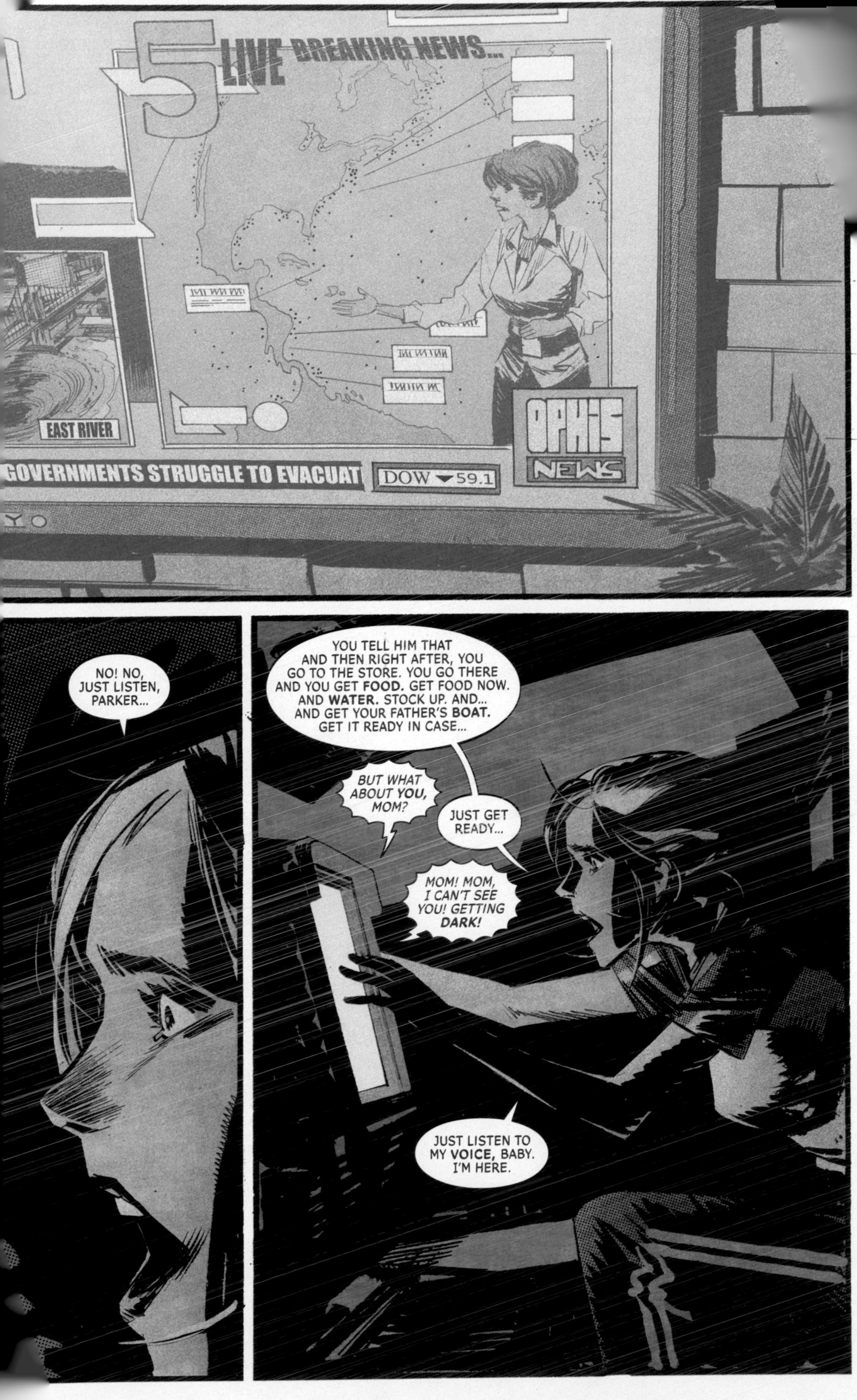
5 LIVE BREAKING NEWS...
EAST RIVER
GOVERNMENTS STRUGGLE TO EVACUAT
DOW 59.1
OPHIS NEWS
NO! NO, JUST LISTEN, PARKER...
YOU TELL HIM THAT AND THEN RIGHT AFTER, YOU GO TO THE STORE. YOU GO THERE AND YOU GET FOOD. GET FOOD NOW. AND WATER. STOCK UP. AND... AND GET YOUR FATHER'S BOAT. GET IT READY IN CASE...
BUT WHAT ABOUT YOU, MOM?
JUST GET READY...
MOM! MOM, I CAN'T SEE YOU! GETTING DARK!
JUST LISTEN TO MY VOICE, BABY. I'M HERE.

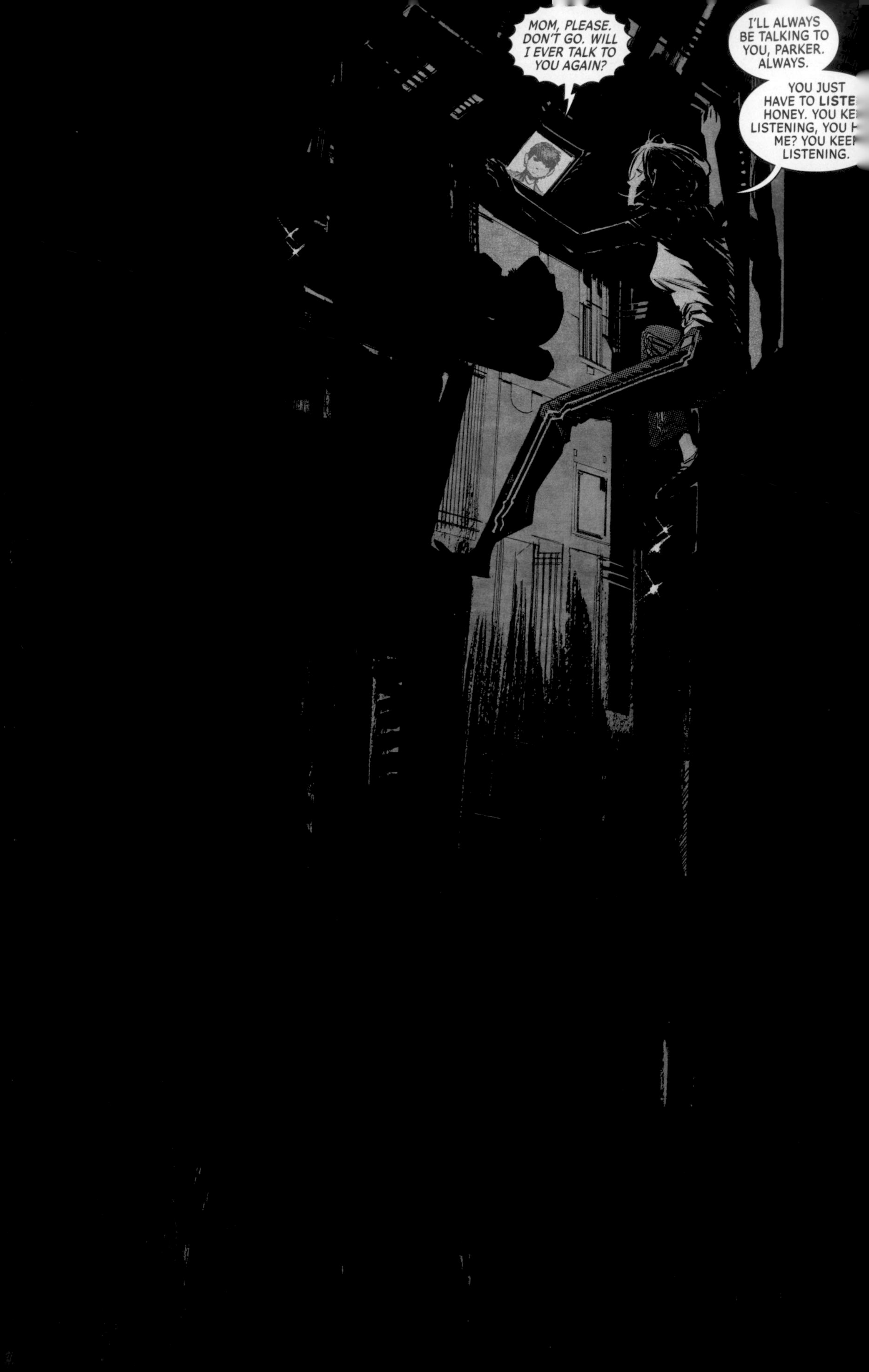

MOM, PLEASE. DON'T GO. WILL I EVER TALK TO YOU AGAIN?
I'LL ALWAYS BE TALKING TO YOU, PARKER. ALWAYS.
YOU JUST HAVE TO LISTE

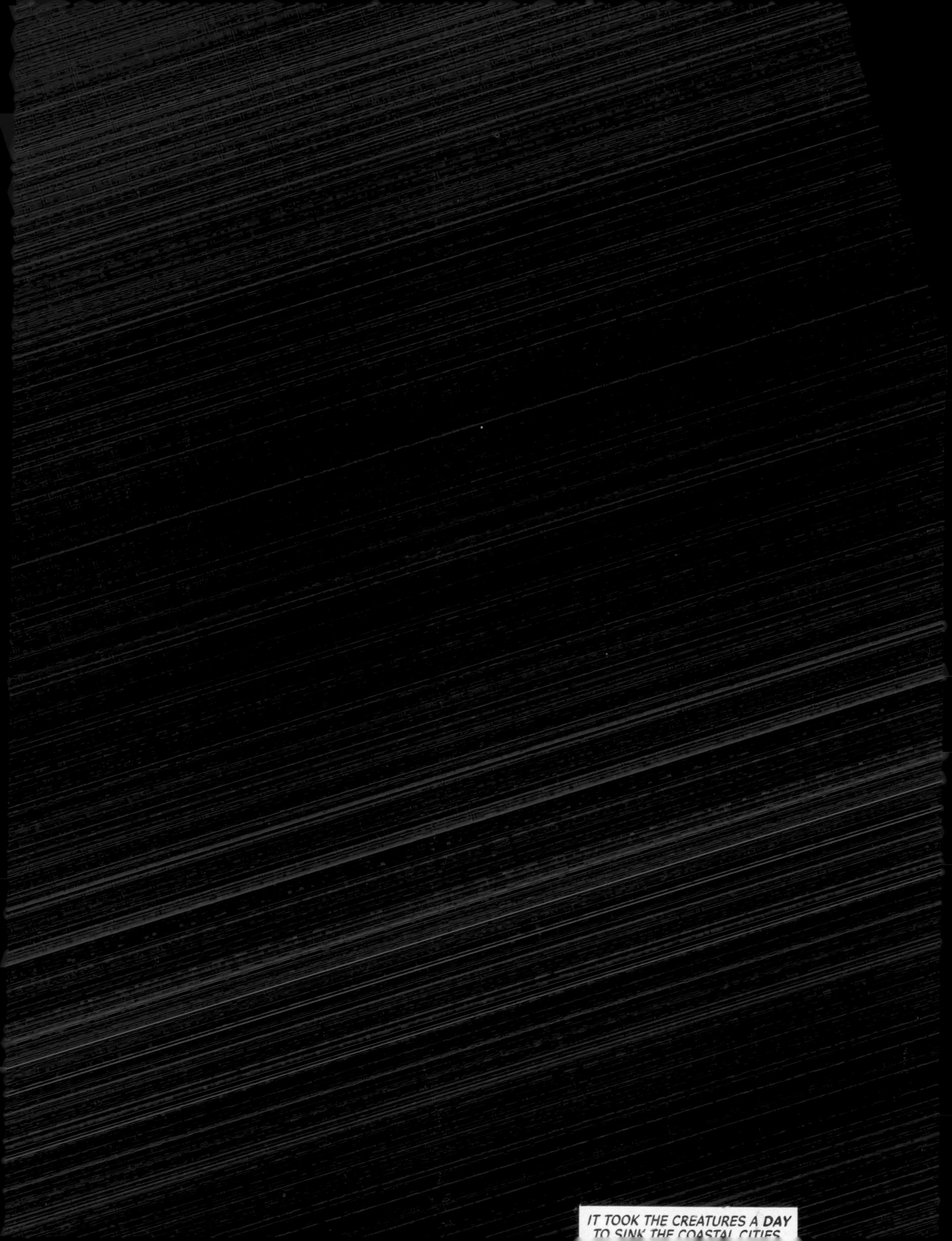
IT TOOK THE CREATURES A **DAY**
TO SINK THE COASTAL CITIES

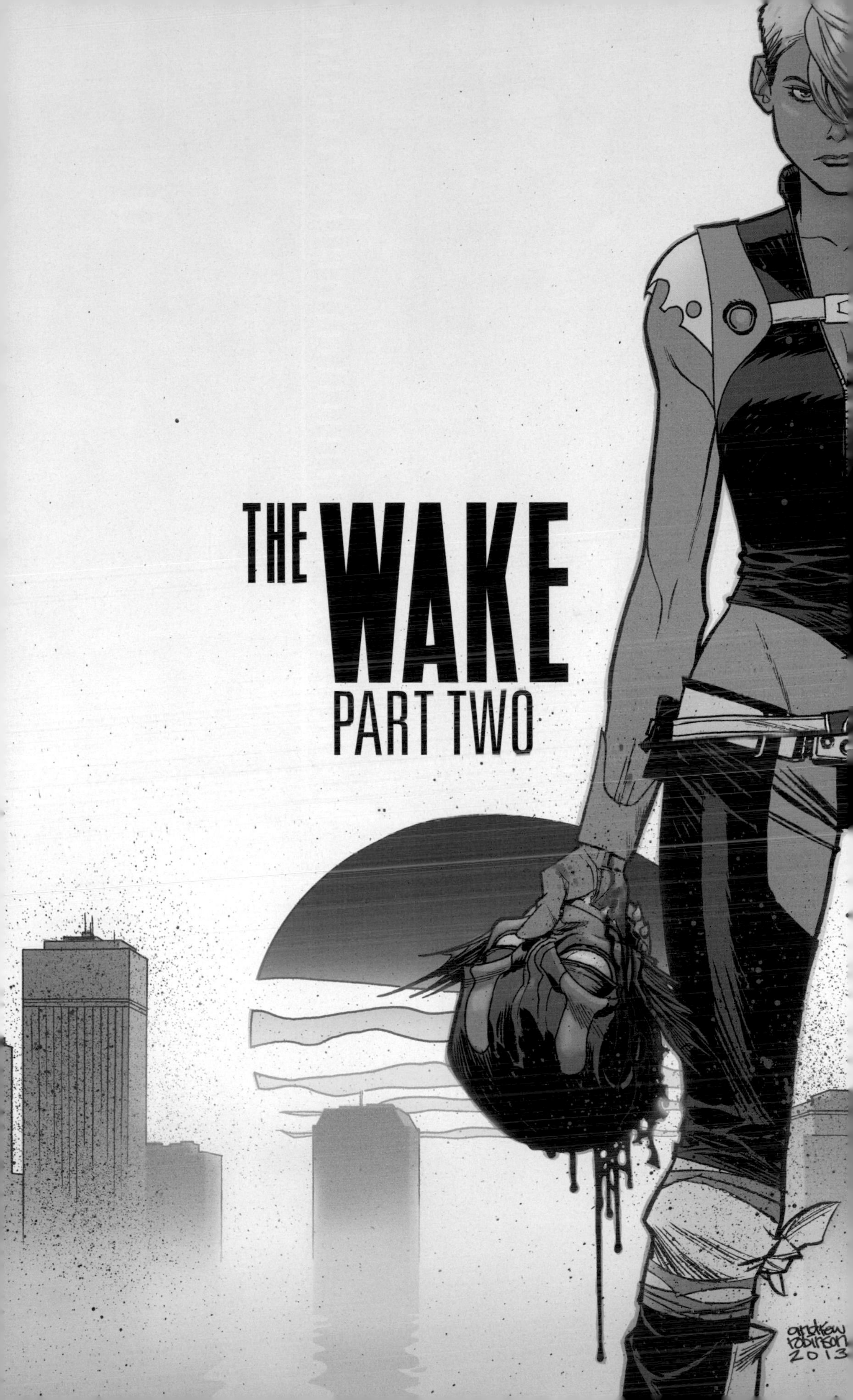
THE WAKE
PART TWO
andrew robinson 2013

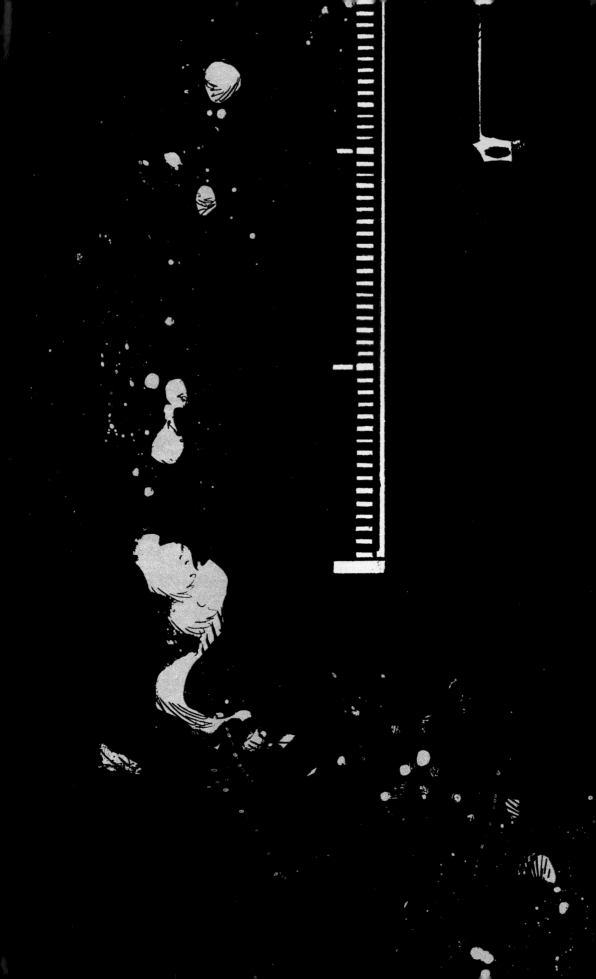

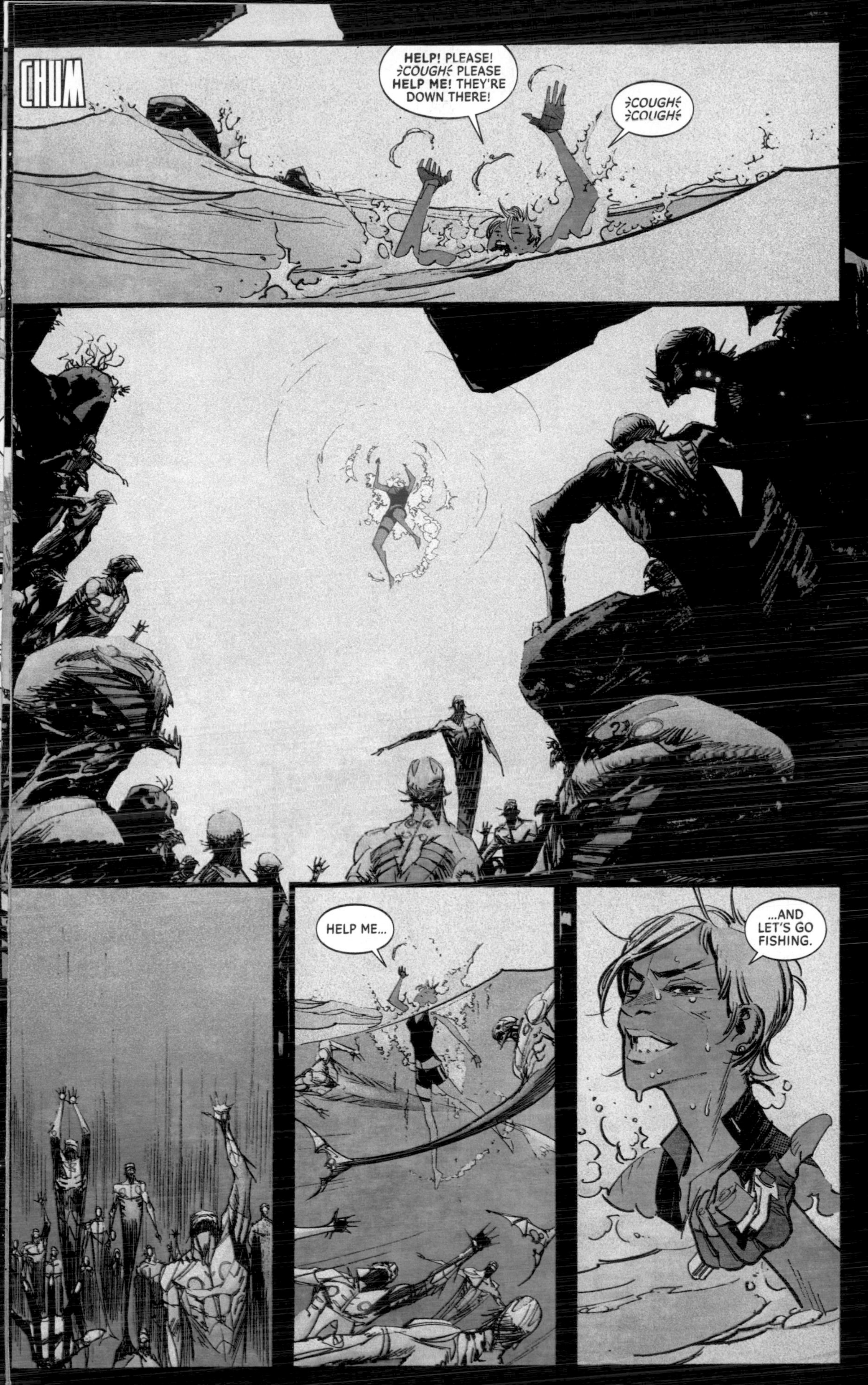
CHUM
HELP! PLEASE! *COUGH* PLEASE HELP ME! THEY'RE DOWN THERE!
COUGH *COUGH*
HELP ME...
...AND LET'S GO FISHING.

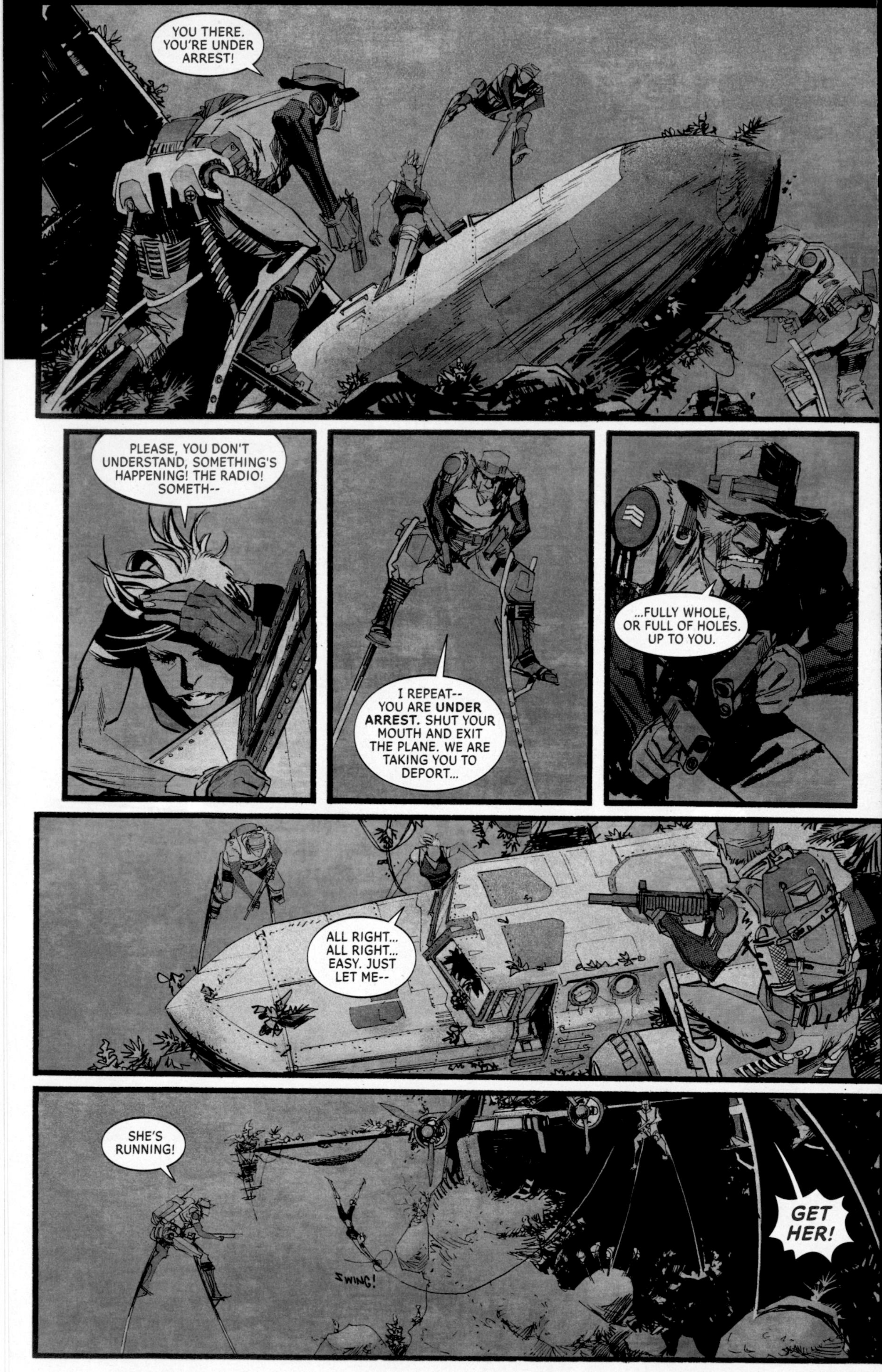
YOU THERE. YOU'RE UNDER ARREST!
PLEASE, YOU DON'T UNDERSTAND, SOMETHING'S HAPPENING! THE RADIO! SOMETH--
I REPEAT-- YOU ARE **UNDER ARREST.** SHUT YOUR MOUTH AND EXIT THE PLANE. WE ARE TAKING YOU TO DEPORT...
...FULLY WHOLE, OR FULL OF HOLES. UP TO YOU.
ALL RIGHT... ALL RIGHT... EASY. JUST LET ME--
SHE'S RUNNING!
SWING!
GET HER!

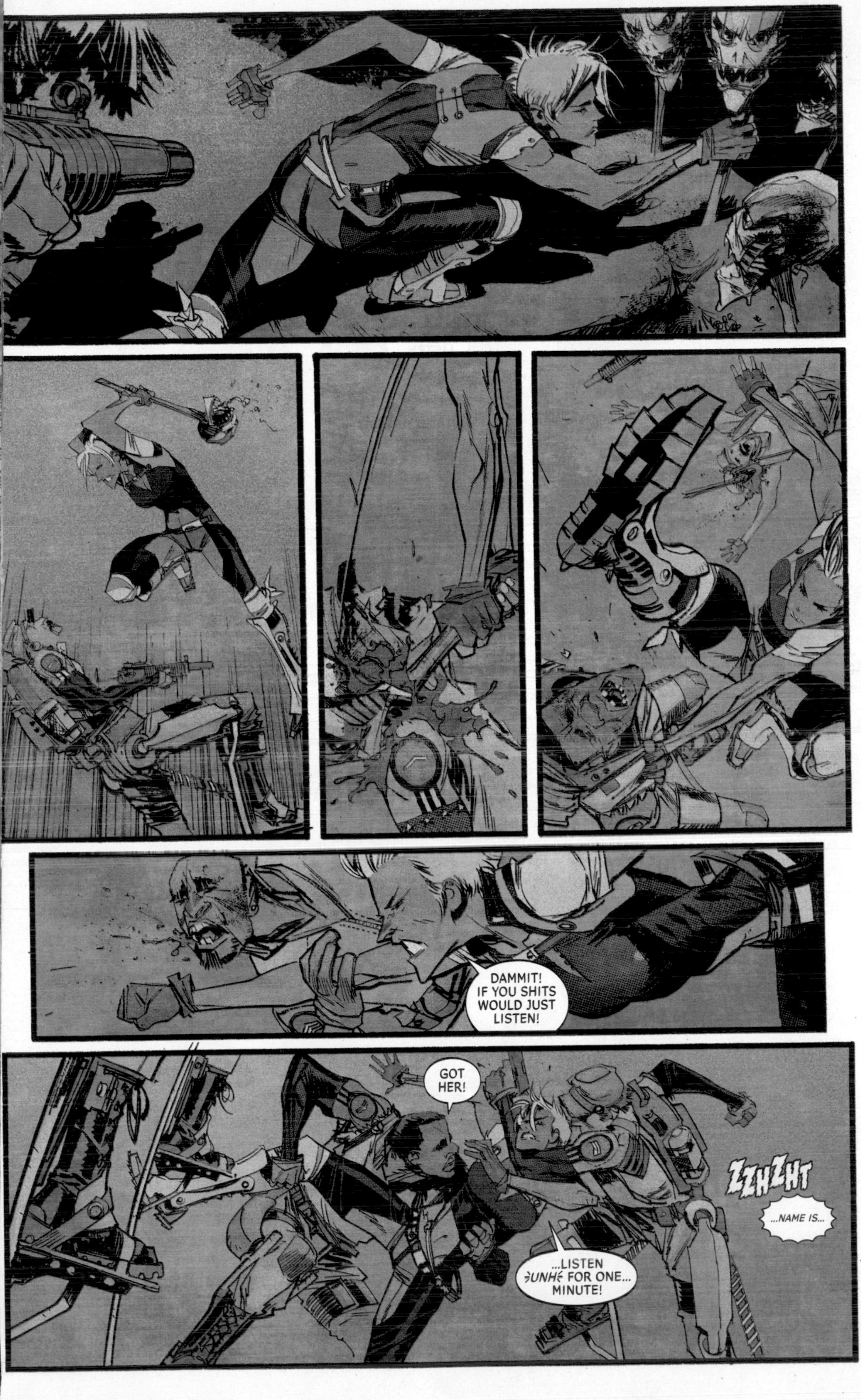
DAMMIT! IF YOU SHITS WOULD JUST LISTEN!
GOT HER!
ZZHZHT
...NAME IS...
...LISTEN UNHF FOR ONE... MINUTE!

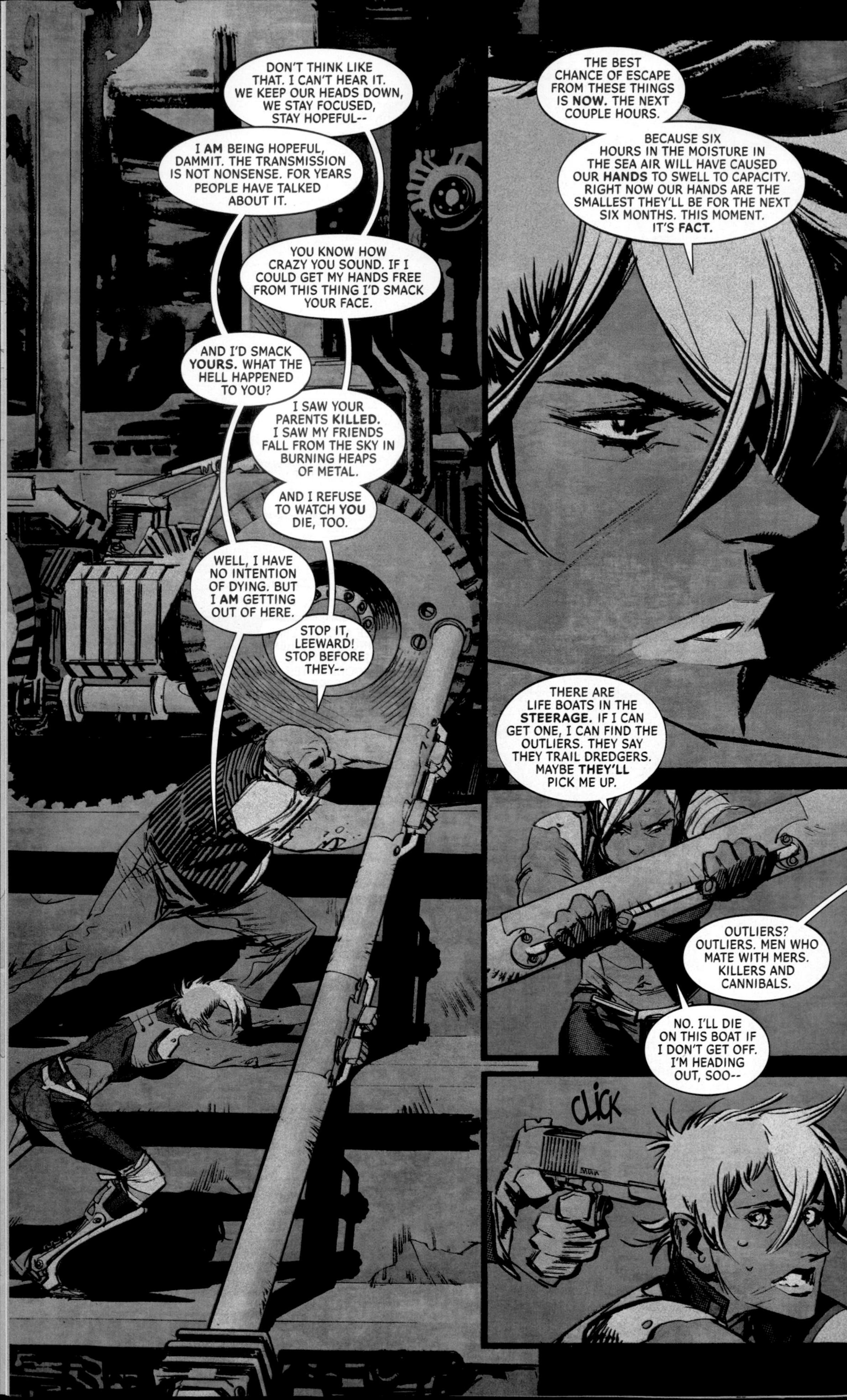
DON'T THINK LIKE THAT. I CAN'T HEAR IT. WE KEEP OUR HEADS DOWN, WE STAY FOCUSED, STAY HOPEFUL--
I AM BEING HOPEFUL, DAMMIT. THE TRANSMISSION IS NOT NONSENSE. FOR YEARS PEOPLE HAVE TALKED ABOUT IT.
YOU KNOW HOW CRAZY YOU SOUND. IF I COULD GET MY HANDS FREE FROM THIS THING I'D SMACK YOUR FACE.
AND I'D SMACK YOURS. WHAT THE HELL HAPPENED TO YOU?
I SAW YOUR PARENTS KILLED. I SAW MY FRIENDS FALL FROM THE SKY IN BURNING HEAPS OF METAL.
AND I REFUSE TO WATCH YOU DIE, TOO.
WELL, I HAVE NO INTENTION OF DYING. BUT I AM GETTING OUT OF HERE.
STOP IT, LEEWARD! STOP BEFORE THEY--
THE BEST CHANCE OF ESCAPE FROM THESE THINGS IS NOW. THE NEXT COUPLE HOURS.
BECAUSE SIX HOURS IN THE MOISTURE IN THE SEA AIR WILL HAVE CAUSED OUR HANDS TO SWELL TO CAPACITY. RIGHT NOW OUR HANDS ARE THE SMALLEST THEY'LL BE FOR THE NEXT SIX MONTHS. THIS MOMENT. IT'S FACT.
THERE ARE LIFE BOATS IN THE STEERAGE. IF I CAN GET ONE, I CAN FIND THE OUTLIERS. THEY SAY THEY TRAIL DREDGERS. MAYBE THEY'LL PICK ME UP.
OUTLIERS? OUTLIERS. MEN WHO MATE WITH MERS. KILLERS AND CANNIBALS.
NO. I'LL DIE ON THIS BOAT IF I DON'T GET OFF. I'M HEADING OUT, SOO--
CLICK

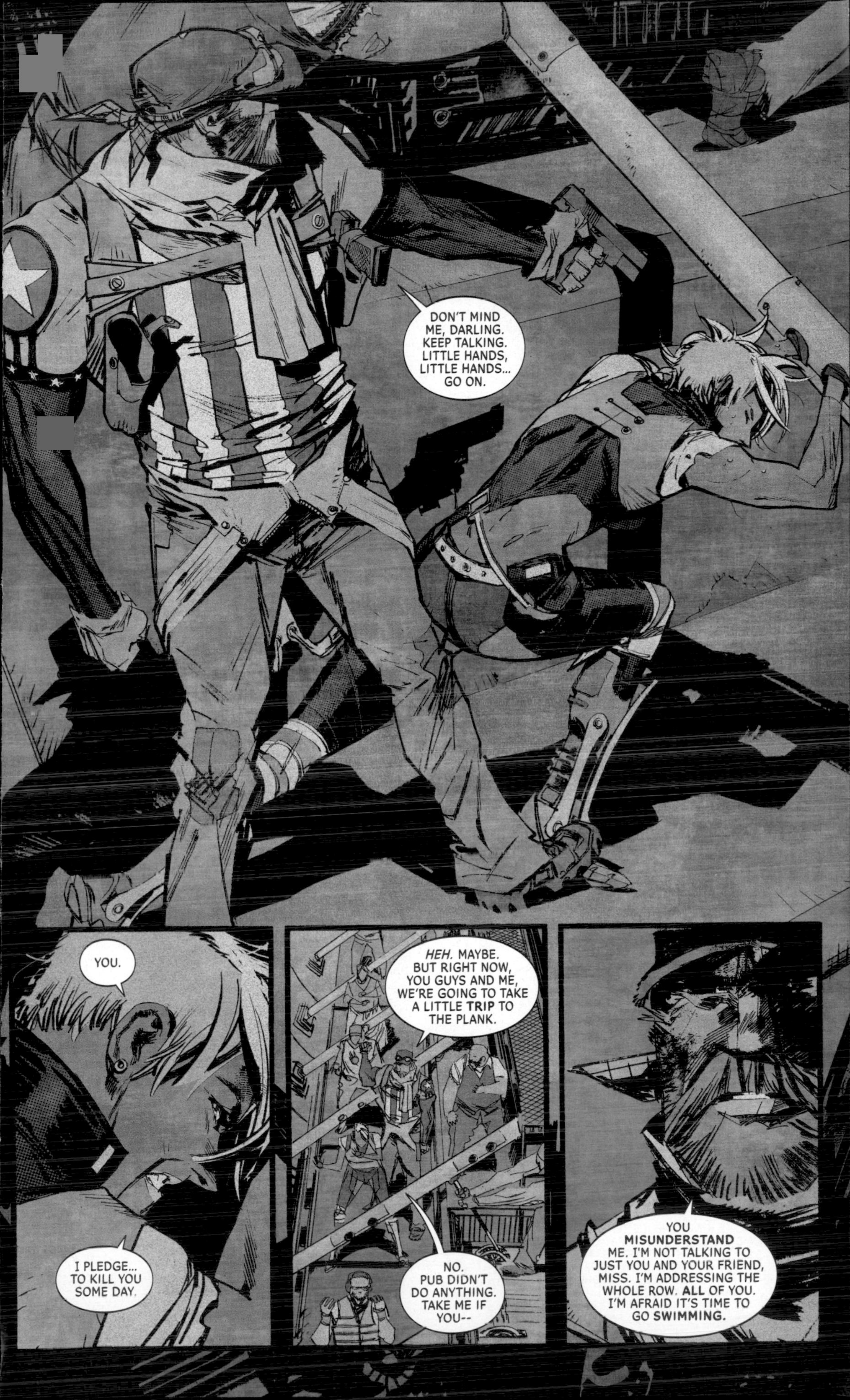
DON'T MIND ME, DARLING. KEEP TALKING. LITTLE HANDS, LITTLE HANDS... GO ON.
YOU.
I PLEDGE... TO KILL YOU SOME DAY.
HEH. MAYBE. BUT RIGHT NOW, YOU GUYS AND ME, WE'RE GOING TO TAKE A LITTLE TRIP TO THE PLANK.
NO. PUB DIDN'T DO ANYTHING. TAKE ME IF YOU--
YOU MISUNDERSTAND ME. I'M NOT TALKING TO JUST YOU AND YOUR FRIEND, MISS. I'M ADDRESSING THE WHOLE ROW. ALL OF YOU. I'M AFRAID IT'S TIME TO GO SWIMMING.

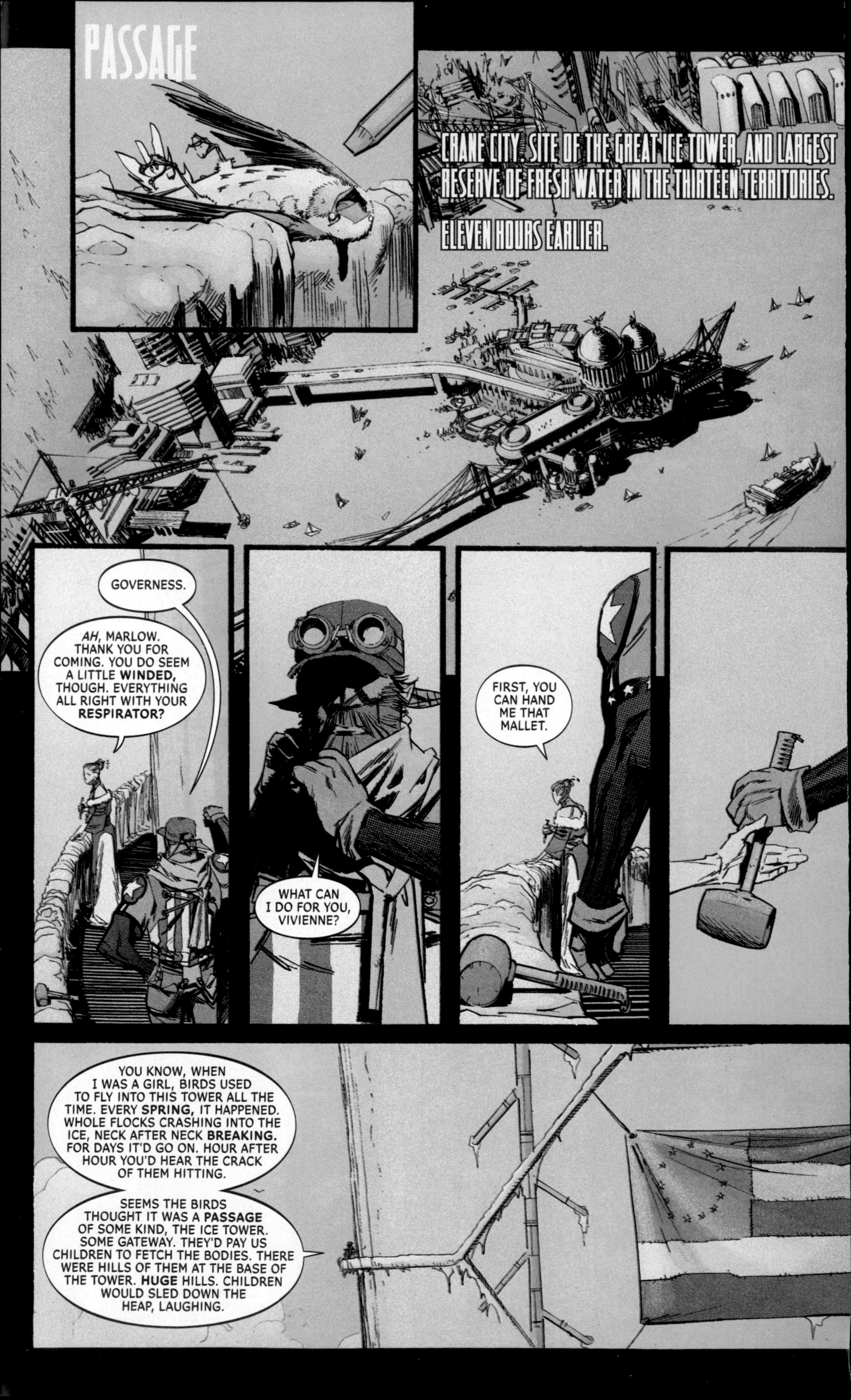
PASSAGE
CRANE CITY. SITE OF THE GREAT ICE TOWER, AND LARGEST RESERVE OF FRESH WATER IN THE THIRTEEN TERRITORIES.
ELEVEN HOURS EARLIER.
GOVERNESS.
AH, MARLOW. THANK YOU FOR COMING. YOU DO SEEM A LITTLE WINDED, THOUGH. EVERYTHING ALL RIGHT WITH YOUR RESPIRATOR?
WHAT CAN I DO FOR YOU, VIVIENNE?
FIRST, YOU CAN HAND ME THAT MALLET.
YOU KNOW, WHEN I WAS A GIRL, BIRDS USED TO FLY INTO THIS TOWER ALL THE TIME. EVERY SPRING, IT HAPPENED. WHOLE FLOCKS CRASHING INTO THE ICE, NECK AFTER NECK BREAKING. FOR DAYS IT'D GO ON. HOUR AFTER HOUR YOU'D HEAR THE CRACK OF THEM HITTING.
SEEMS THE BIRDS THOUGHT IT WAS A PASSAGE OF SOME KIND, THE ICE TOWER. SOME GATEWAY. THEY'D PAY US CHILDREN TO FETCH THE BODIES. THERE WERE HILLS OF THEM AT THE BASE OF THE TOWER. HUGE HILLS. CHILDREN WOULD SLED DOWN THE HEAP, LAUGHING.

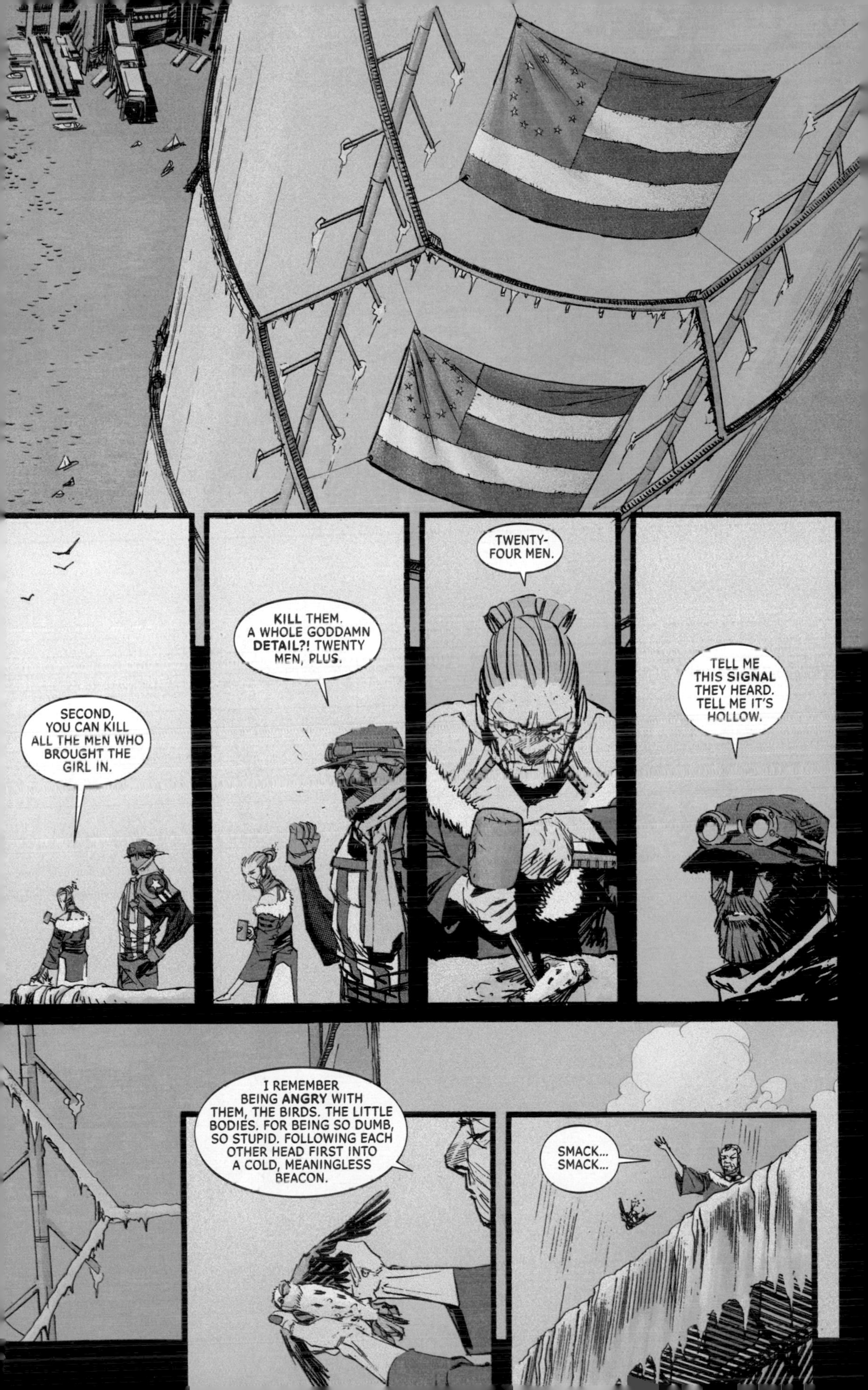
SECOND, YOU CAN KILL ALL THE MEN WHO BROUGHT THE GIRL IN.
KILL THEM. A WHOLE GODDAMN DETAIL?! TWENTY MEN, PLUS.
TWENTY-FOUR MEN.
TELL ME THIS SIGNAL THEY HEARD. TELL ME IT'S HOLLOW.
I REMEMBER BEING ANGRY WITH THEM, THE BIRDS. THE LITTLE BODIES. FOR BEING SO DUMB, SO STUPID. FOLLOWING EACH OTHER HEAD FIRST INTO A COLD, MEANINGLESS BEACON.
SMACK... SMACK...

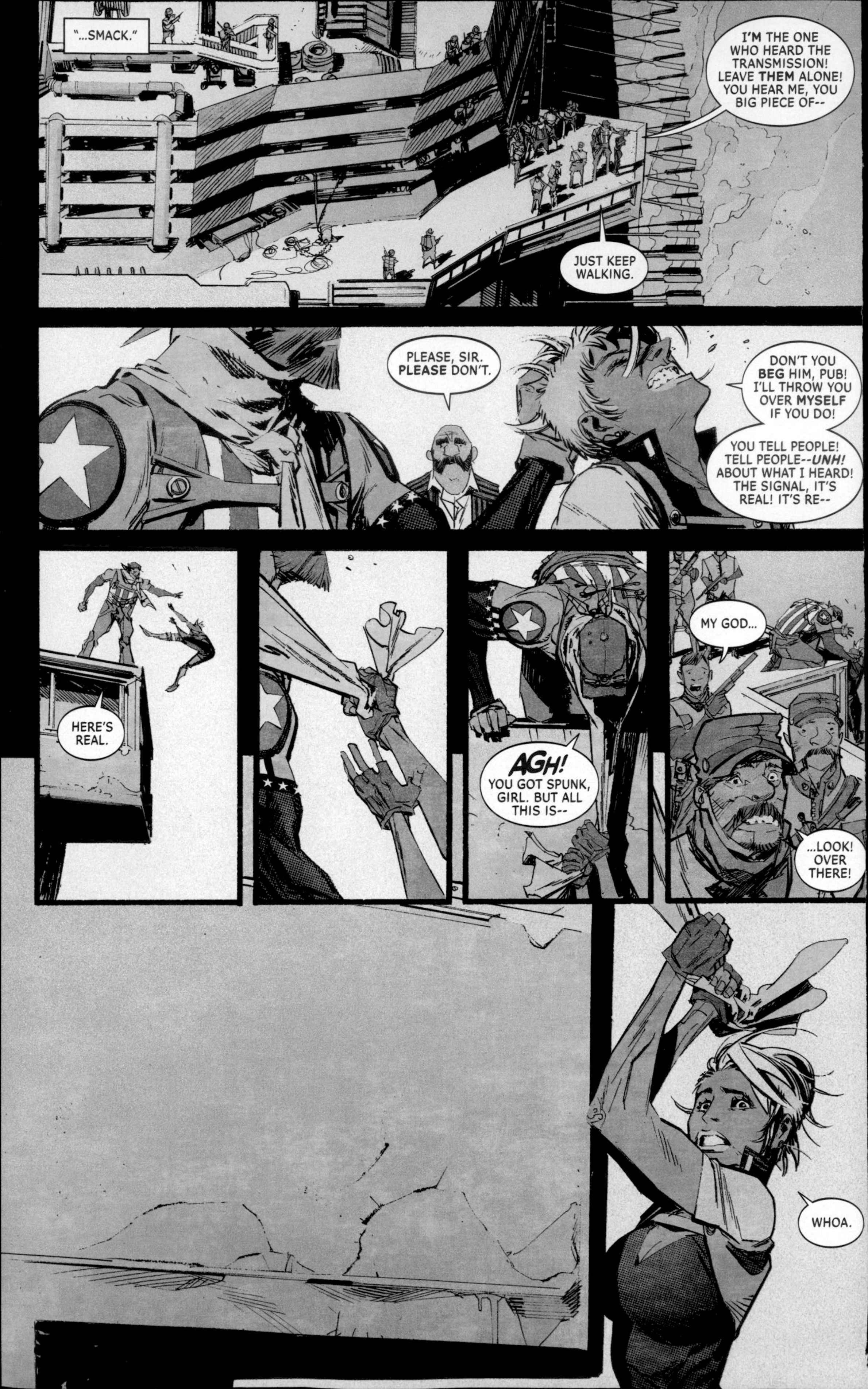
"...SMACK."
I'M THE ONE WHO HEARD THE TRANSMISSION! LEAVE THEM ALONE! YOU HEAR ME, YOU BIG PIECE OF--
JUST KEEP WALKING.
PLEASE, SIR. PLEASE DON'T.
DON'T YOU BEG HIM, PUB! I'LL THROW YOU OVER MYSELF IF YOU DO!
YOU TELL PEOPLE! TELL PEOPLE--UNH! ABOUT WHAT I HEARD! THE SIGNAL, IT'S REAL! IT'S RE--
HERE'S REAL.
AGH! YOU GOT SPUNK, GIRL. BUT ALL THIS IS--
MY GOD...
...LOOK! OVER THERE!
WHOA.

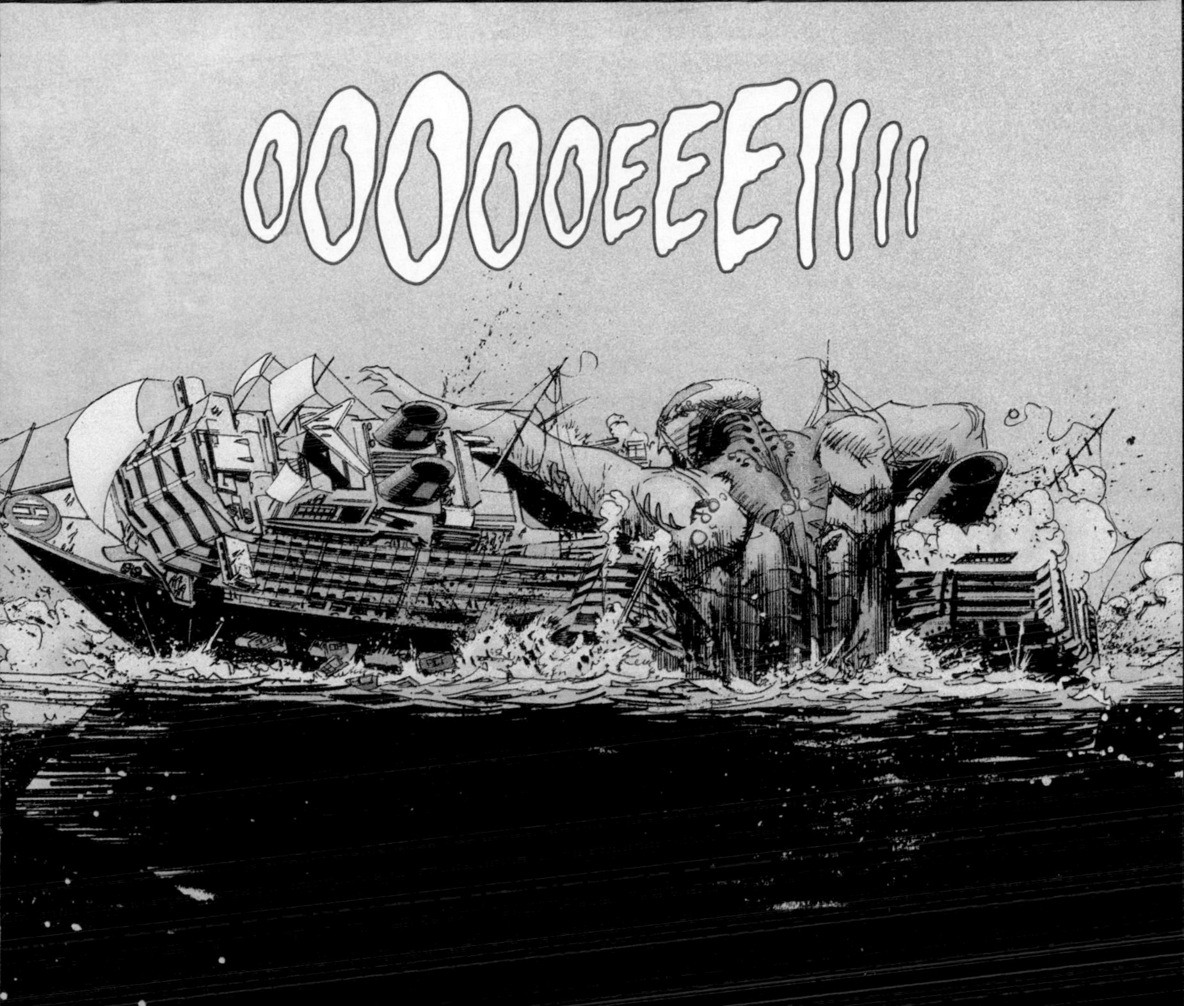
OOOOOEEEIIII

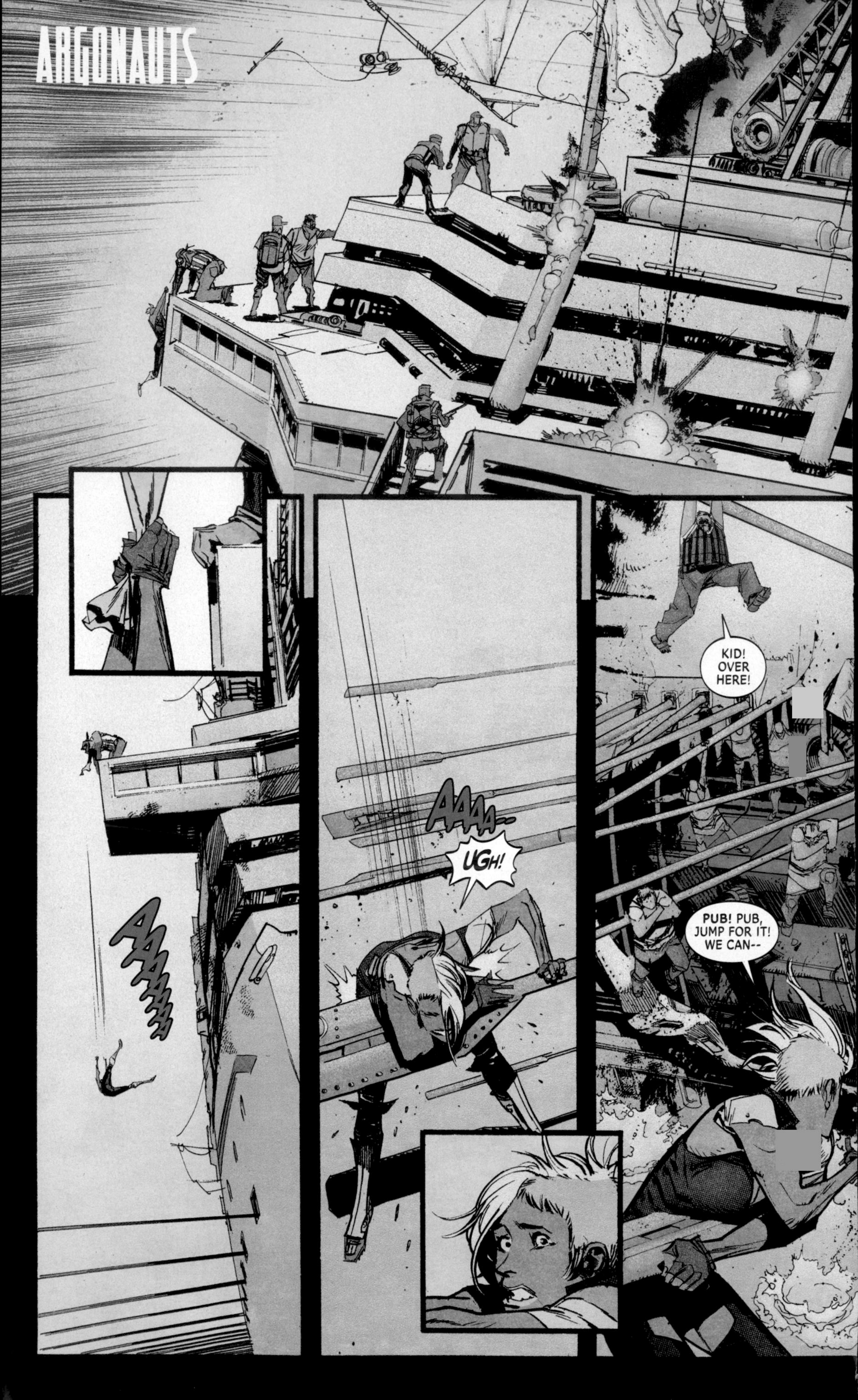
ARGONAUTS
AAAAAAAA
AAAA--
UGH!
KID! OVER HERE!
PUB! PUB, JUMP FOR IT! WE CAN--

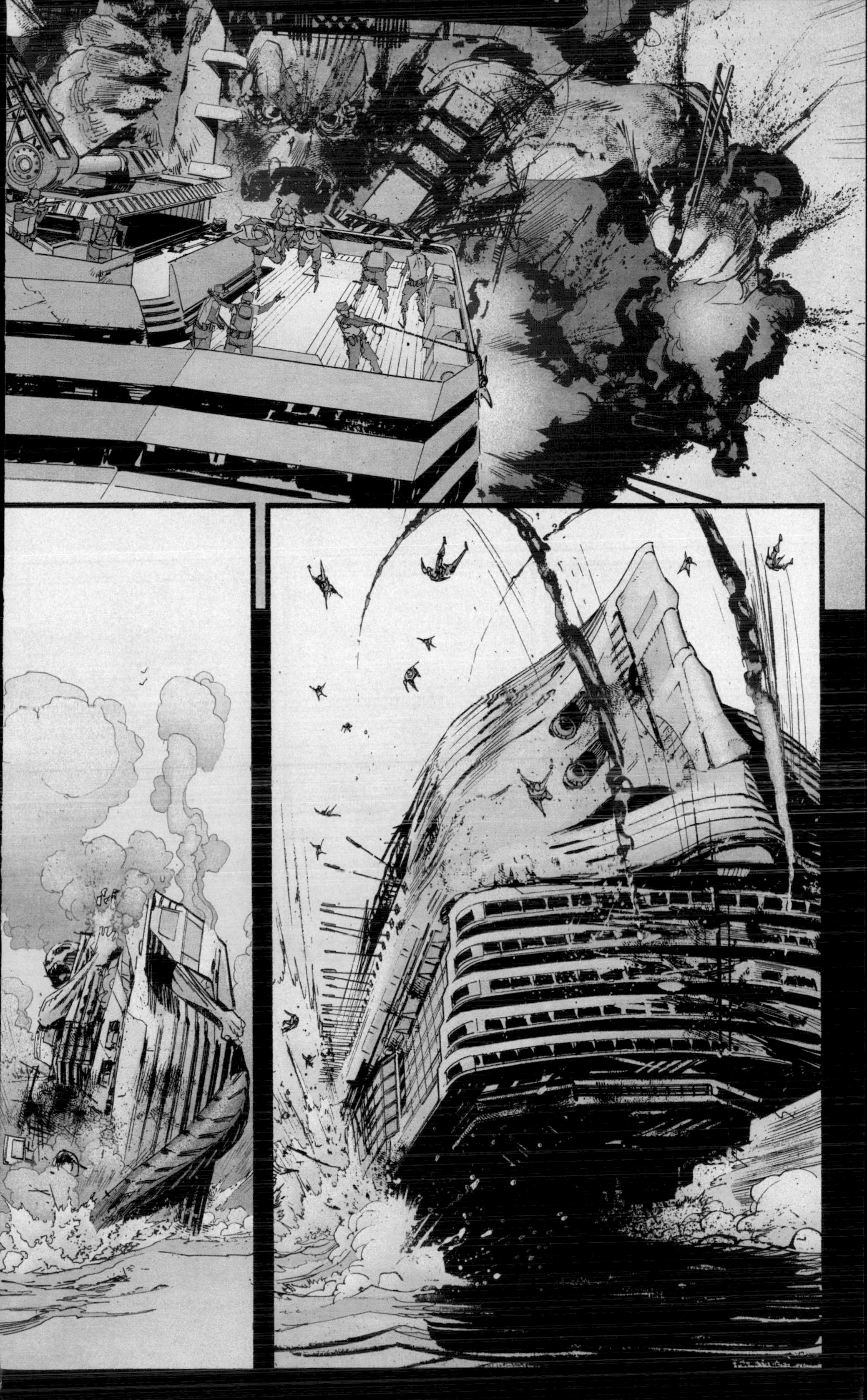

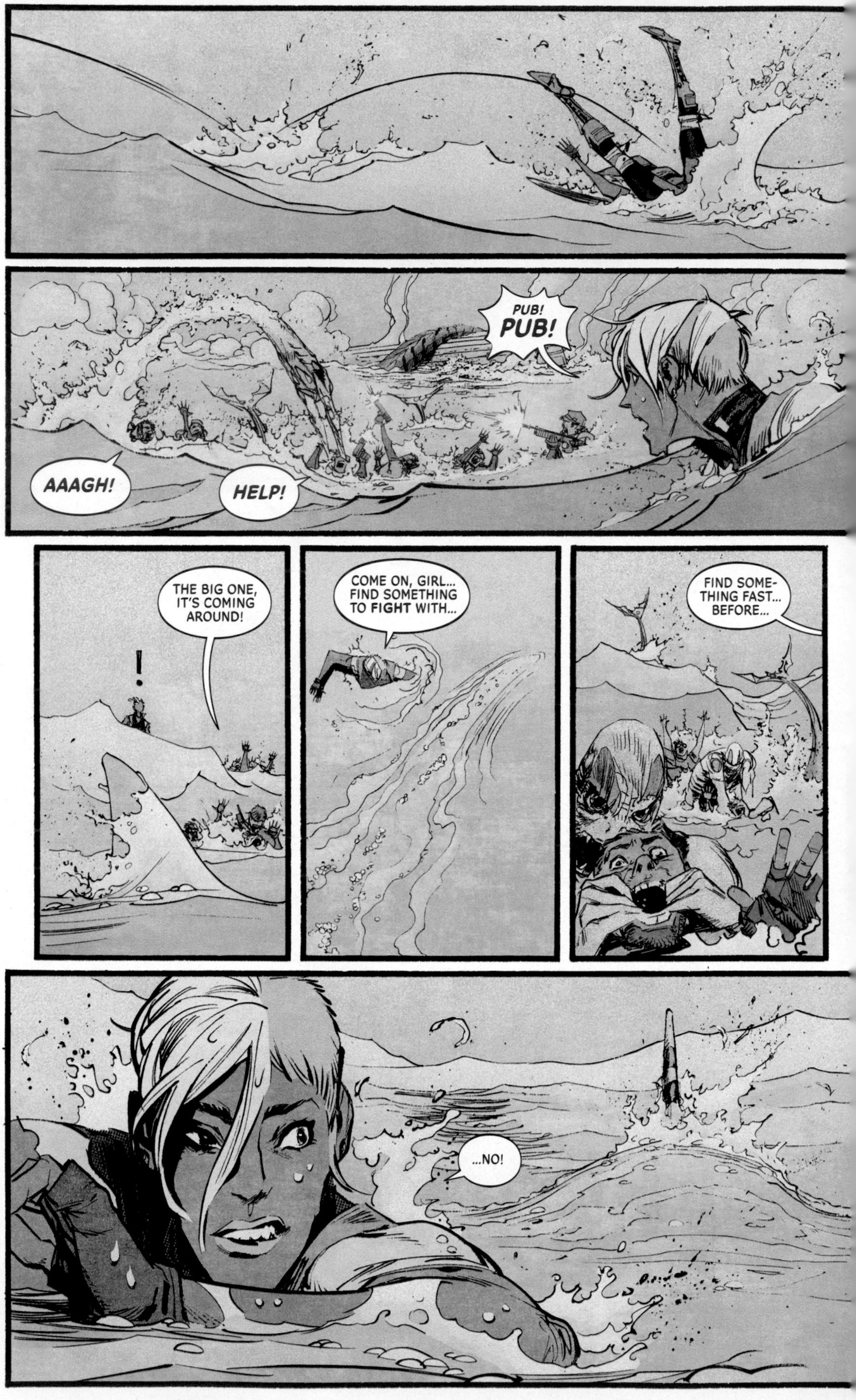
PUB! PUB!
AAAGH!
HELP!
THE BIG ONE, IT'S COMING AROUND!
!
COME ON, GIRL... FIND SOMETHING TO FIGHT WITH...
FIND SOMETHING FAST... BEFORE...
...NO!

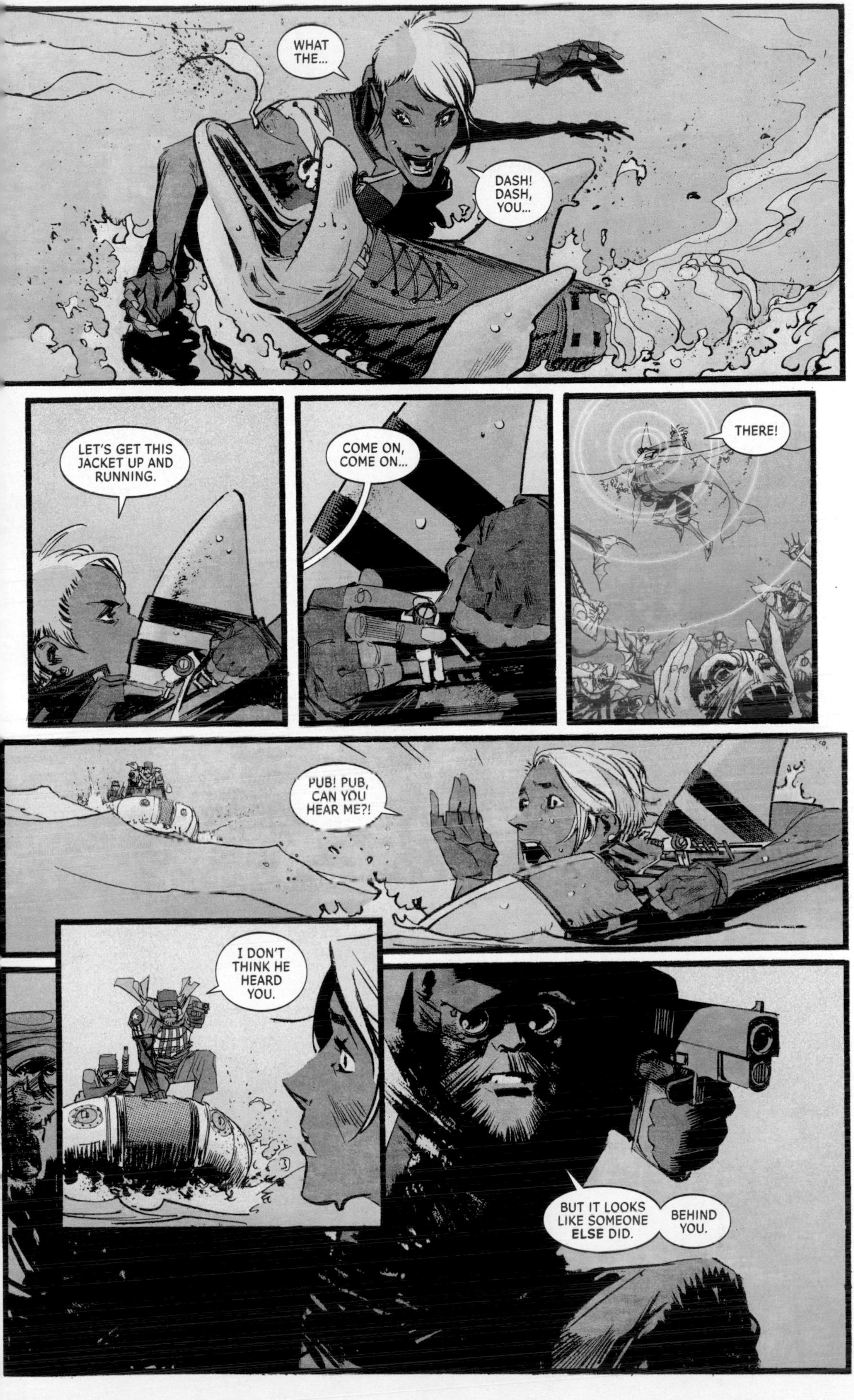
WHAT THE...
DASH! DASH, YOU...
LET'S GET THIS JACKET UP AND RUNNING.
COME ON, COME ON...
THERE!
PUB! PUB, CAN YOU HEAR ME?!
I DON'T THINK HE HEARD YOU.
BUT IT LOOKS LIKE SOMEONE **ELSE** DID.
BEHIND YOU.

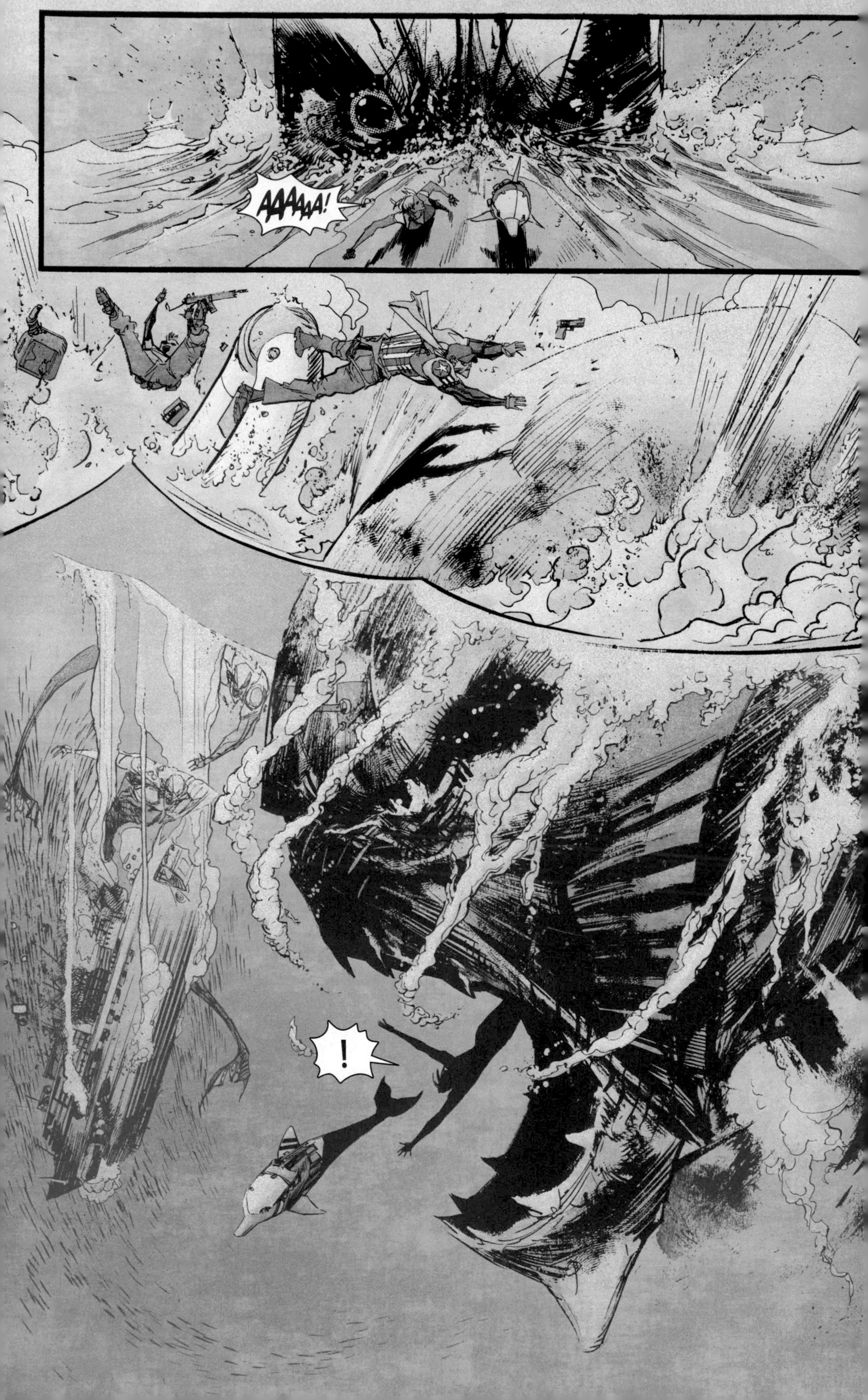
AAAAAA!
!

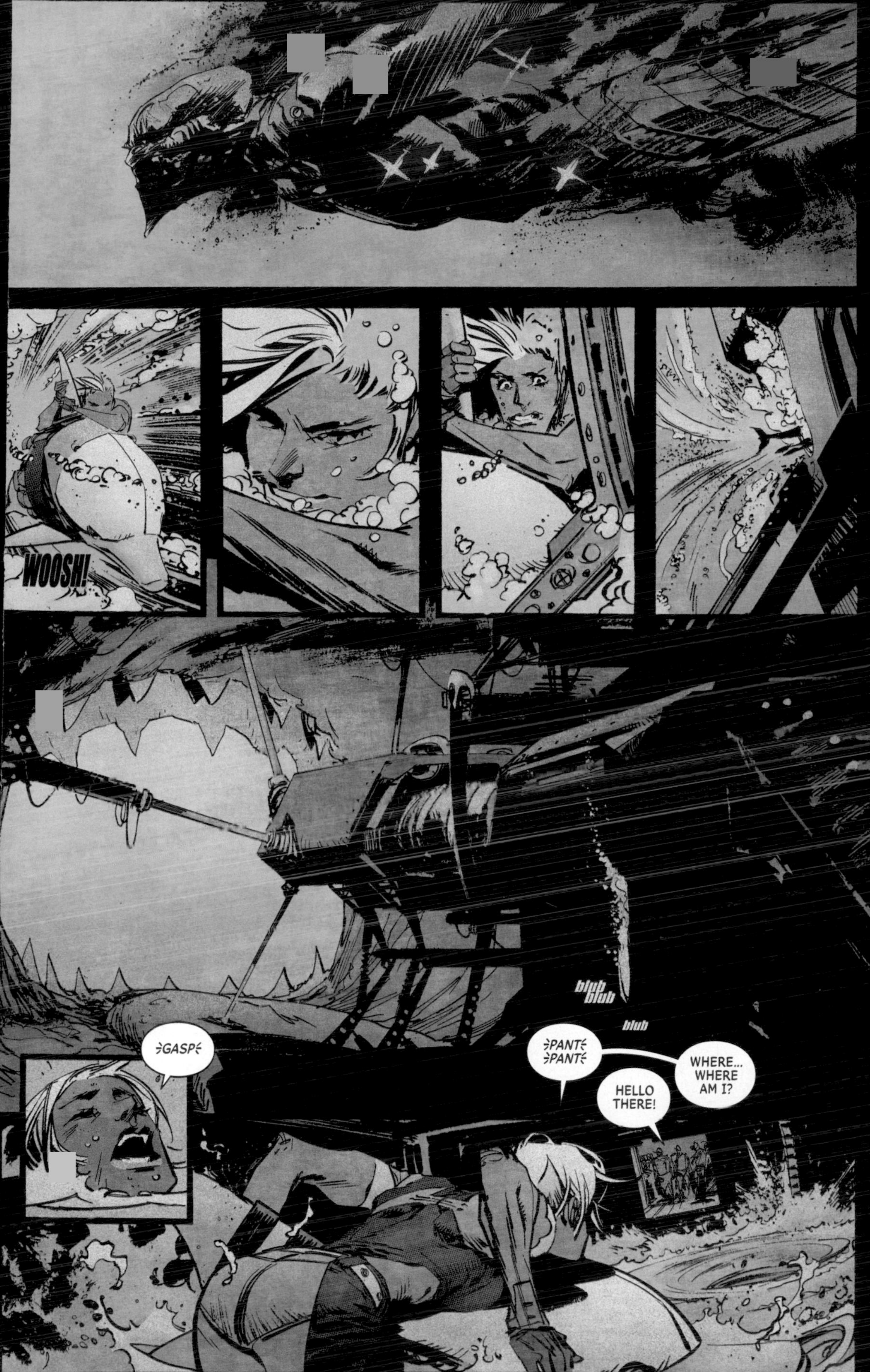
WOOSH!
blub blub
blub
GASP
PANT PANT
WHERE... WHERE AM I?
HELLO THERE!

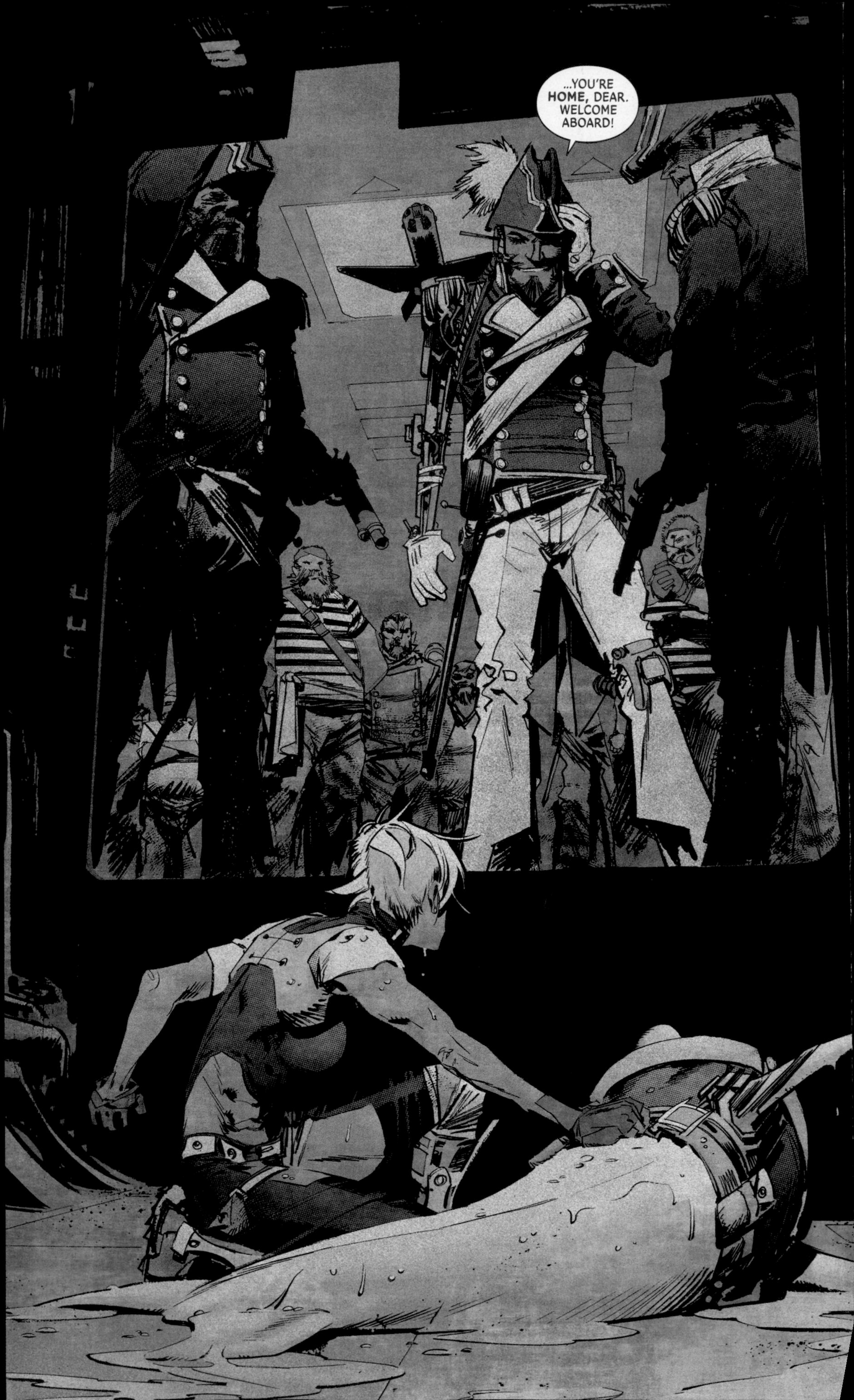
...YOU'RE HOME, DEAR. WELCOME ABOARD!

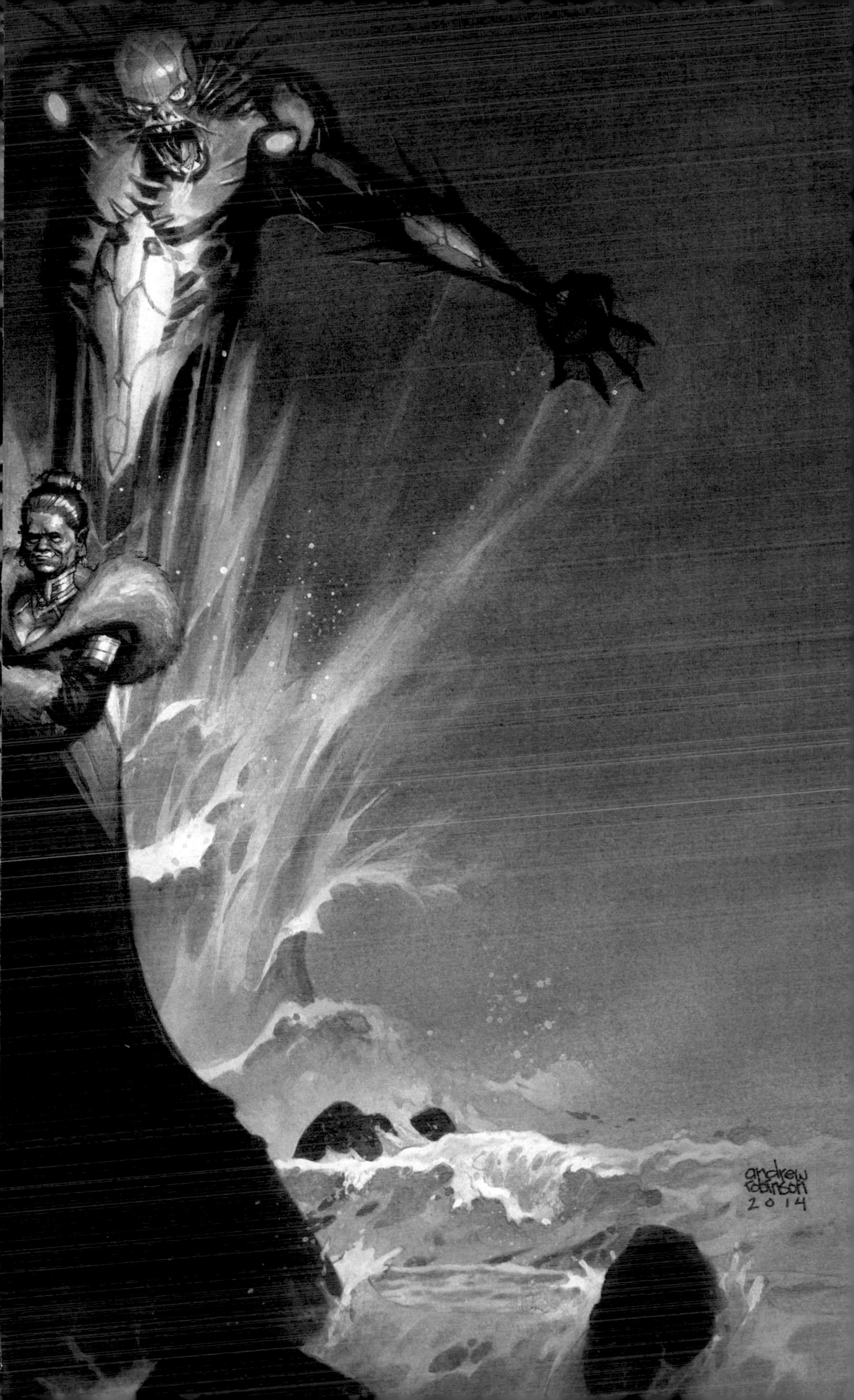
andrew robinson 2014

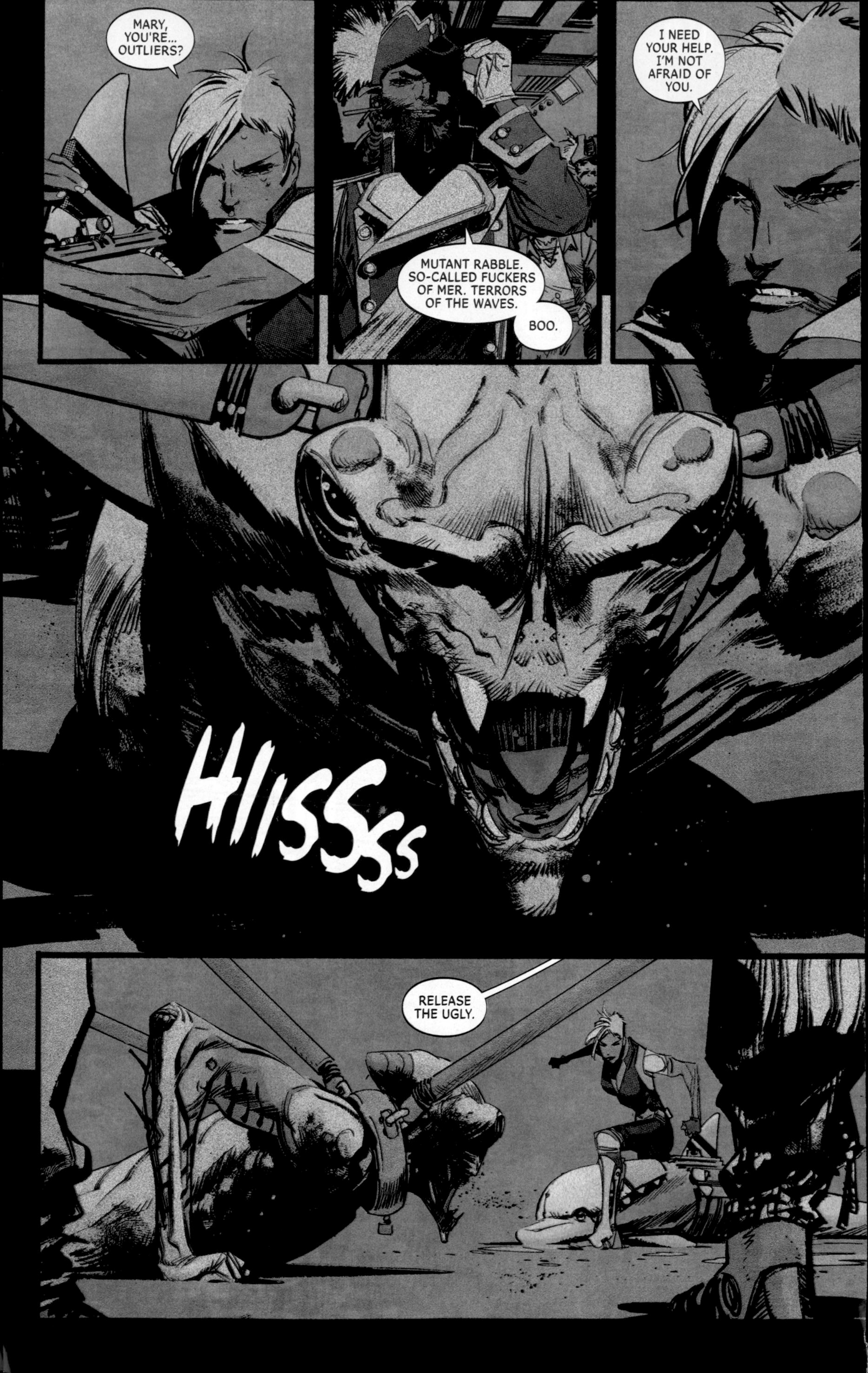
MARY, YOU'RE... OUTLIERS?
MUTANT RABBLE. SO-CALLED FUCKERS OF MER. TERRORS OF THE WAVES.
BOO.
I NEED YOUR HELP. I'M NOT AFRAID OF YOU.
HISSSss
RELEASE THE UGLY.

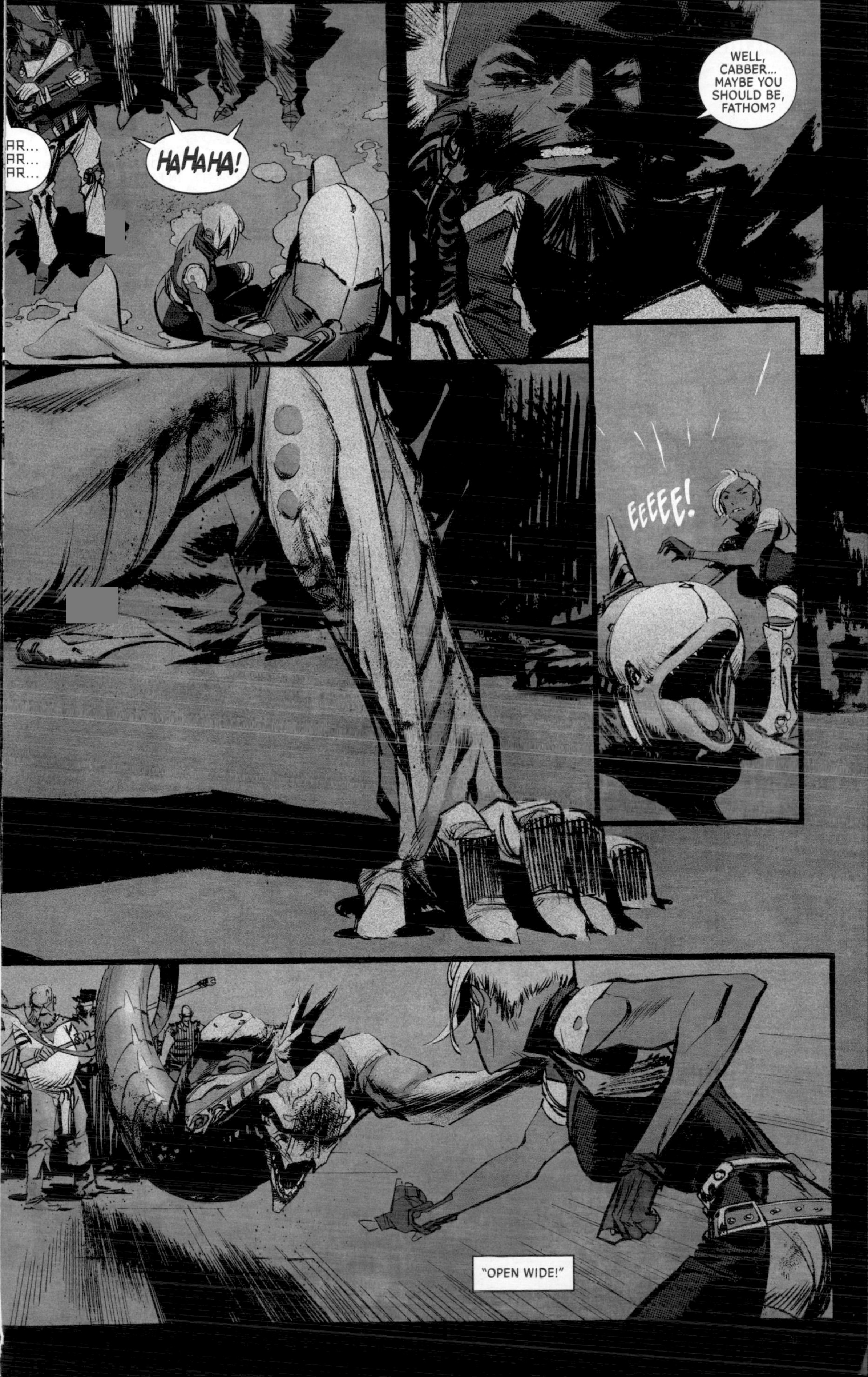
AR...
AR...
AR...
HAHAHA!
WELL, CABBER... MAYBE YOU SHOULD BE, FATHOM?
EEEEE!
"OPEN WIDE!"

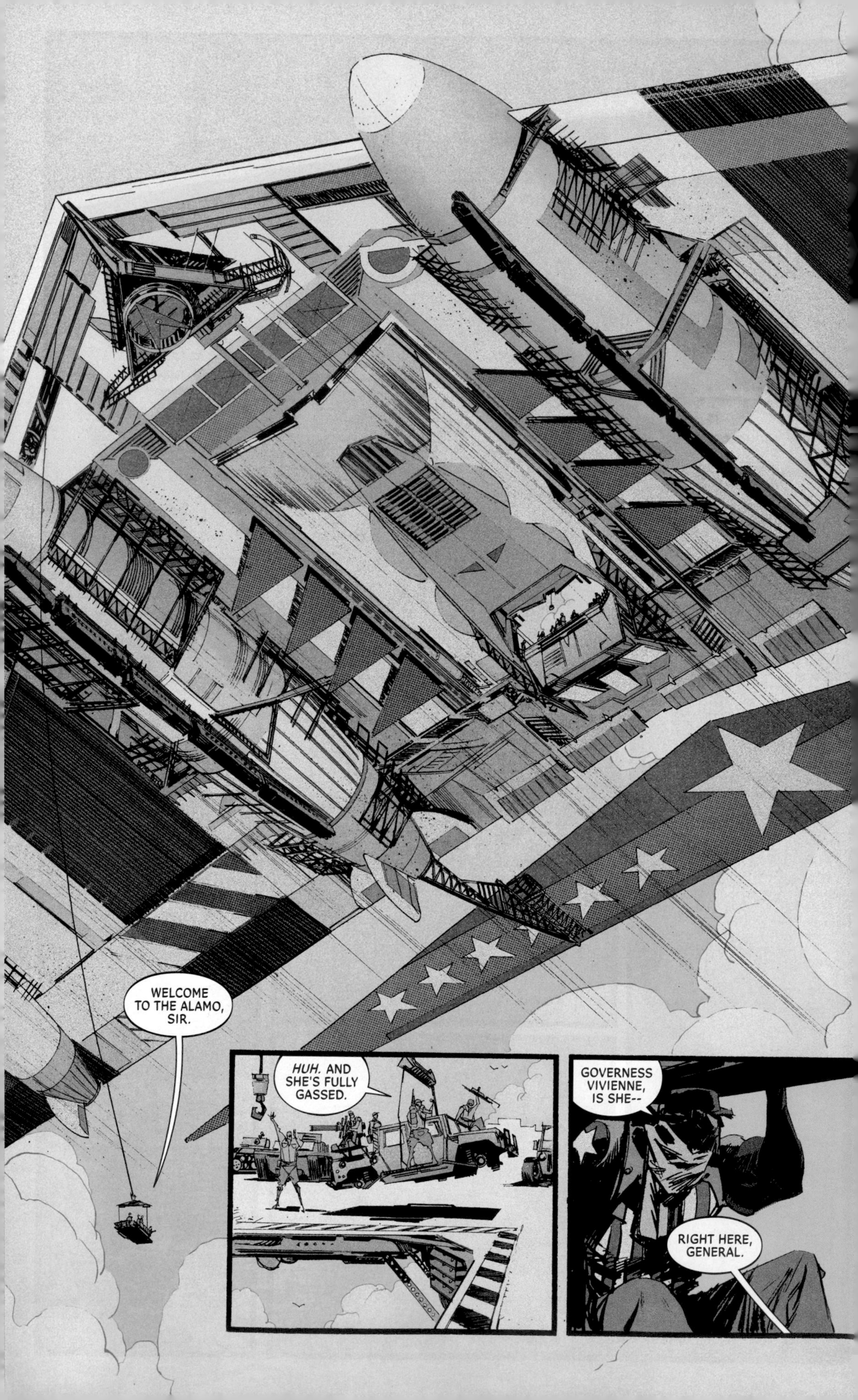
WELCOME TO THE ALAMO, SIR.
HUH. AND SHE'S FULLY GASSED.
GOVERNESS VIVIENNE, IS SHE--
RIGHT HERE, GENERAL.

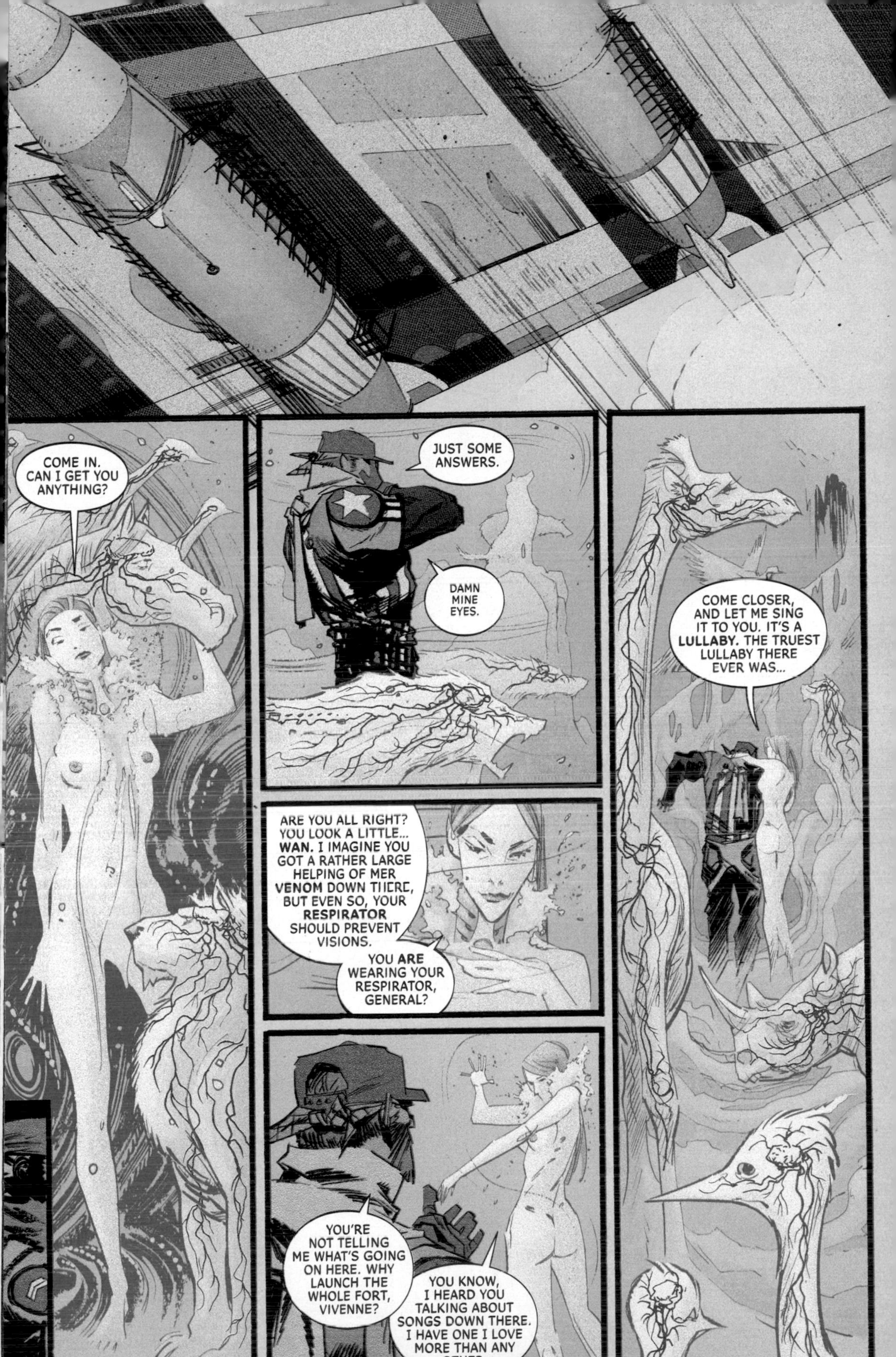
COME IN. CAN I GET YOU ANYTHING?
JUST SOME ANSWERS.
DAMN MINE EYES.
ARE YOU ALL RIGHT? YOU LOOK A LITTLE... WAN. I IMAGINE YOU GOT A RATHER LARGE HELPING OF MER VENOM DOWN THERE, BUT EVEN SO, YOUR RESPIRATOR SHOULD PREVENT VISIONS.
YOU ARE WEARING YOUR RESPIRATOR, GENERAL?
YOU'RE NOT TELLING ME WHAT'S GOING ON HERE. WHY LAUNCH THE WHOLE FORT, VIVENNE?
YOU KNOW, I HEARD YOU TALKING ABOUT SONGS DOWN THERE. I HAVE ONE I LOVE MORE THAN ANY OTHER.
COME CLOSER, AND LET ME SING IT TO YOU. IT'S A LULLABY. THE TRUEST LULLABY THERE EVER WAS...

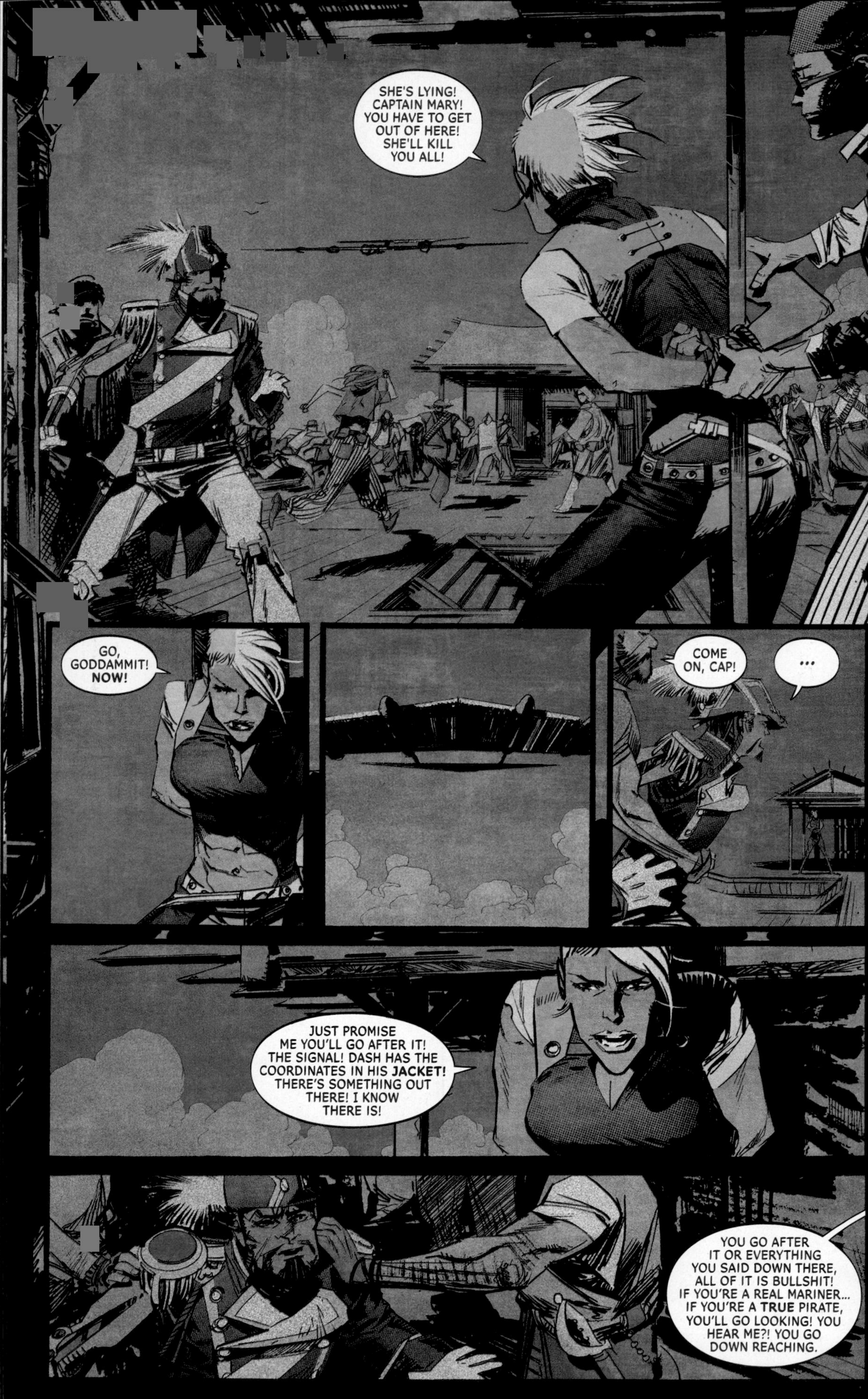
SHE'S LYING! CAPTAIN MARY! YOU HAVE TO GET OUT OF HERE! SHE'LL KILL YOU ALL!
GO, GODDAMMIT! **NOW!**
COME ON, CAP!
...
JUST PROMISE ME YOU'LL GO AFTER IT! THE SIGNAL! DASH HAS THE COORDINATES IN HIS **JACKET!** THERE'S SOMETHING OUT THERE! I KNOW THERE IS!
YOU GO AFTER IT OR EVERYTHING YOU SAID DOWN THERE, ALL OF IT IS BULLSHIT! IF YOU'RE A REAL MARINER... IF YOU'RE A **TRUE** PIRATE, YOU'LL GO LOOKING! YOU HEAR ME?! YOU GO DOWN REACHING.

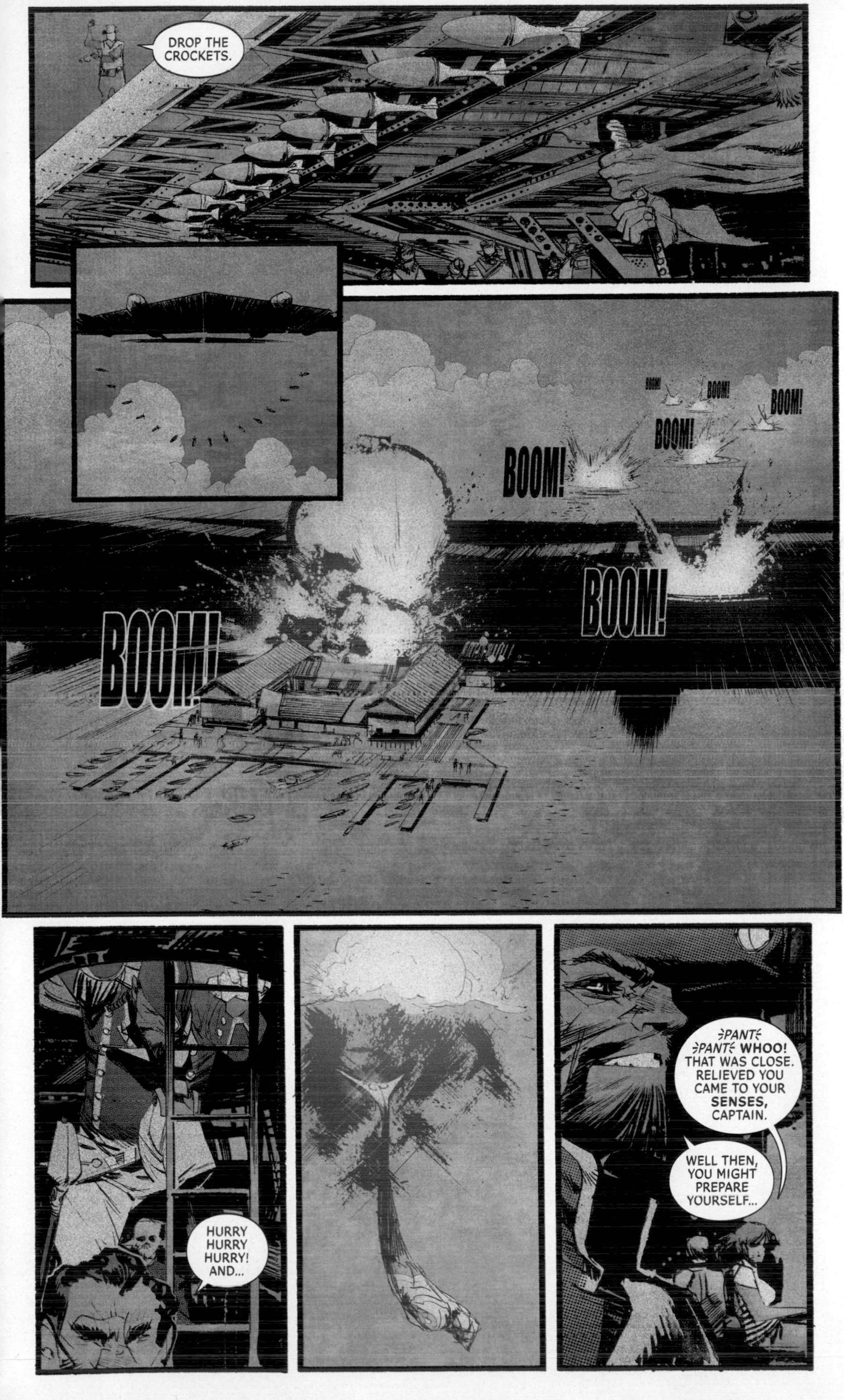
DROP THE CROCKETS.
BOOM!
BOOM!
BOOM!
BOOM!
BOOM!
BOOM!
BOOM!
HURRY HURRY HURRY! AND...
PANT PANT WHOO! THAT WAS CLOSE. RELIEVED YOU CAME TO YOUR SENSES, CAPTAIN.
WELL THEN, YOU MIGHT PREPARE YOURSELF...

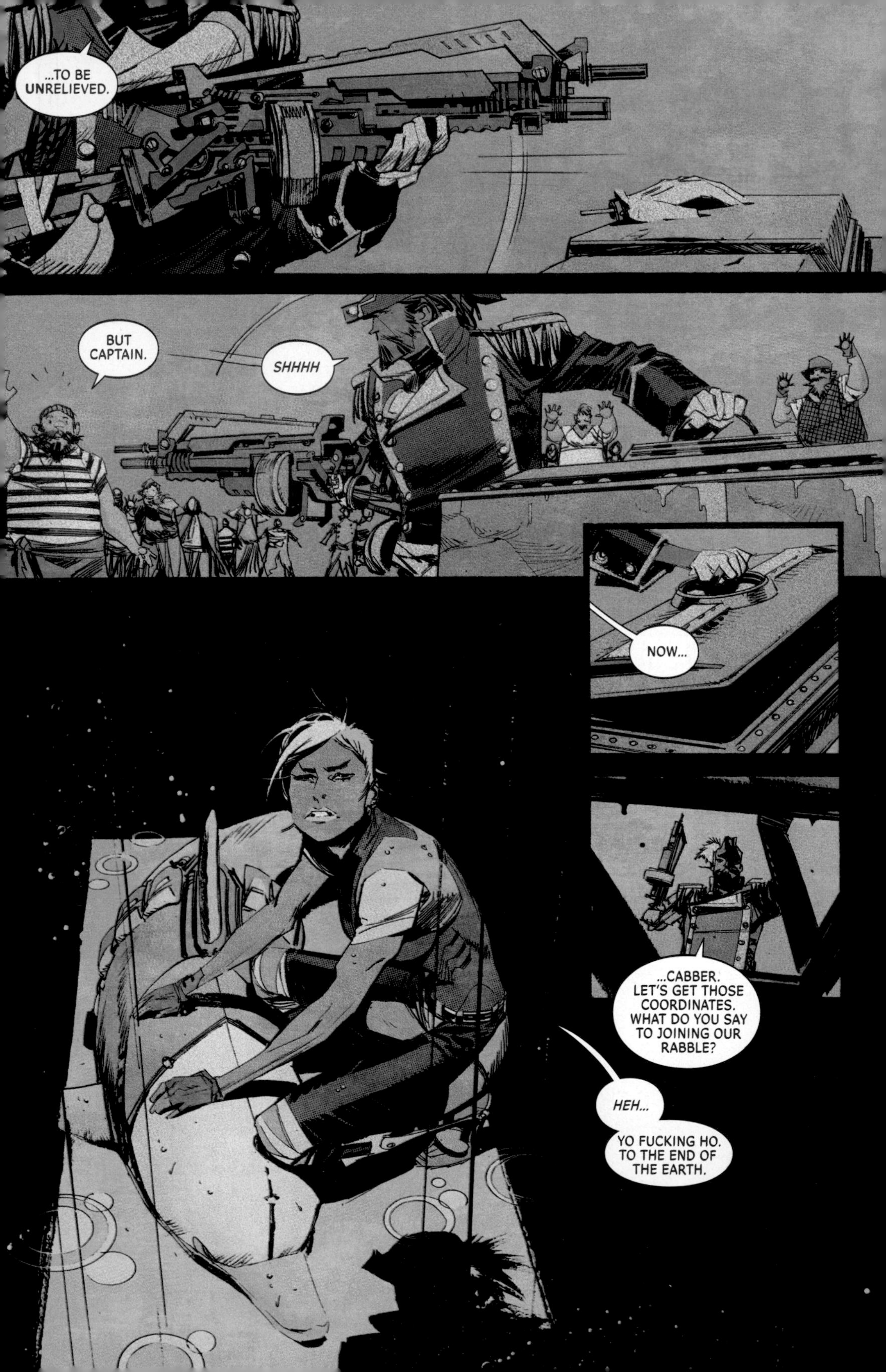
...TO BE UNRELIEVED.
BUT CAPTAIN.
SHHHH
NOW...
...CABBER. LET'S GET THOSE COORDINATES. WHAT DO YOU SAY TO JOINING OUR RABBLE?
HEH...
YO FUCKING HO. TO THE END OF THE EARTH.

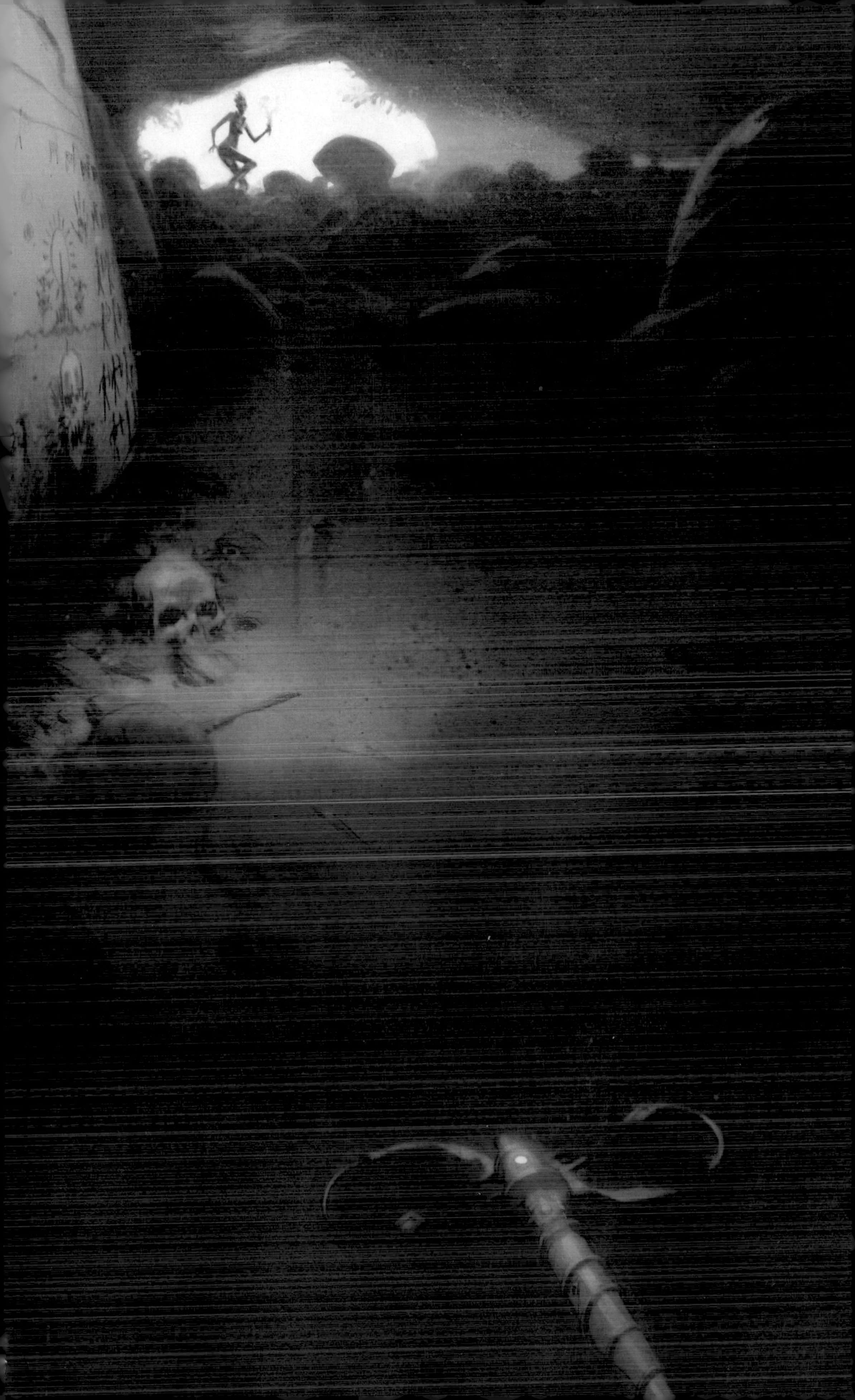

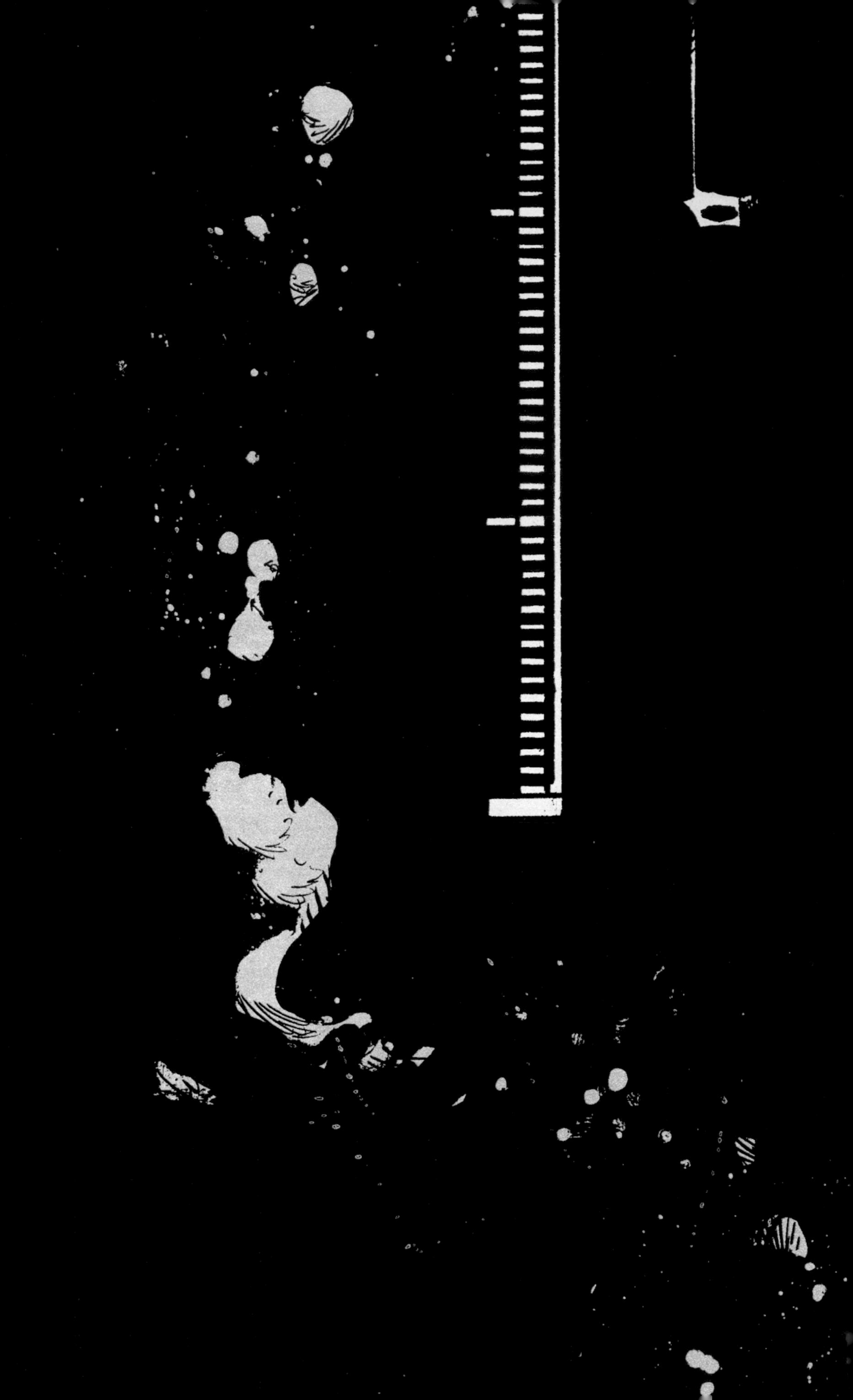

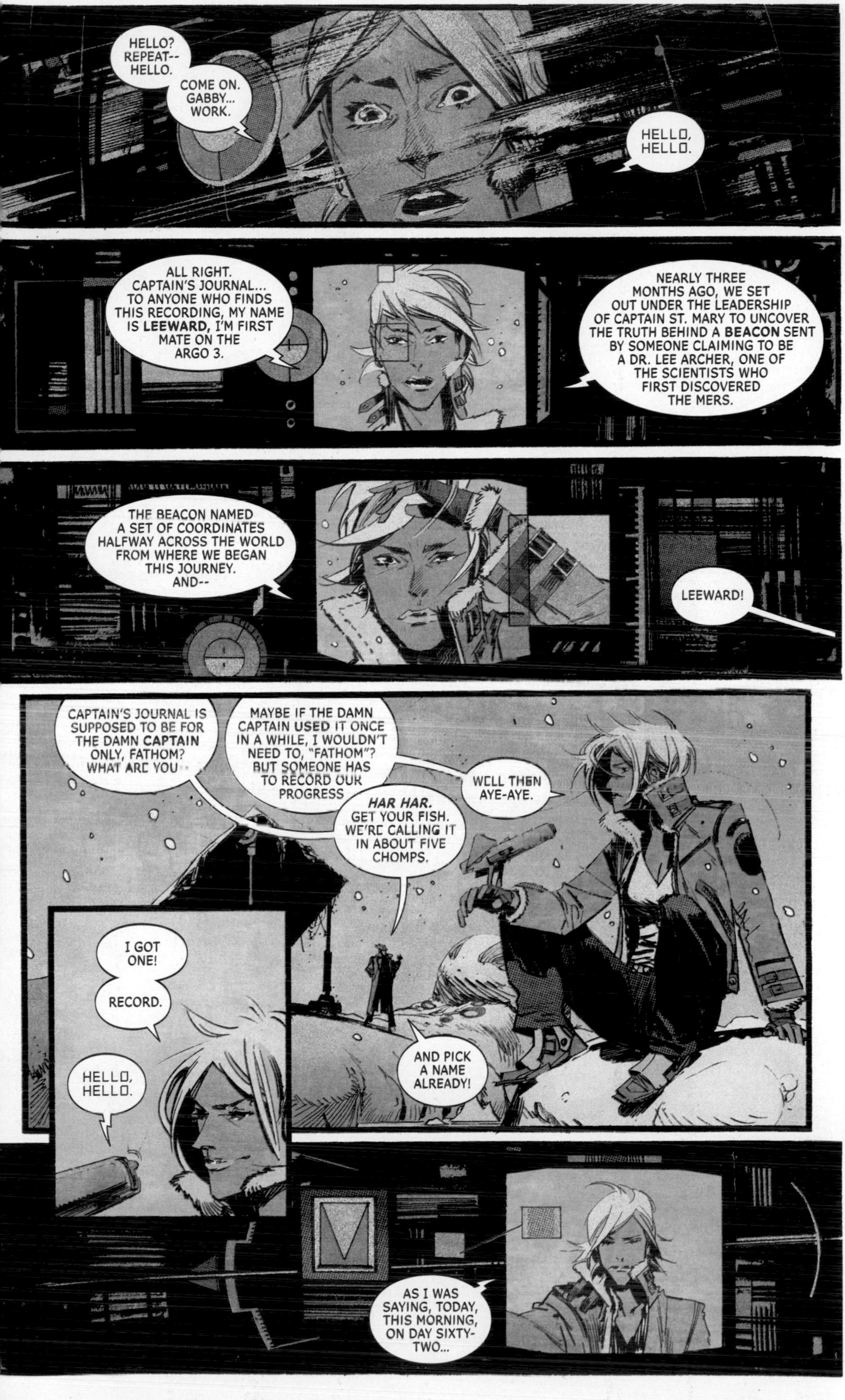
HELLO? REPEAT-- HELLO.
COME ON. GABBY... WORK.
HELLO, HELLO.
ALL RIGHT. CAPTAIN'S JOURNAL... TO ANYONE WHO FINDS THIS RECORDING, MY NAME IS **LEEWARD,** I'M FIRST MATE ON THE ARGO 3.
NEARLY THREE MONTHS AGO, WE SET OUT UNDER THE LEADERSHIP OF CAPTAIN ST. MARY TO UNCOVER THE TRUTH BEHIND A **BEACON** SENT BY SOMEONE CLAIMING TO BE A DR. LEE ARCHER, ONE OF THE SCIENTISTS WHO FIRST DISCOVERED THE MERS.
THE BEACON NAMED A SET OF COORDINATES HALFWAY ACROSS THE WORLD FROM WHERE WE BEGAN THIS JOURNEY. AND--
LEEWARD!
CAPTAIN'S JOURNAL IS SUPPOSED TO BE FOR THE DAMN **CAPTAIN** ONLY, FATHOM? WHAT ARE YOU--
MAYBE IF THE DAMN CAPTAIN **USED** IT ONCE IN A WHILE, I WOULDN'T NEED TO, "FATHOM"? BUT SOMEONE HAS TO RECORD OUR PROGRESS
WELL THEN AYE-AYE.
HAR HAR. GET YOUR FISH. WE'RE CALLING IT IN ABOUT FIVE CHOMPS.
AND PICK A NAME ALREADY!
I GOT ONE!
RECORD.
HELLO, HELLO.
AS I WAS SAYING, TODAY, THIS MORNING, ON DAY SIXTY-TWO...

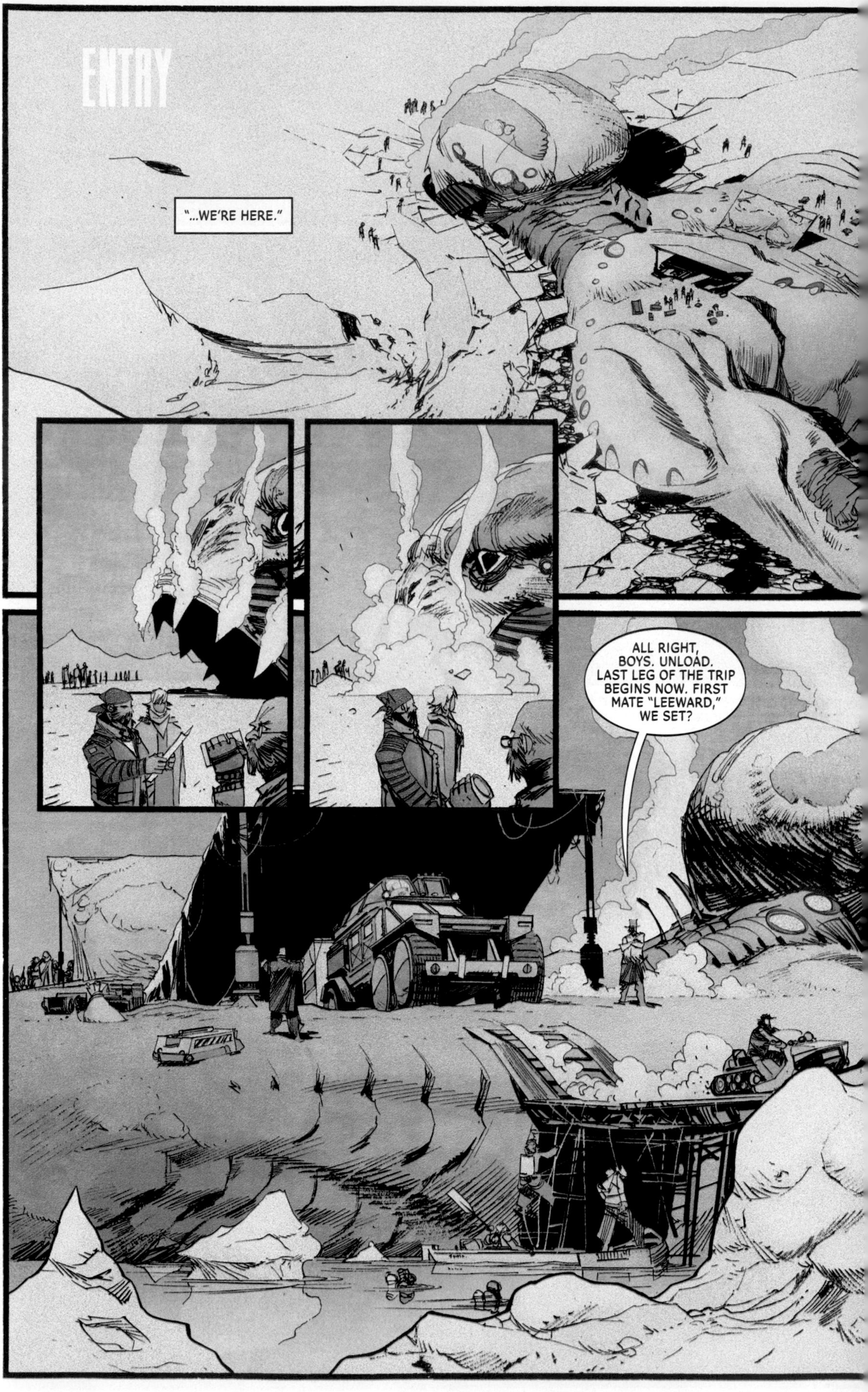
ENTRY
"...WE'RE HERE."
ALL RIGHT, BOYS. UNLOAD. LAST LEG OF THE TRIP BEGINS NOW. FIRST MATE "LEEWARD," WE SET?

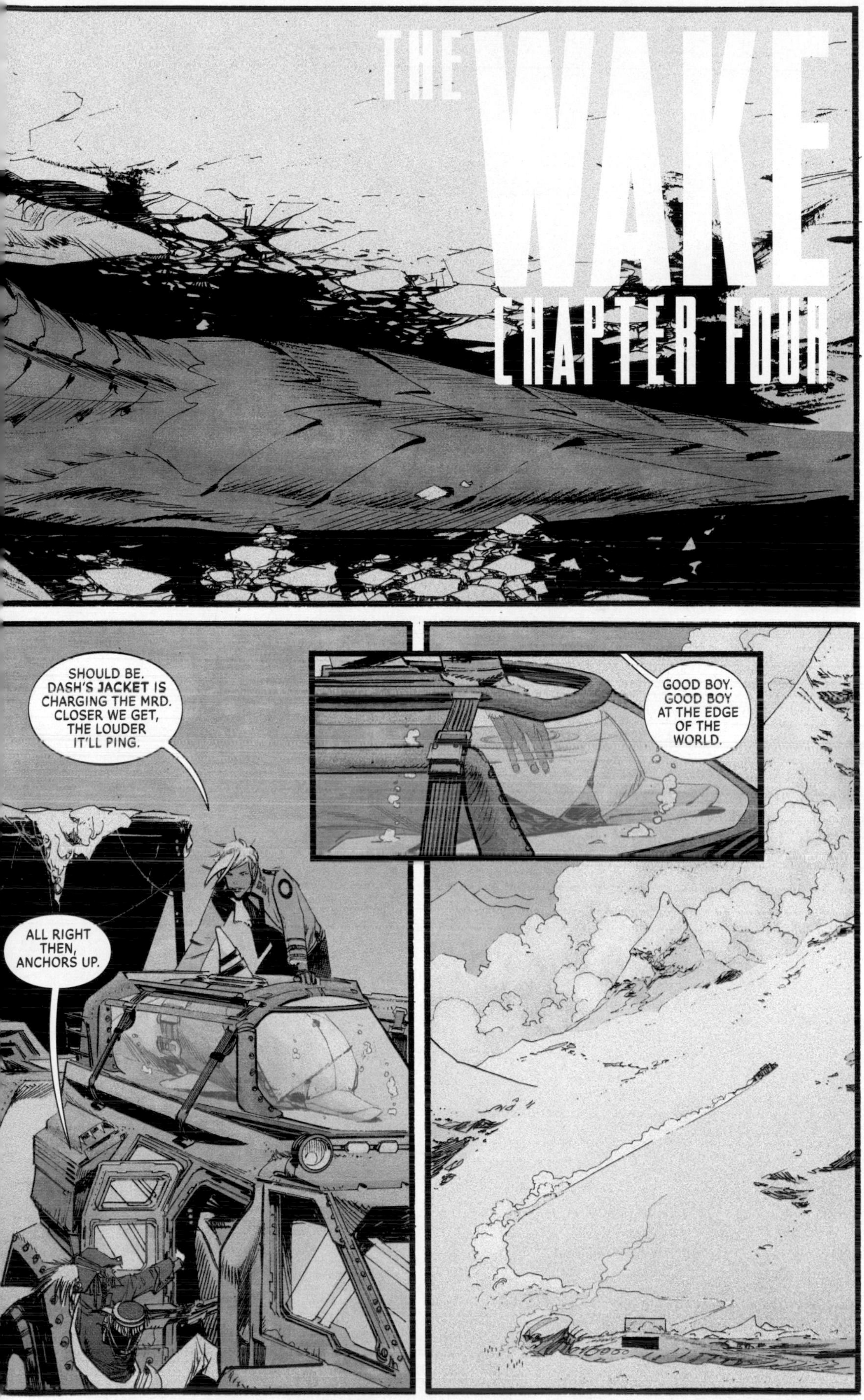
THE WAKE
CHAPTER FOUR
SHOULD BE. DASH'S JACKET IS CHARGING THE MRD. CLOSER WE GET, THE LOUDER IT'LL PING.
ALL RIGHT THEN, ANCHORS UP.
GOOD BOY. GOOD BOY AT THE EDGE OF THE WORLD.

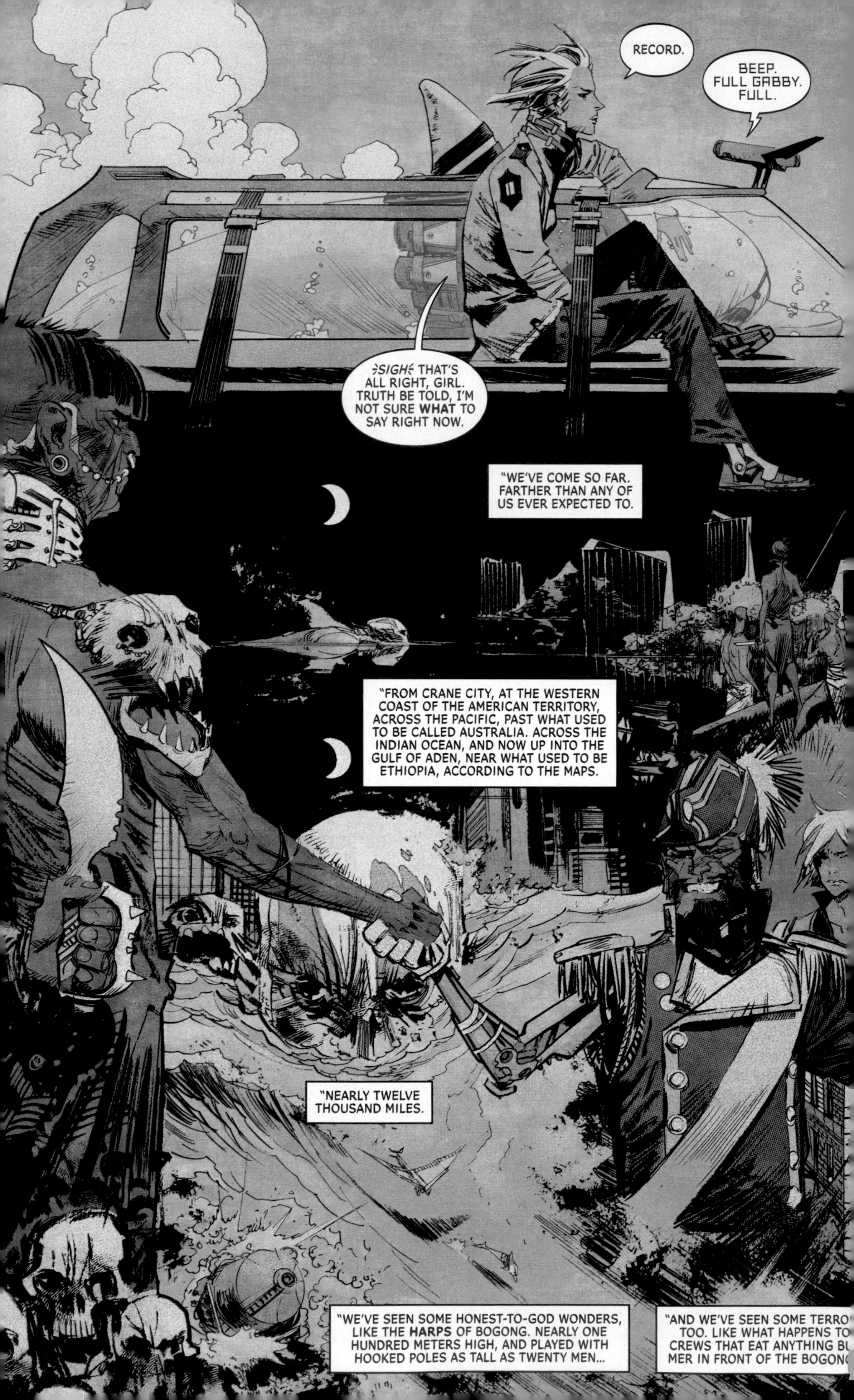
RECORD.
BEEP. FULL GABBY. FULL.
SIGH THAT'S ALL RIGHT, GIRL. TRUTH BE TOLD, I'M NOT SURE **WHAT** TO SAY RIGHT NOW.
"WE'VE COME SO FAR. FARTHER THAN ANY OF US EVER EXPECTED TO.
"FROM CRANE CITY, AT THE WESTERN COAST OF THE AMERICAN TERRITORY, ACROSS THE PACIFIC, PAST WHAT USED TO BE CALLED AUSTRALIA. ACROSS THE INDIAN OCEAN, AND NOW UP INTO THE GULF OF ADEN, NEAR WHAT USED TO BE ETHIOPIA, ACCORDING TO THE MAPS.
"NEARLY TWELVE THOUSAND MILES.
"WE'VE SEEN SOME HONEST-TO-GOD WONDERS, LIKE THE **HARPS** OF BOGONG. NEARLY ONE HUNDRED METERS HIGH, AND PLAYED WITH HOOKED POLES AS TALL AS TWENTY MEN...
"AND WE'VE SEEN SOME TERRO
TOO. LIKE WHAT HAPPENS TO
CREWS THAT EAT ANYTHING BU
MER IN FRONT OF THE BOGON

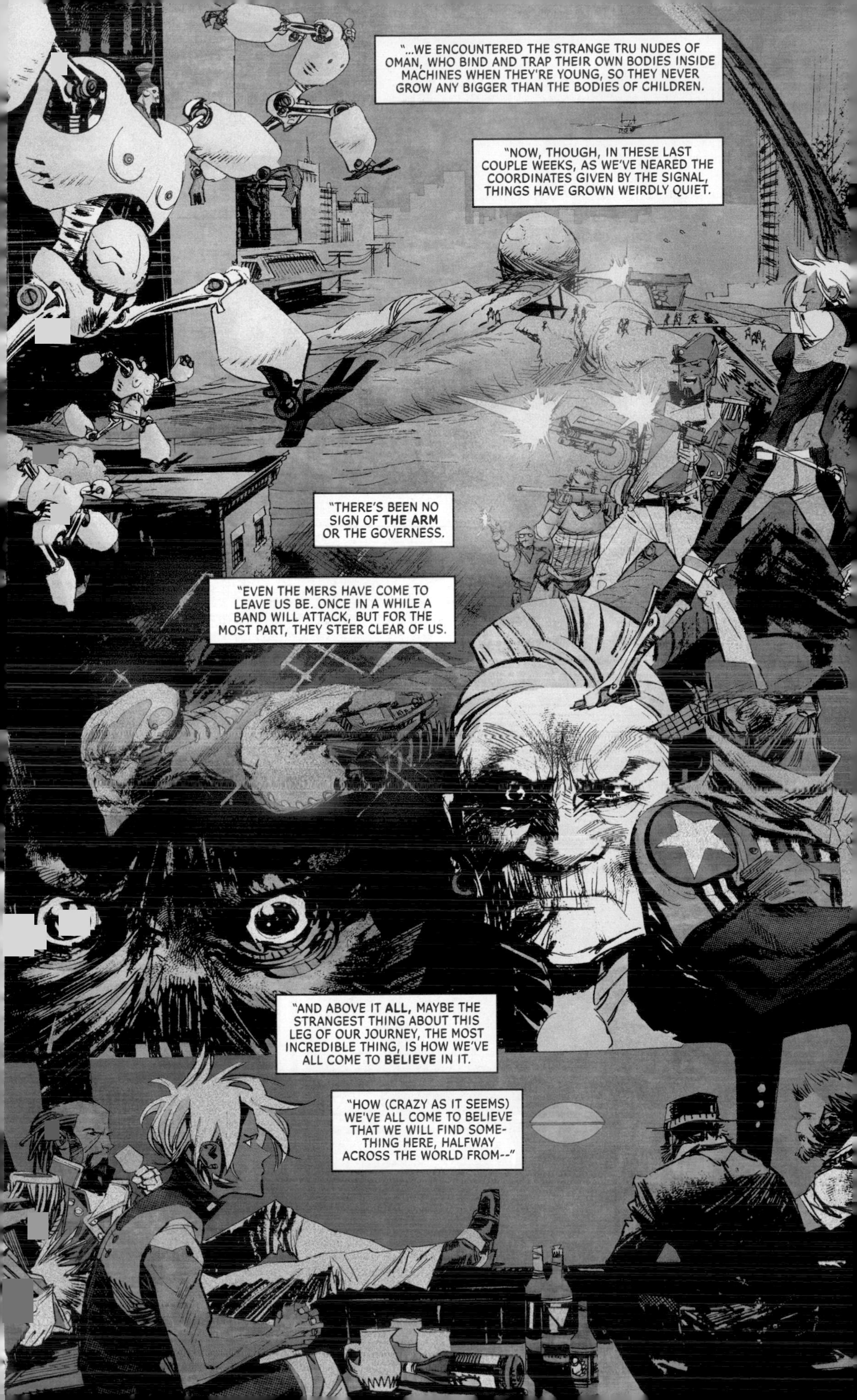
"...WE ENCOUNTERED THE STRANGE TRU NUDES OF OMAN, WHO BIND AND TRAP THEIR OWN BODIES INSIDE MACHINES WHEN THEY'RE YOUNG, SO THEY NEVER GROW ANY BIGGER THAN THE BODIES OF CHILDREN.
"NOW, THOUGH, IN THESE LAST COUPLE WEEKS, AS WE'VE NEARED THE COORDINATES GIVEN BY THE SIGNAL, THINGS HAVE GROWN WEIRDLY QUIET.
"THERE'S BEEN NO SIGN OF **THE ARM** OR THE GOVERNESS.
"EVEN THE MERS HAVE COME TO LEAVE US BE. ONCE IN A WHILE A BAND WILL ATTACK, BUT FOR THE MOST PART, THEY STEER CLEAR OF US.
"AND ABOVE IT **ALL,** MAYBE THE STRANGEST THING ABOUT THIS LEG OF OUR JOURNEY, THE MOST INCREDIBLE THING, IS HOW WE'VE ALL COME TO **BELIEVE** IN IT.
"HOW (CRAZY AS IT SEEMS) WE'VE ALL COME TO BELIEVE THAT WE WILL FIND SOMETHING HERE, HALFWAY ACROSS THE WORLD FROM--"

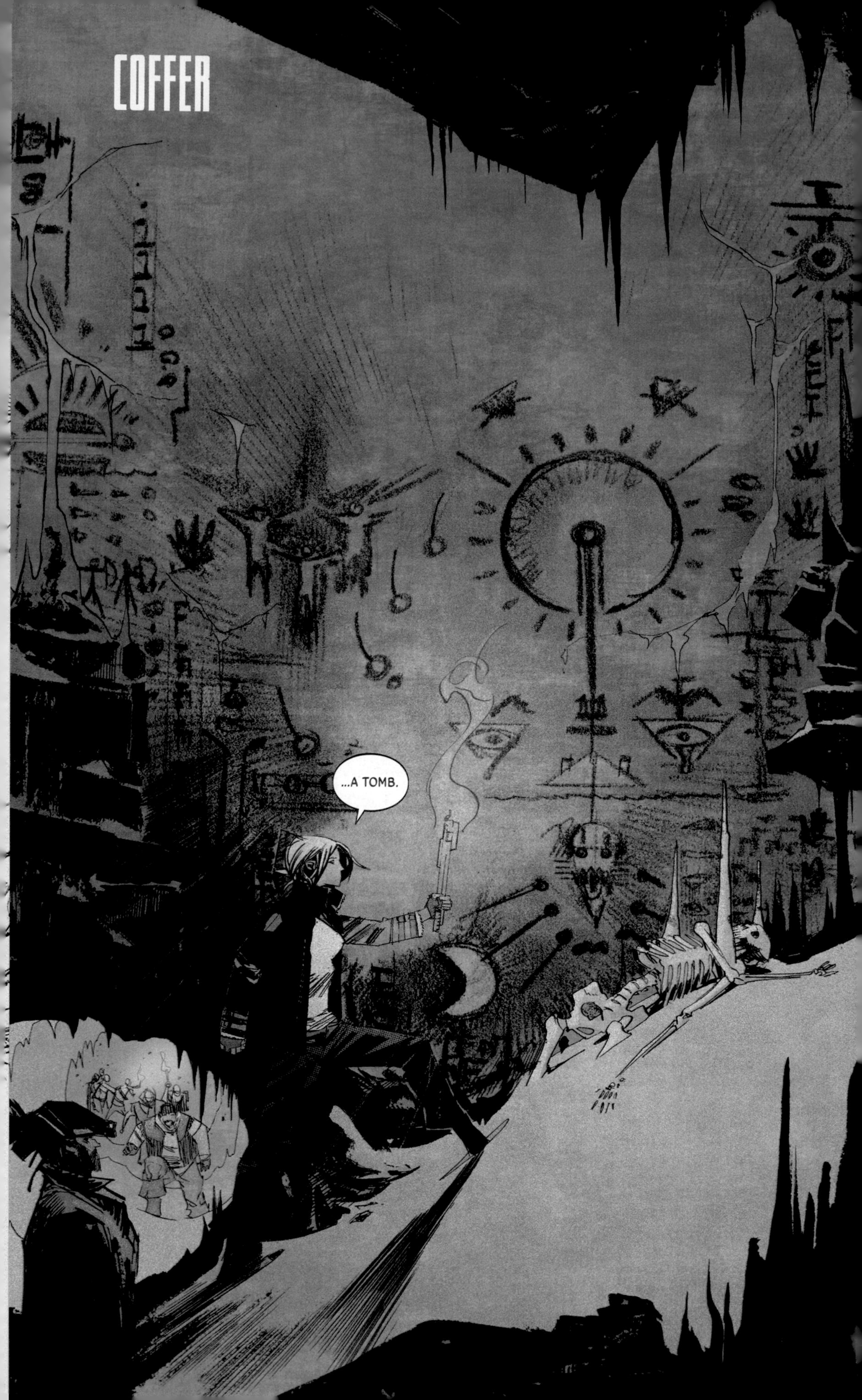
COFFER
...A TOMB.

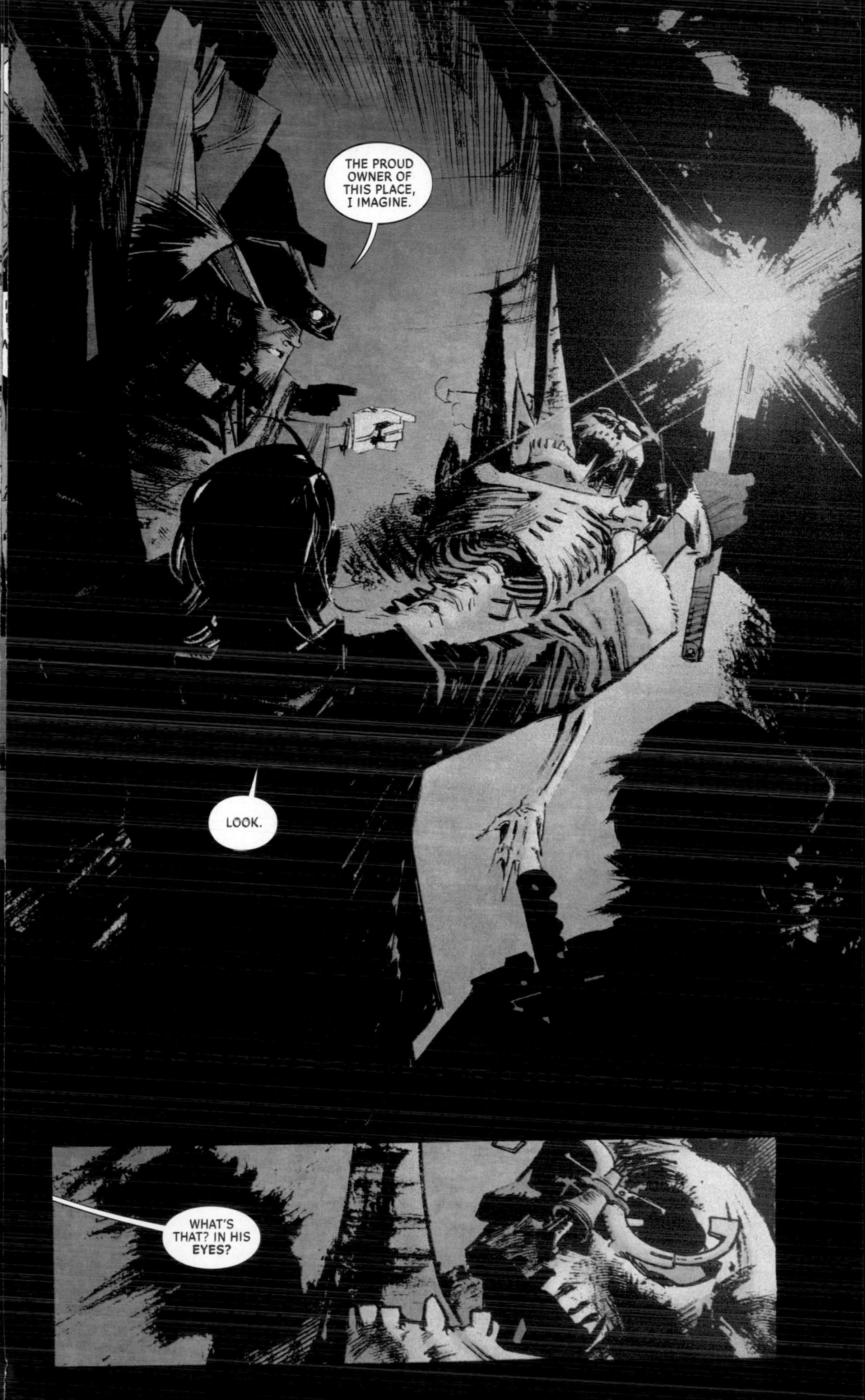
THE PROUD OWNER OF THIS PLACE, I IMAGINE.
LOOK.
WHAT'S THAT? IN HIS EYES?

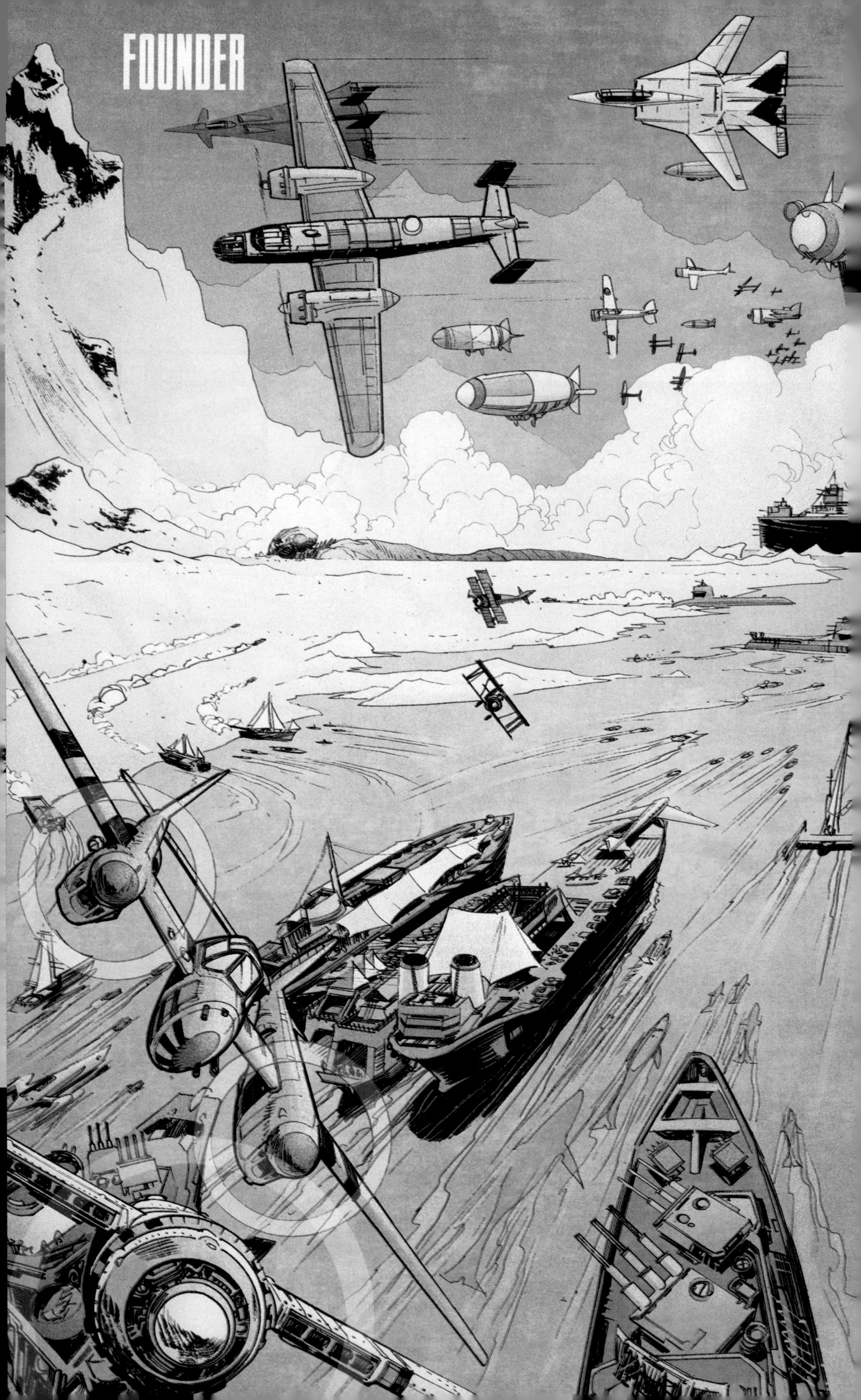
FOUNDER

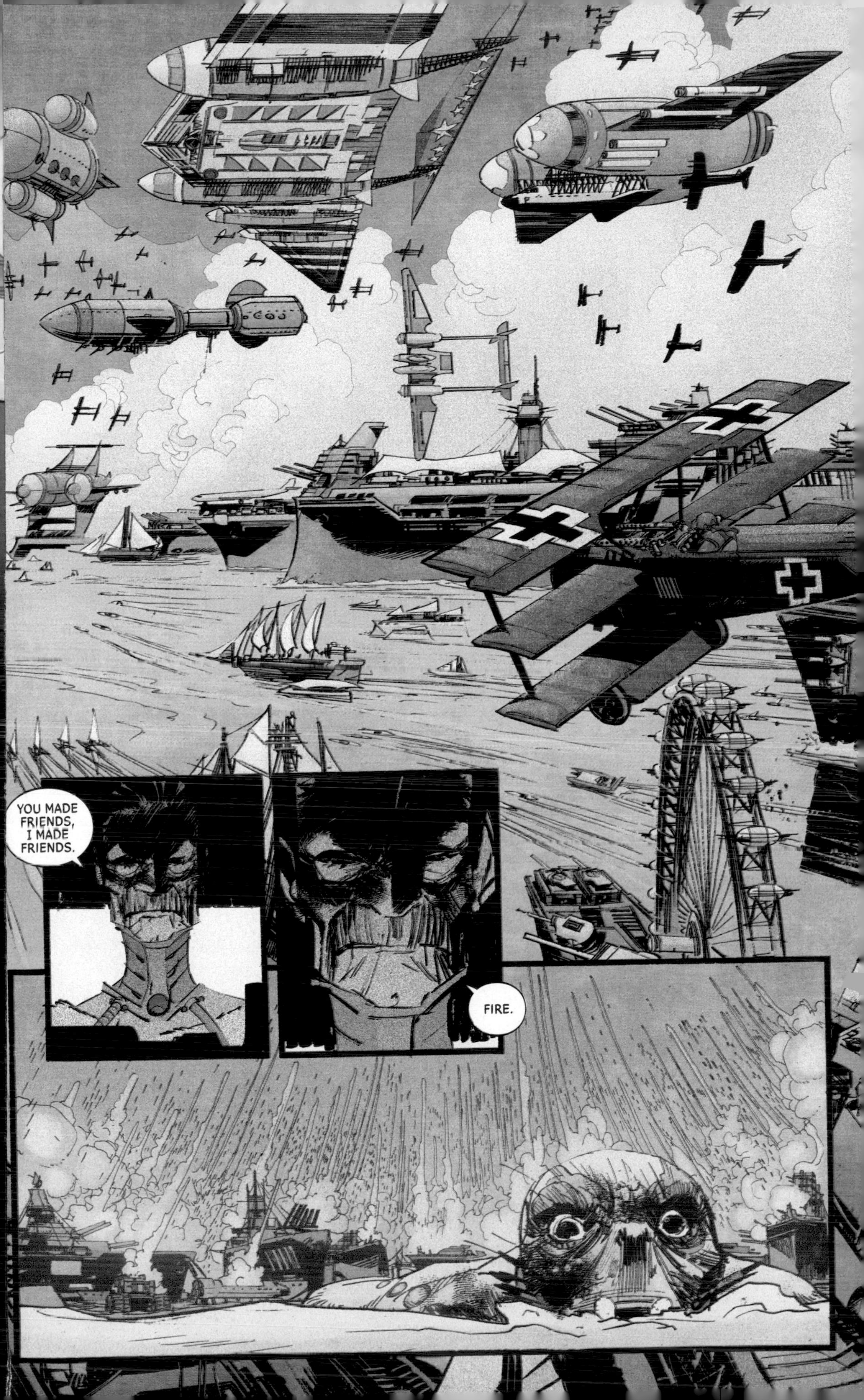
YOU MADE FRIENDS, I MADE FRIENDS.
FIRE.

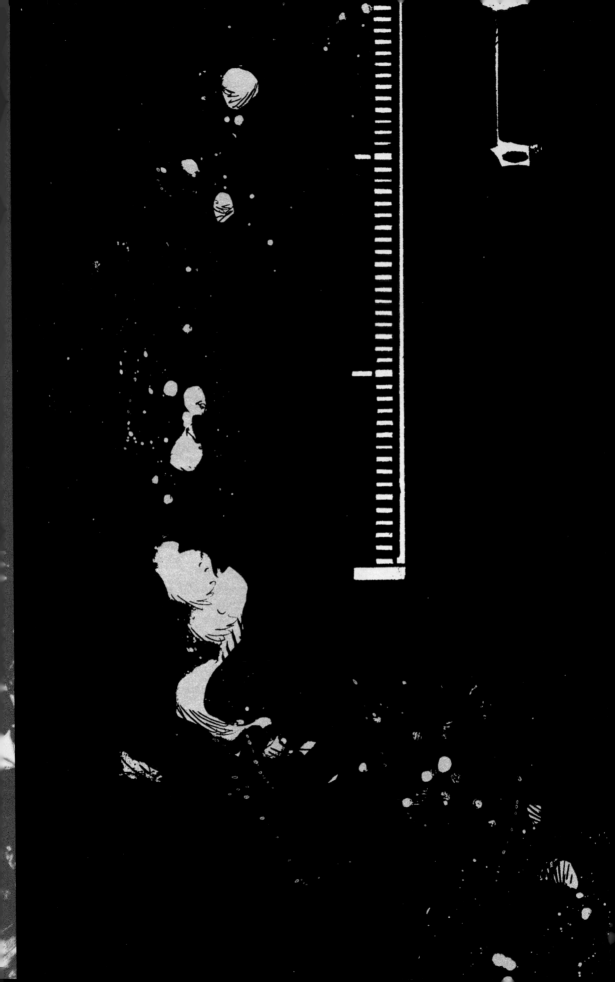

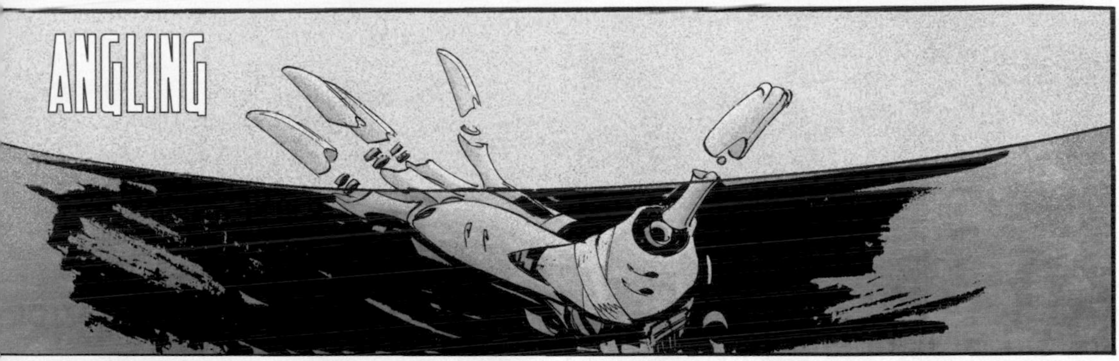
ANGLING

THE WAKE

CHAPTER FIVE

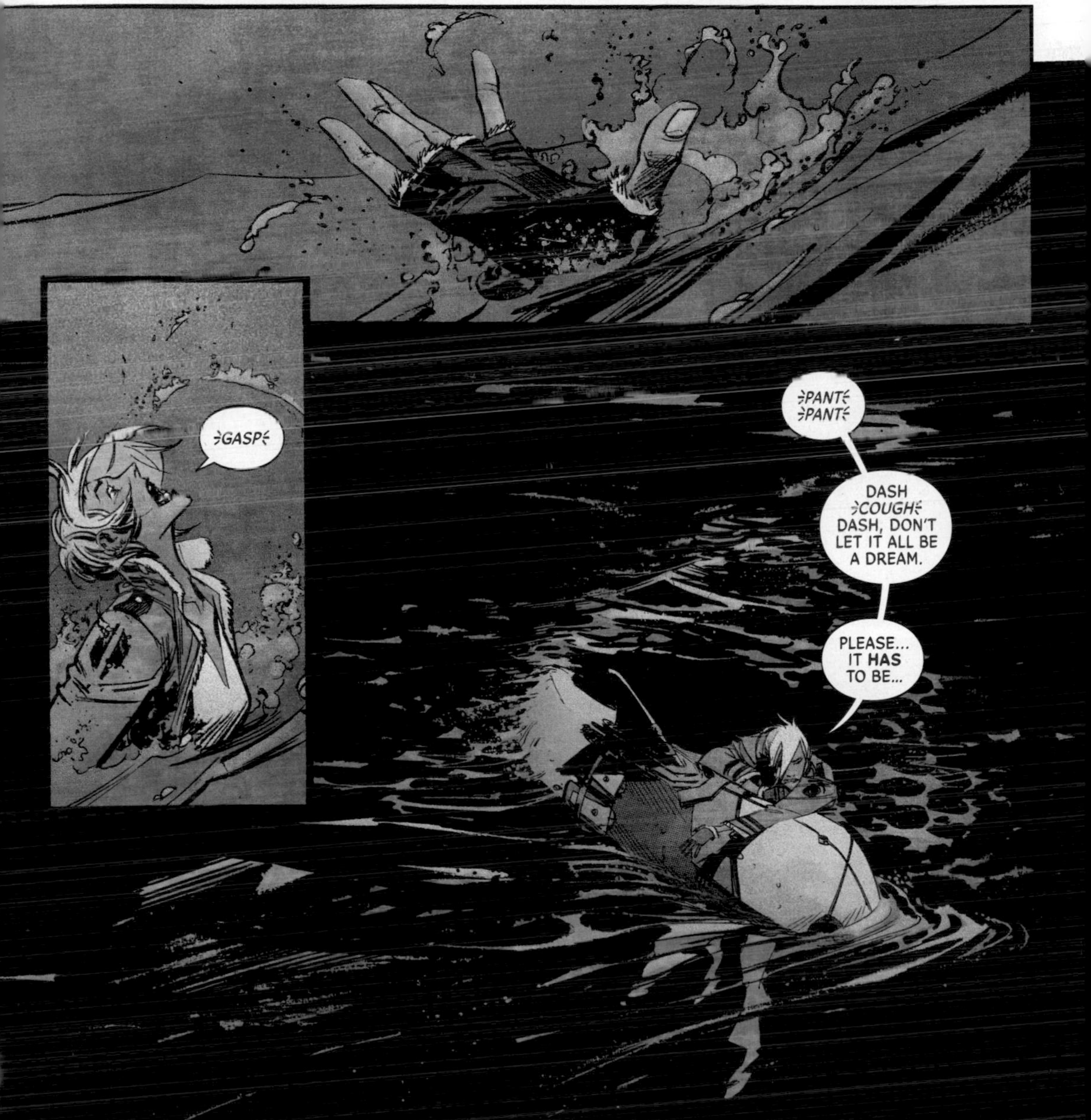
GASP
PANT PANT
DASH COUGH DASH, DON'T LET IT ALL BE A DREAM.
PLEASE... IT **HAS** TO BE...

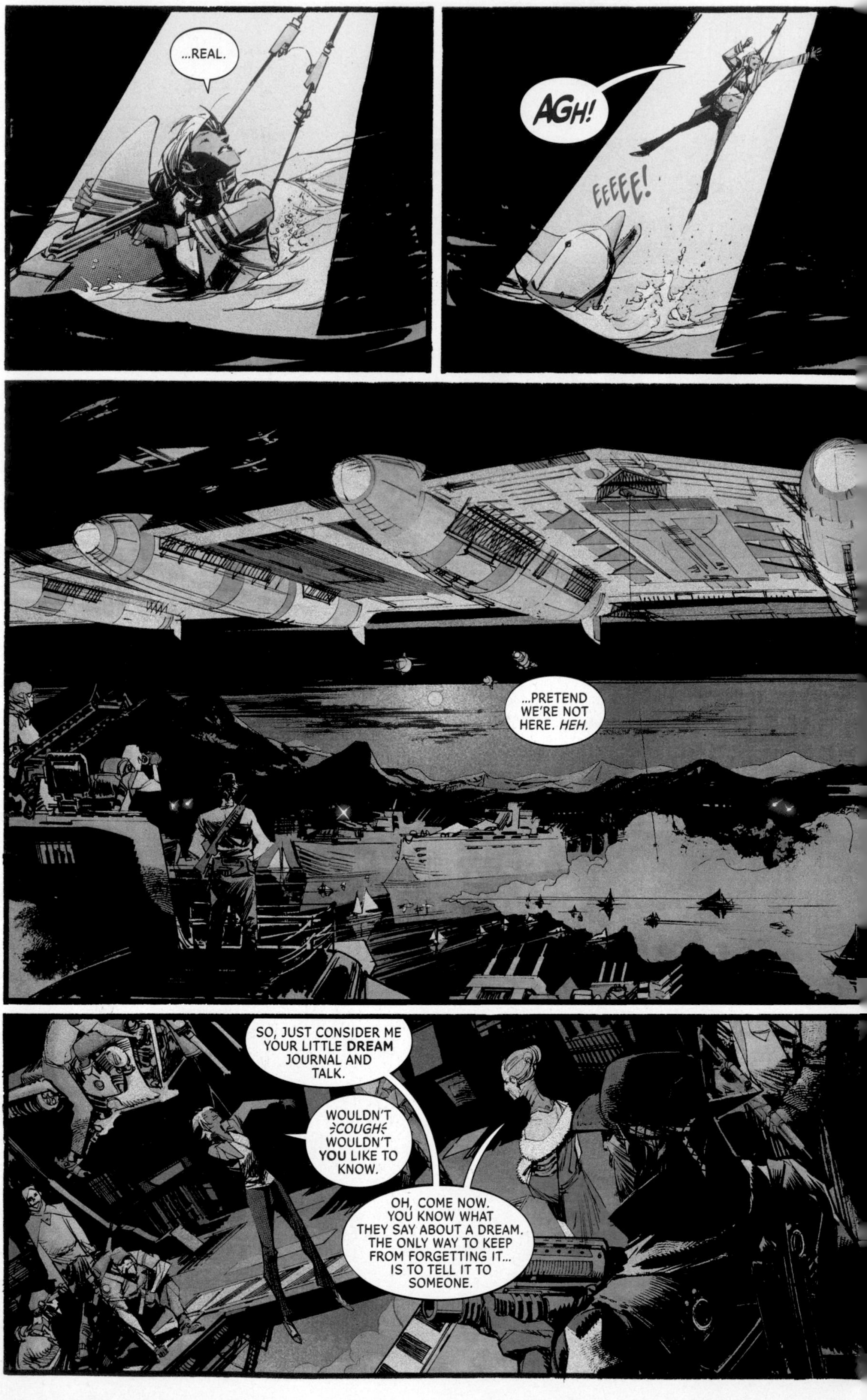
...REAL.
AGH!
EEEEE!
...PRETEND WE'RE NOT HERE. *HEH.*
SO, JUST CONSIDER ME YOUR LITTLE **DREAM** JOURNAL AND TALK.
WOULDN'T *COUGH* WOULDN'T **YOU** LIKE TO KNOW.
OH, COME NOW. YOU KNOW WHAT THEY SAY ABOUT A DREAM. THE ONLY WAY TO KEEP FROM FORGETTING IT... IS TO TELL IT TO SOMEONE.

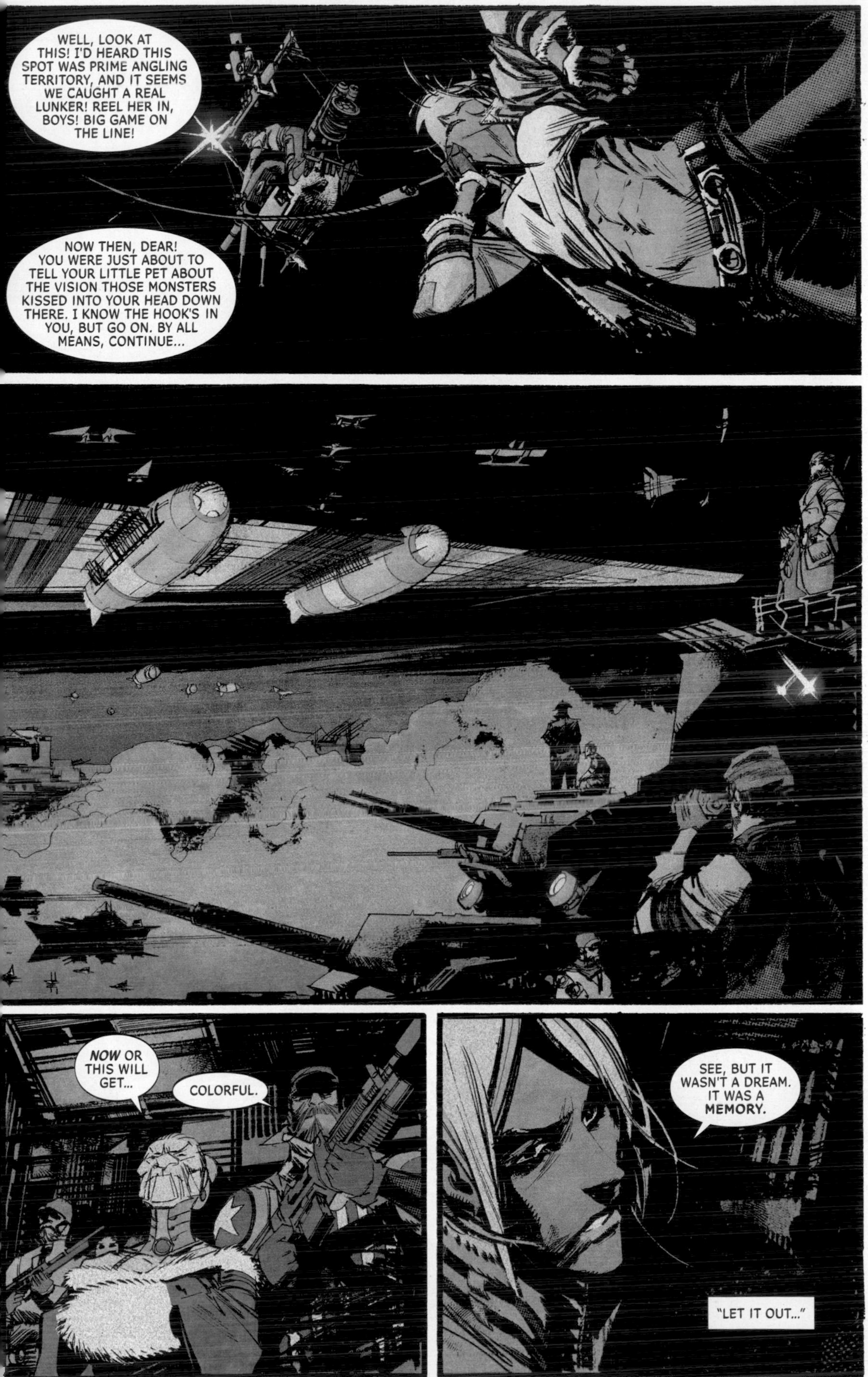
WELL, LOOK AT THIS! I'D HEARD THIS SPOT WAS PRIME ANGLING TERRITORY, AND IT SEEMS WE CAUGHT A REAL LUNKER! REEL HER IN, BOYS! BIG GAME ON THE LINE!
NOW THEN, DEAR! YOU WERE JUST ABOUT TO TELL YOUR LITTLE PET ABOUT THE VISION THOSE MONSTERS KISSED INTO YOUR HEAD DOWN THERE. I KNOW THE HOOK'S IN YOU, BUT GO ON. BY ALL MEANS, CONTINUE...
NOW OR THIS WILL GET...
COLORFUL.
SEE, BUT IT WASN'T A DREAM. IT WAS A **MEMORY.**
"LET IT OUT..."

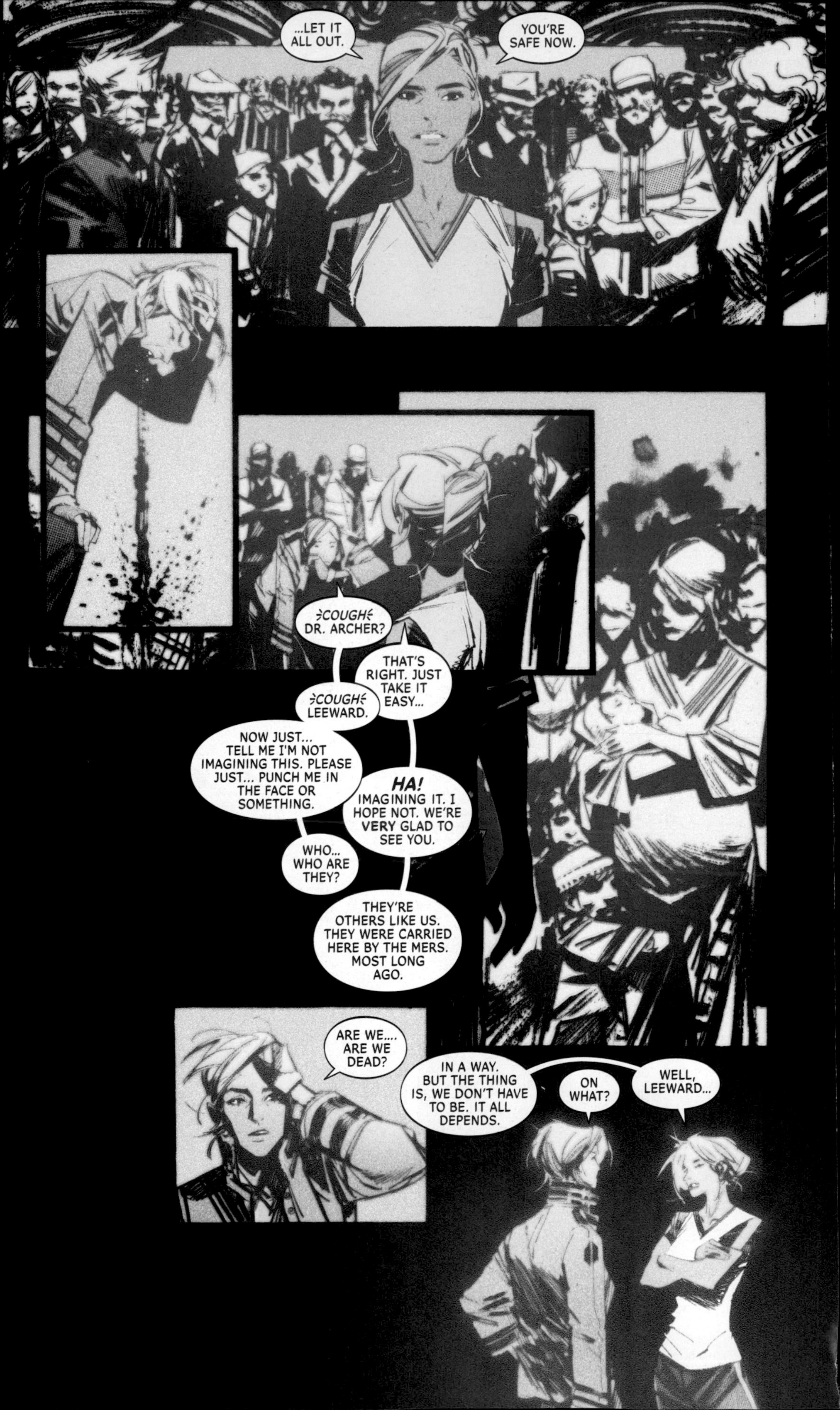
...LET IT ALL OUT.
YOU'RE SAFE NOW.
COUGH DR. ARCHER?
THAT'S RIGHT. JUST TAKE IT EASY...
COUGH LEEWARD.
NOW JUST... TELL ME I'M NOT IMAGINING THIS. PLEASE JUST... PUNCH ME IN THE FACE OR SOMETHING.
HA! IMAGINING IT. I HOPE NOT. WE'RE VERY GLAD TO SEE YOU.
WHO... WHO ARE THEY?
THEY'RE OTHERS LIKE US. THEY WERE CARRIED HERE BY THE MERS. MOST LONG AGO.
ARE WE.... ARE WE DEAD?
WELL, LEEWARD...
IN A WAY. BUT THE THING IS, WE DON'T HAVE TO BE. IT ALL DEPENDS.
ON WHAT?

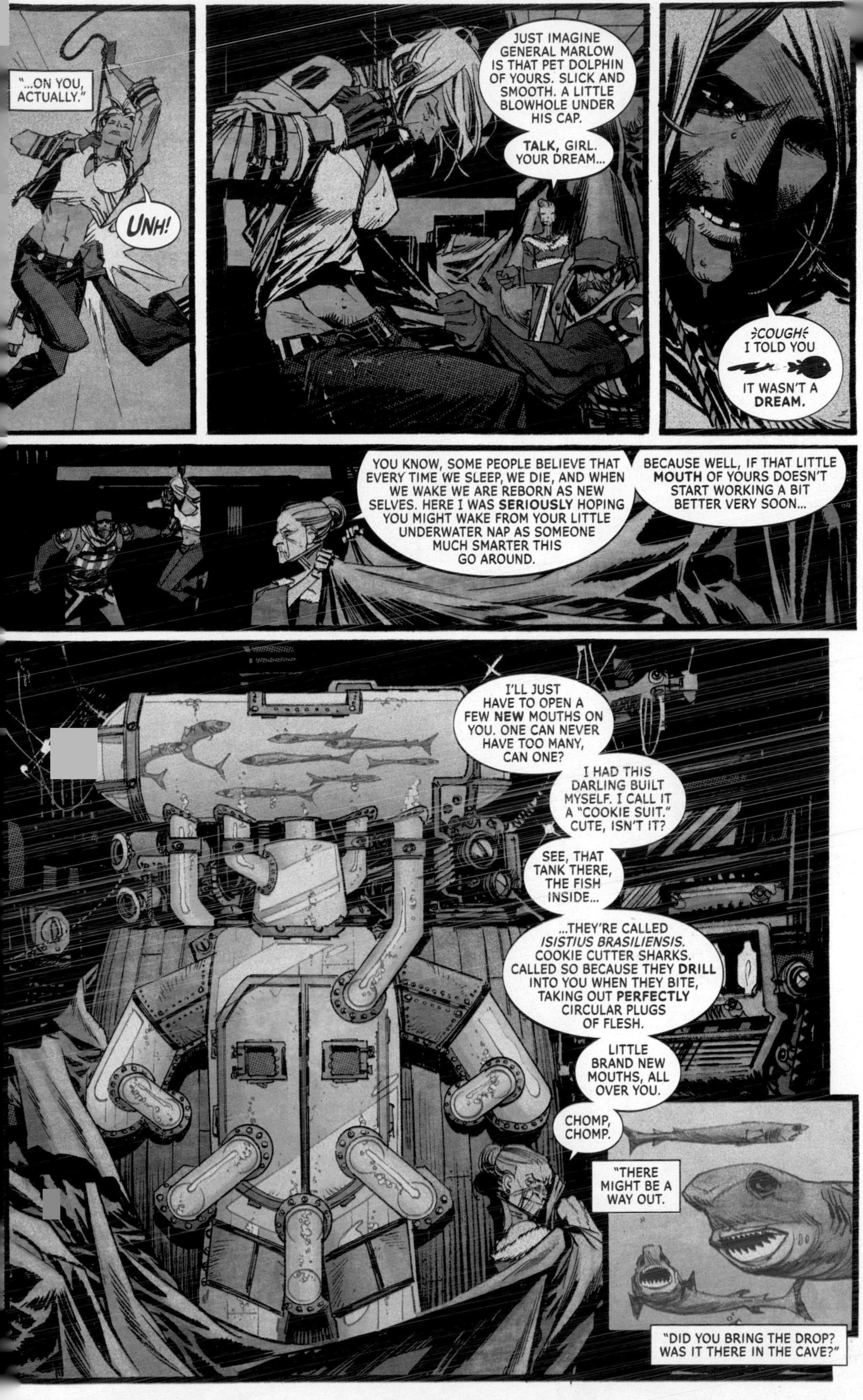
"...ON YOU, ACTUALLY."
UNH!
JUST IMAGINE GENERAL MARLOW IS THAT PET DOLPHIN OF YOURS. SLICK AND SMOOTH. A LITTLE BLOWHOLE UNDER HIS CAP.
TALK, GIRL. YOUR DREAM...
COUGH I TOLD YOU
IT WASN'T A DREAM.
YOU KNOW, SOME PEOPLE BELIEVE THAT EVERY TIME WE SLEEP, WE DIE, AND WHEN WE WAKE WE ARE REBORN AS NEW SELVES. HERE I WAS SERIOUSLY HOPING YOU MIGHT WAKE FROM YOUR LITTLE UNDERWATER NAP AS SOMEONE MUCH SMARTER THIS GO AROUND.
BECAUSE WELL, IF THAT LITTLE MOUTH OF YOURS DOESN'T START WORKING A BIT BETTER VERY SOON...
I'LL JUST HAVE TO OPEN A FEW NEW MOUTHS ON YOU. ONE CAN NEVER HAVE TOO MANY, CAN ONE?
I HAD THIS DARLING BUILT MYSELF. I CALL IT A "COOKIE SUIT." CUTE, ISN'T IT?
SEE, THAT TANK THERE, THE FISH INSIDE...
...THEY'RE CALLED ISISTIUS BRASILIENSIS. COOKIE CUTTER SHARKS. CALLED SO BECAUSE THEY DRILL INTO YOU WHEN THEY BITE, TAKING OUT PERFECTLY CIRCULAR PLUGS OF FLESH.
LITTLE BRAND NEW MOUTHS, ALL OVER YOU.
CHOMP, CHOMP.
"THERE MIGHT BE A WAY OUT.
"DID YOU BRING THE DROP? WAS IT THERE IN THE CAVE?"

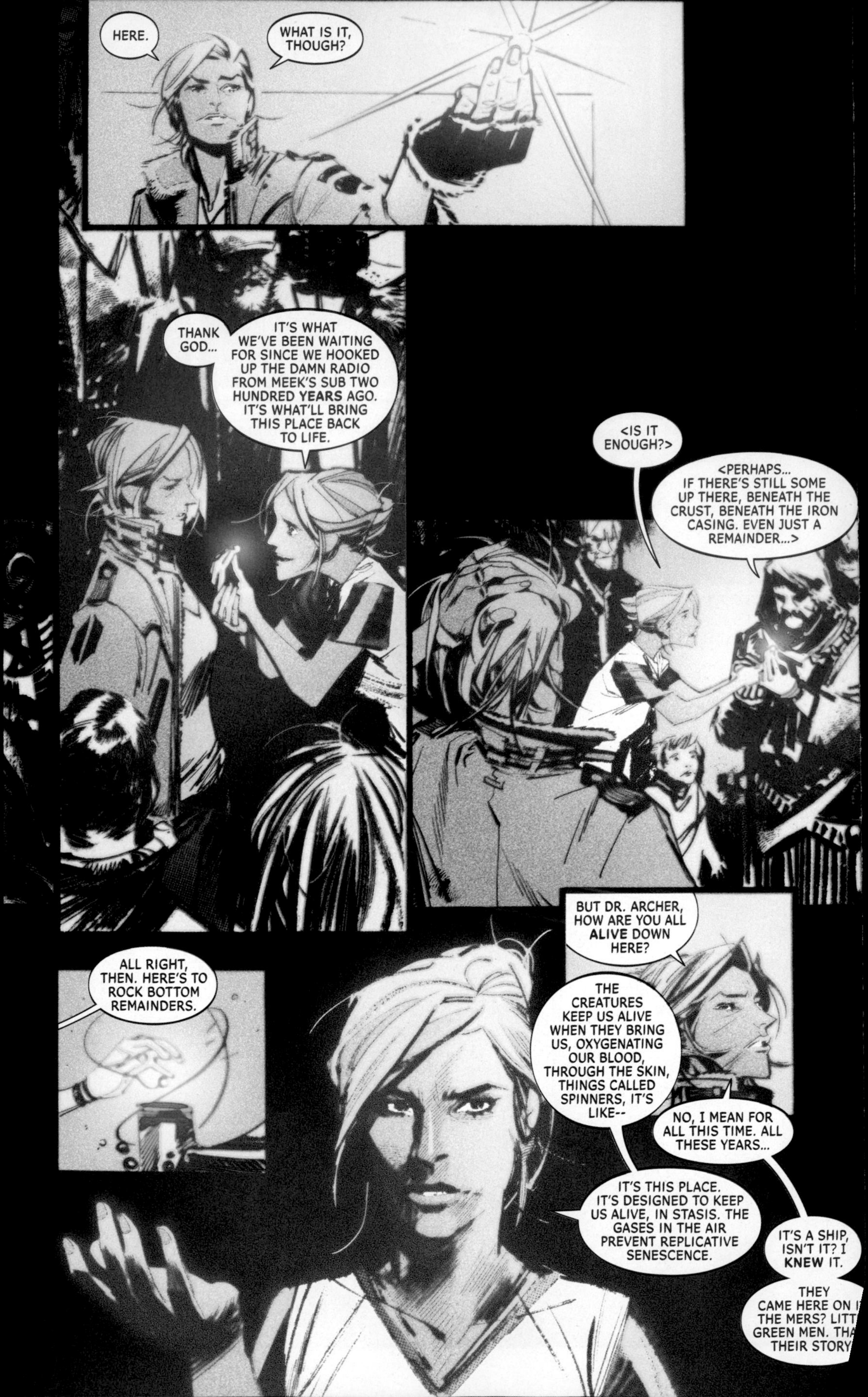
HERE.
WHAT IS IT, THOUGH?
THANK GOD...
IT'S WHAT WE'VE BEEN WAITING FOR SINCE WE HOOKED UP THE DAMN RADIO FROM MEEK'S SUB TWO HUNDRED YEARS AGO. IT'S WHAT'LL BRING THIS PLACE BACK TO LIFE.
<IS IT ENOUGH?>
<PERHAPS... IF THERE'S STILL SOME UP THERE, BENEATH THE CRUST, BENEATH THE IRON CASING. EVEN JUST A REMAINDER...>
ALL RIGHT, THEN. HERE'S TO ROCK BOTTOM REMAINDERS.
BUT DR. ARCHER, HOW ARE YOU ALL ALIVE DOWN HERE?
THE CREATURES KEEP US ALIVE WHEN THEY BRING US, OXYGENATING OUR BLOOD, THROUGH THE SKIN, THINGS CALLED SPINNERS, IT'S LIKE--
NO, I MEAN FOR ALL THIS TIME. ALL THESE YEARS...
IT'S THIS PLACE. IT'S DESIGNED TO KEEP US ALIVE, IN STASIS. THE GASES IN THE AIR PREVENT REPLICATIVE SENESCENCE.
IT'S A SHIP, ISN'T IT? I KNEW IT.

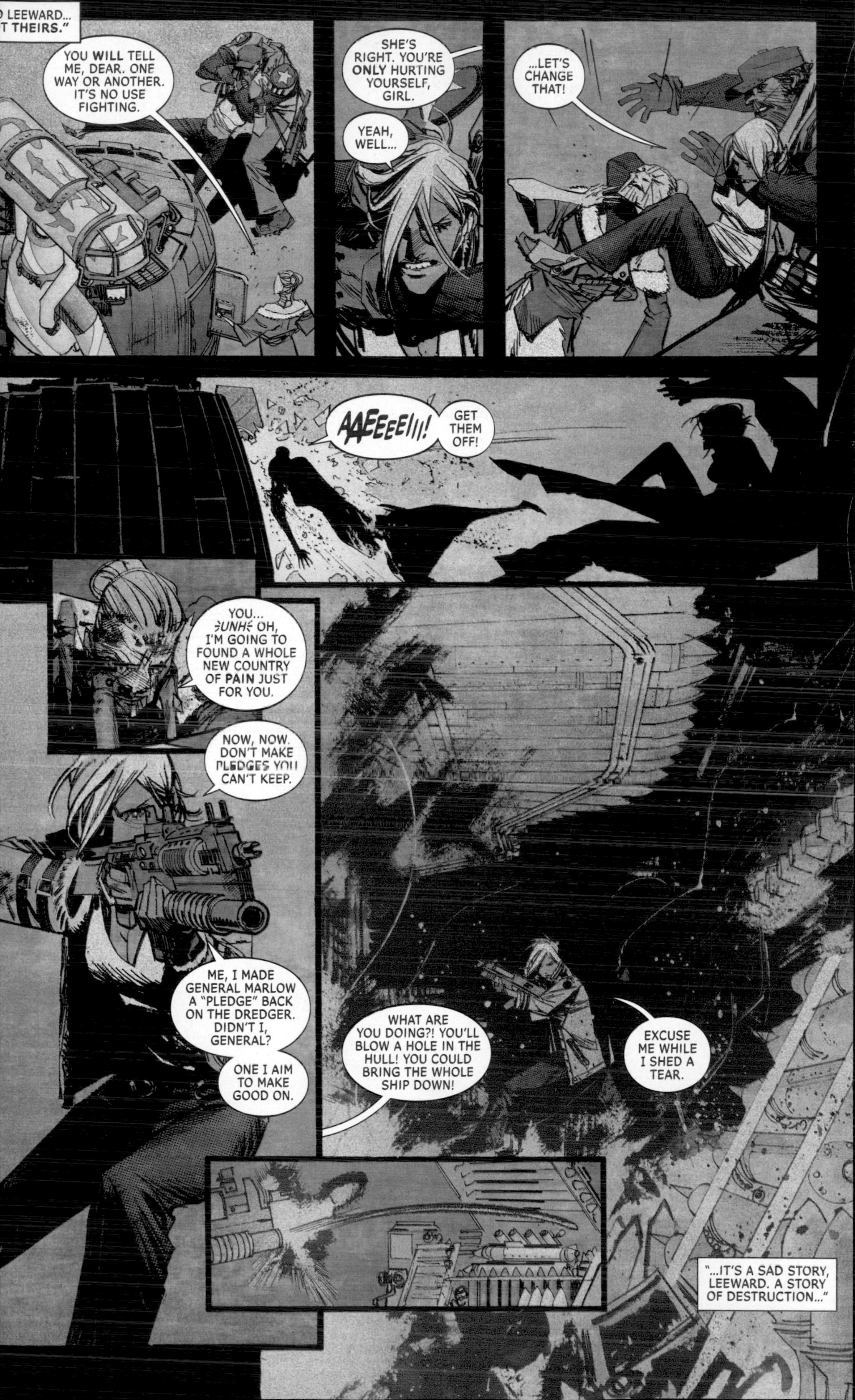
...D LEEWARD...
...T THEIRS."
YOU WILL TELL ME, DEAR. ONE WAY OR ANOTHER. IT'S NO USE FIGHTING.
SHE'S RIGHT. YOU'RE ONLY HURTING YOURSELF, GIRL.
YEAH, WELL...
...LET'S CHANGE THAT!
AAEEEE!!!!
GET THEM OFF!
YOU... UNH OH, I'M GOING TO FOUND A WHOLE NEW COUNTRY OF PAIN JUST FOR YOU.
NOW, NOW. DON'T MAKE PLEDGES YOU CAN'T KEEP.
ME, I MADE GENERAL MARLOW A "PLEDGE" BACK ON THE DREDGER. DIDN'T I, GENERAL?
ONE I AIM TO MAKE GOOD ON.
WHAT ARE YOU DOING?! YOU'LL BLOW A HOLE IN THE HULL! YOU COULD BRING THE WHOLE SHIP DOWN!
EXCUSE ME WHILE I SHED A TEAR.
"...IT'S A SAD STORY, LEEWARD. A STORY OF DESTRUCTION..."

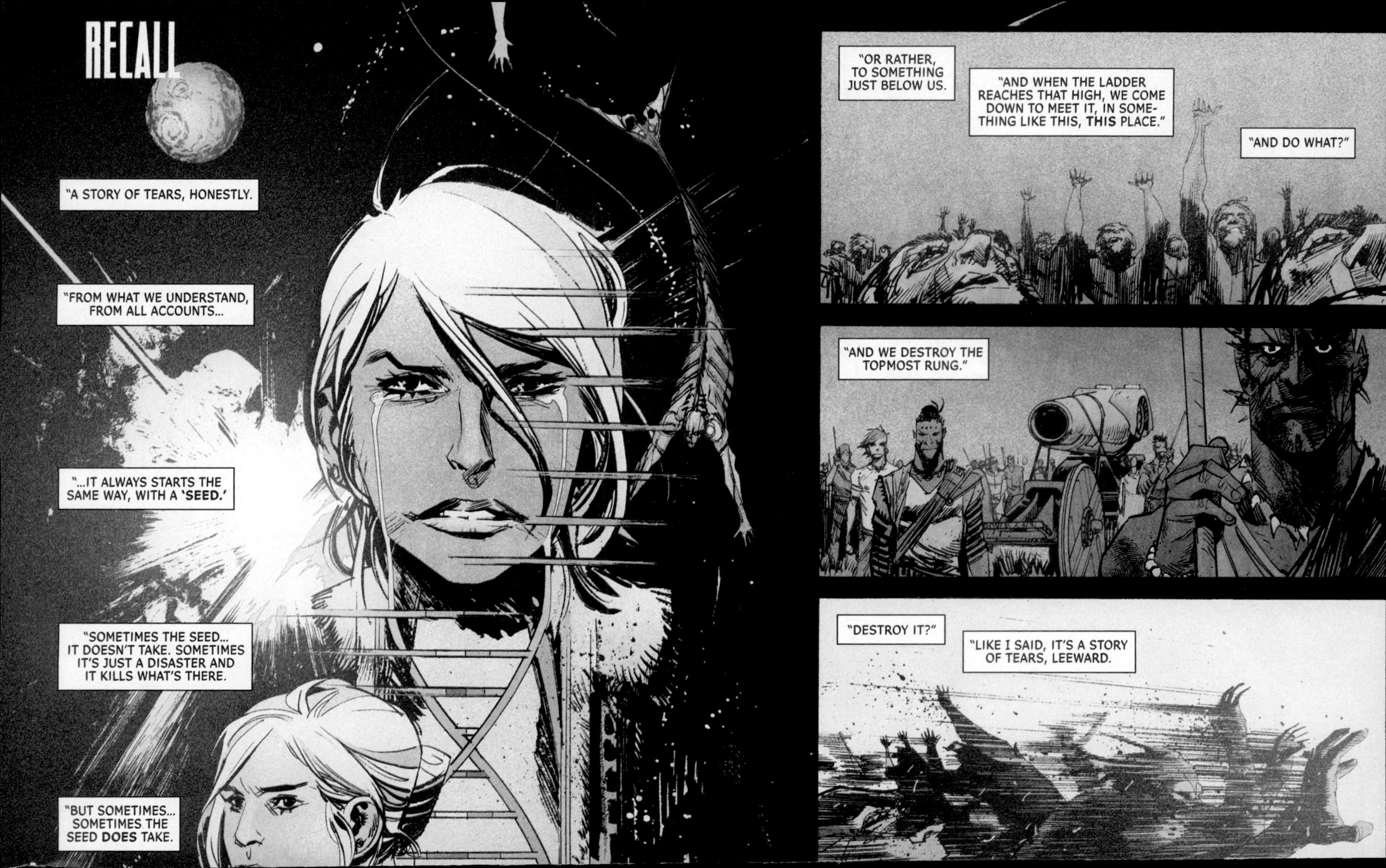
RECALL
"A STORY OF TEARS, HONESTLY.
"FROM WHAT WE UNDERSTAND, FROM ALL ACCOUNTS...
"...IT ALWAYS STARTS THE SAME WAY, WITH A **'SEED.'**
"SOMETIMES THE SEED... IT DOESN'T TAKE. SOMETIMES IT'S JUST A DISASTER AND IT KILLS WHAT'S THERE.
"BUT SOMETIMES... SOMETIMES THE SEED **DOES** TAKE.
"OR RATHER, TO SOMETHING JUST BELOW US.
"AND WHEN THE LADDER REACHES THAT HIGH, WE COME DOWN TO MEET IT, IN SOMETHING LIKE THIS, **THIS** PLACE."
"AND DO WHAT?"
"AND WE DESTROY THE TOPMOST RUNG."
"DESTROY IT?"
"LIKE I SAID, IT'S A STORY OF TEARS, LEEWARD.

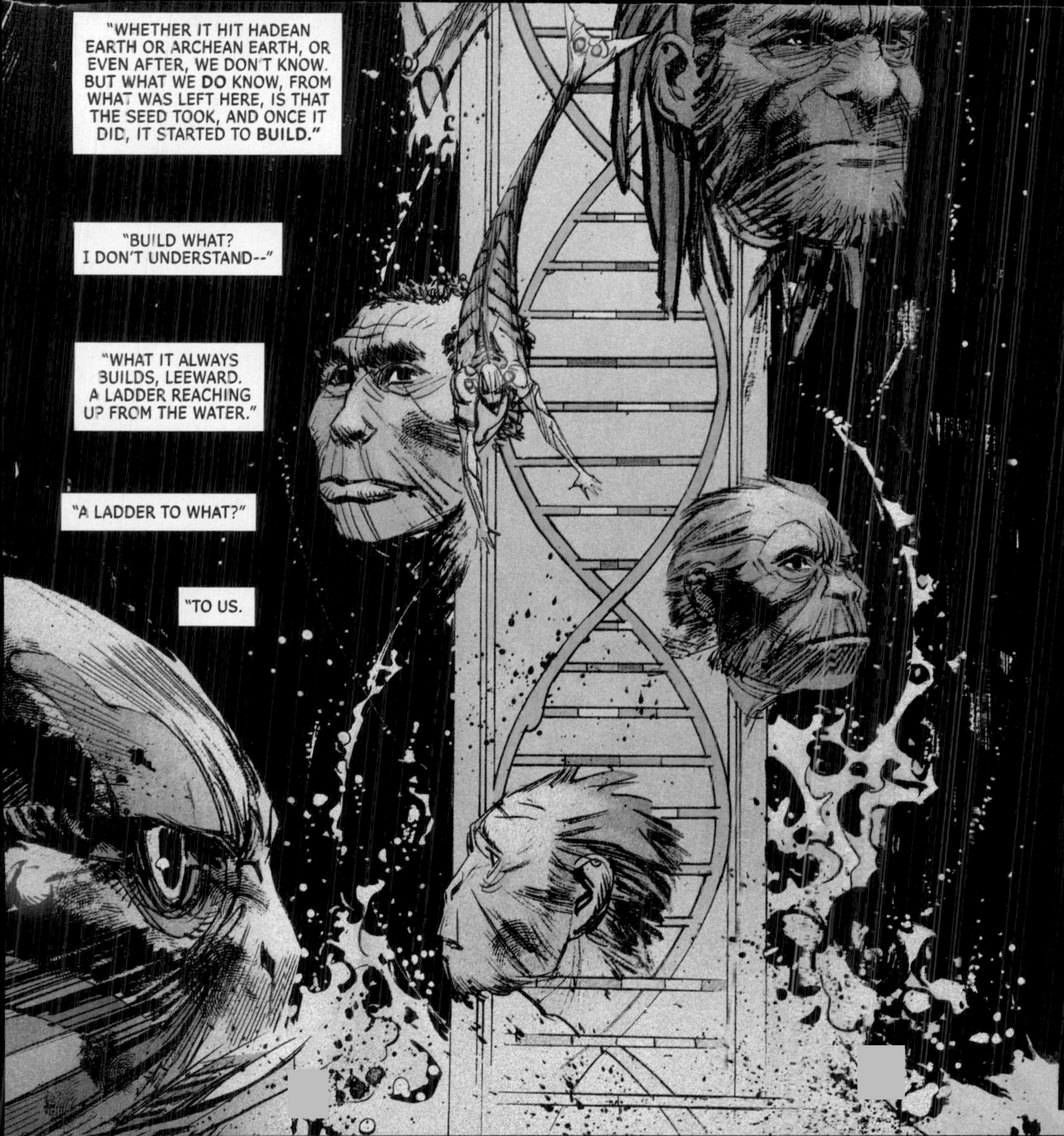
"WHETHER IT HIT HADEAN EARTH OR ARCHEAN EARTH, OR EVEN AFTER, WE DON'T KNOW. BUT WHAT WE DO KNOW, FROM WHAT WAS LEFT HERE, IS THAT THE SEED TOOK, AND ONCE IT DID, IT STARTED TO BUILD."
"BUILD WHAT? I DON'T UNDERSTAND--"
"WHAT IT ALWAYS BUILDS, LEEWARD. A LADDER REACHING UP FROM THE WATER."
"A LADDER TO WHAT?"
"TO US.

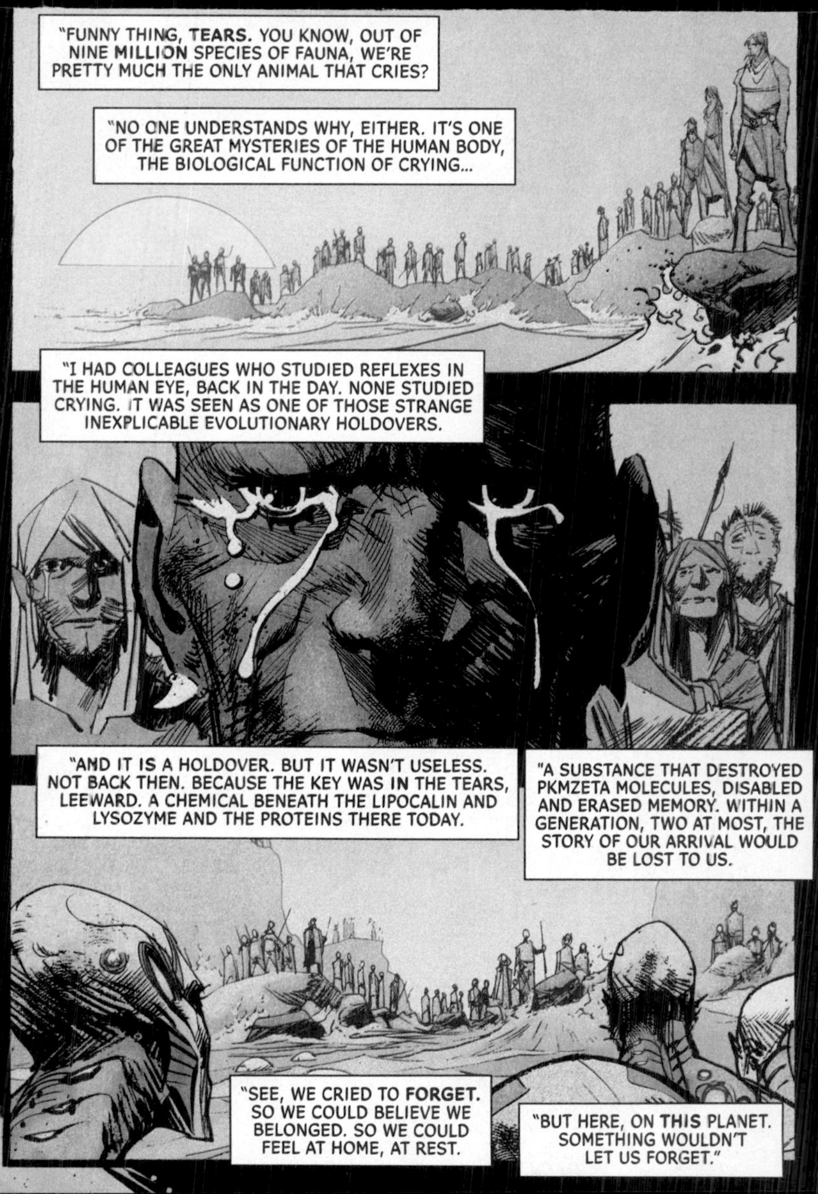
"FUNNY THING, TEARS. YOU KNOW, OUT OF NINE MILLION SPECIES OF FAUNA, WE'RE PRETTY MUCH THE ONLY ANIMAL THAT CRIES?
"NO ONE UNDERSTANDS WHY, EITHER. IT'S ONE OF THE GREAT MYSTERIES OF THE HUMAN BODY, THE BIOLOGICAL FUNCTION OF CRYING...
"I HAD COLLEAGUES WHO STUDIED REFLEXES IN THE HUMAN EYE, BACK IN THE DAY. NONE STUDIED CRYING. IT WAS SEEN AS ONE OF THOSE STRANGE INEXPLICABLE EVOLUTIONARY HOLDOVERS.
"AND IT IS A HOLDOVER. BUT IT WASN'T USELESS. NOT BACK THEN. BECAUSE THE KEY WAS IN THE TEARS, LEEWARD. A CHEMICAL BENEATH THE LIPOCALIN AND LYSOZYME AND THE PROTEINS THERE TODAY.
"A SUBSTANCE THAT DESTROYED PKMZETA MOLECULES, DISABLED AND ERASED MEMORY. WITHIN A GENERATION, TWO AT MOST, THE STORY OF OUR ARRIVAL WOULD BE LOST TO US.
"SEE, WE CRIED TO FORGET. SO WE COULD BELIEVE WE BELONGED. SO WE COULD FEEL AT HOME, AT REST.
"BUT HERE, ON THIS PLANET. SOMETHING WOULDN'T LET US FORGET."

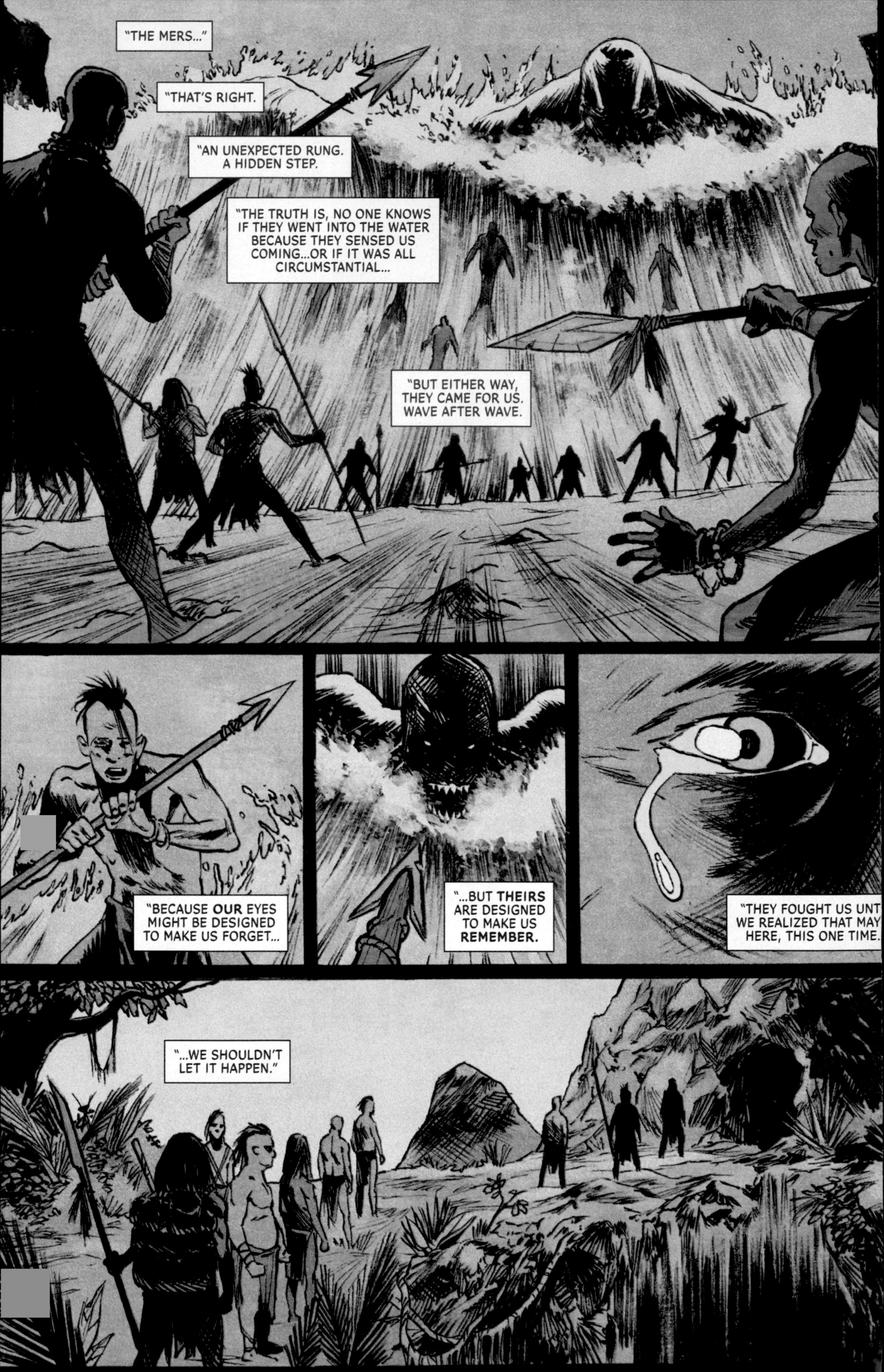
"THE MERS..."
"THAT'S RIGHT.
"AN UNEXPECTED RUNG. A HIDDEN STEP.
"THE TRUTH IS, NO ONE KNOWS IF THEY WENT INTO THE WATER BECAUSE THEY SENSED US COMING...OR IF IT WAS ALL CIRCUMSTANTIAL...
"BUT EITHER WAY, THEY CAME FOR US. WAVE AFTER WAVE.
"BECAUSE OUR EYES MIGHT BE DESIGNED TO MAKE US FORGET...
"...BUT THEIRS ARE DESIGNED TO MAKE US REMEMBER.
"THEY FOUGHT US UNT WE REALIZED THAT MAY HERE, THIS ONE TIME.
"...WE SHOULDN'T LET IT HAPPEN."

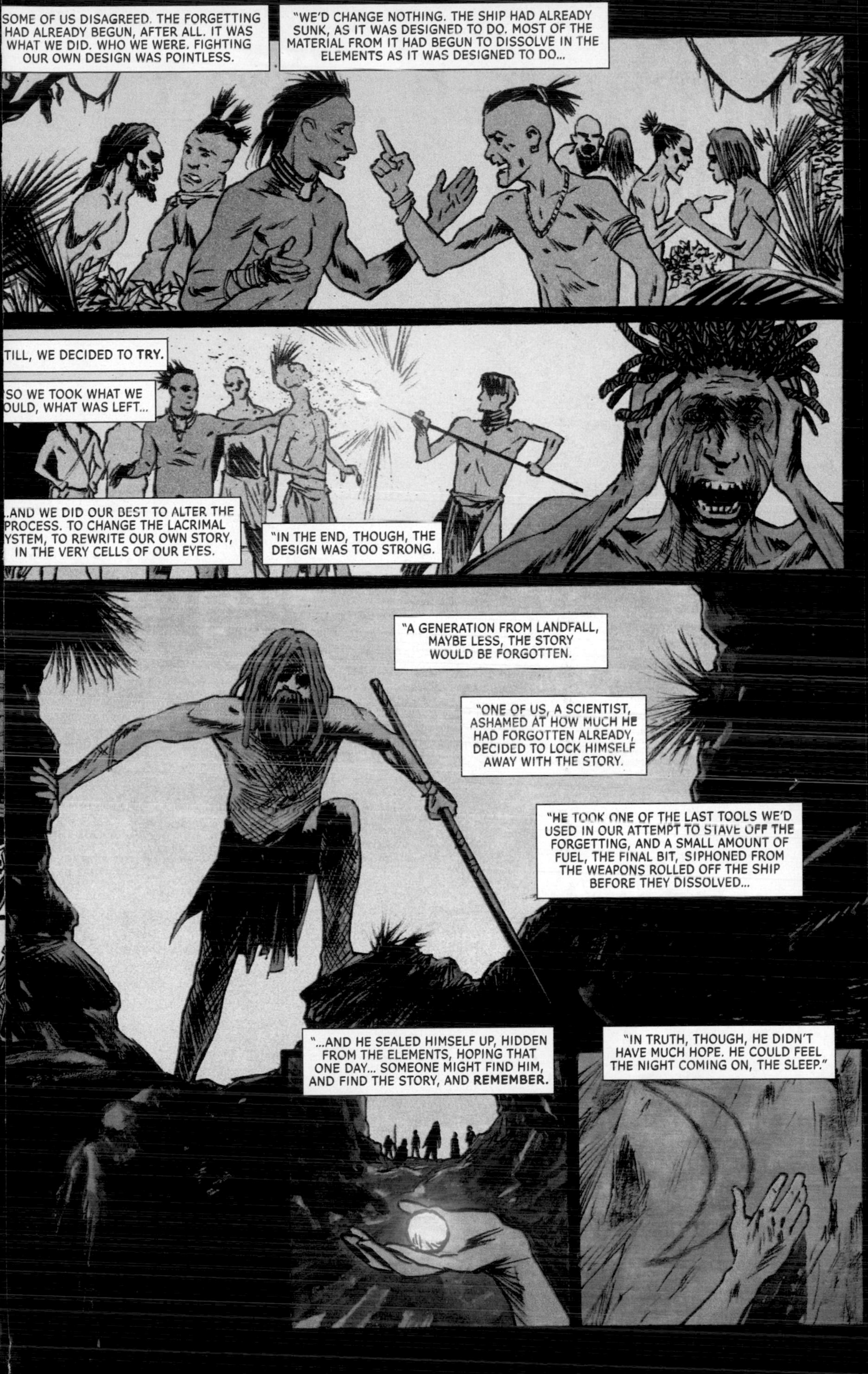
SOME OF US DISAGREED. THE FORGETTING HAD ALREADY BEGUN, AFTER ALL. IT WAS WHAT WE DID. WHO WE WERE. FIGHTING OUR OWN DESIGN WAS POINTLESS.
"WE'D CHANGE NOTHING. THE SHIP HAD ALREADY SUNK, AS IT WAS DESIGNED TO DO. MOST OF THE MATERIAL FROM IT HAD BEGUN TO DISSOLVE IN THE ELEMENTS AS IT WAS DESIGNED TO DO...
TILL, WE DECIDED TO **TRY**.
SO WE TOOK WHAT WE OULD, WHAT WAS LEFT...
..AND WE DID OUR BEST TO ALTER THE PROCESS. TO CHANGE THE LACRIMAL YSTEM, TO REWRITE OUR OWN STORY, IN THE VERY CELLS OF OUR EYES.
"IN THE END, THOUGH, THE DESIGN WAS TOO STRONG.
"A GENERATION FROM LANDFALL, MAYBE LESS, THE STORY WOULD BE FORGOTTEN.
"ONE OF US, A SCIENTIST, ASHAMED AT HOW MUCH HE HAD FORGOTTEN ALREADY, DECIDED TO LOCK HIMSELF AWAY WITH THE STORY.
"HE TOOK ONE OF THE LAST TOOLS WE'D USED IN OUR ATTEMPT TO STAVE OFF THE FORGETTING, AND A SMALL AMOUNT OF FUEL, THE FINAL BIT, SIPHONED FROM THE WEAPONS ROLLED OFF THE SHIP BEFORE THEY DISSOLVED...
"...AND HE SEALED HIMSELF UP, HIDDEN FROM THE ELEMENTS, HOPING THAT ONE DAY... SOMEONE MIGHT FIND HIM, AND FIND THE STORY, AND **REMEMBER**.
"IN TRUTH, THOUGH, HE DIDN'T HAVE MUCH HOPE. HE COULD FEEL THE NIGHT COMING ON, THE SLEEP."

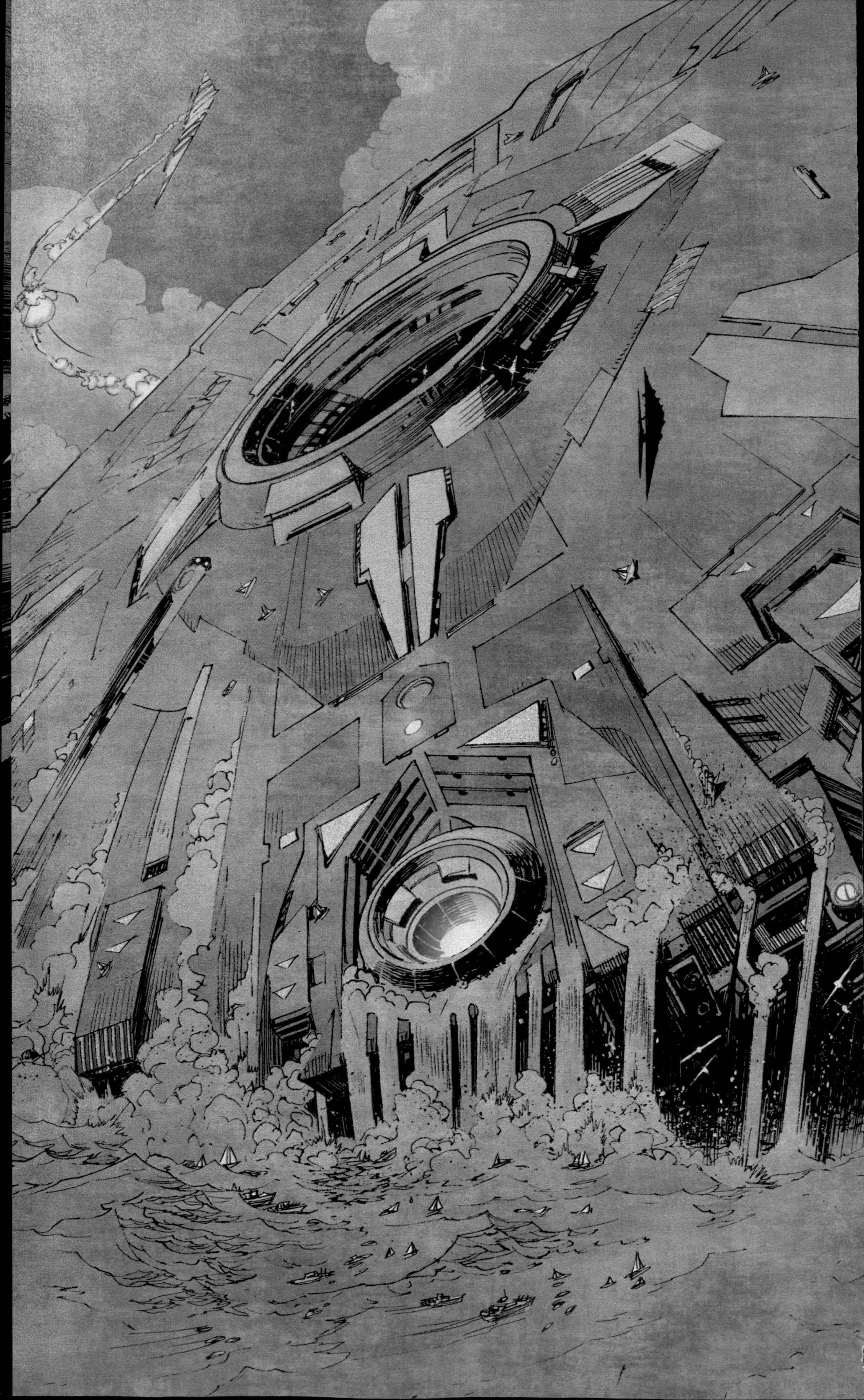

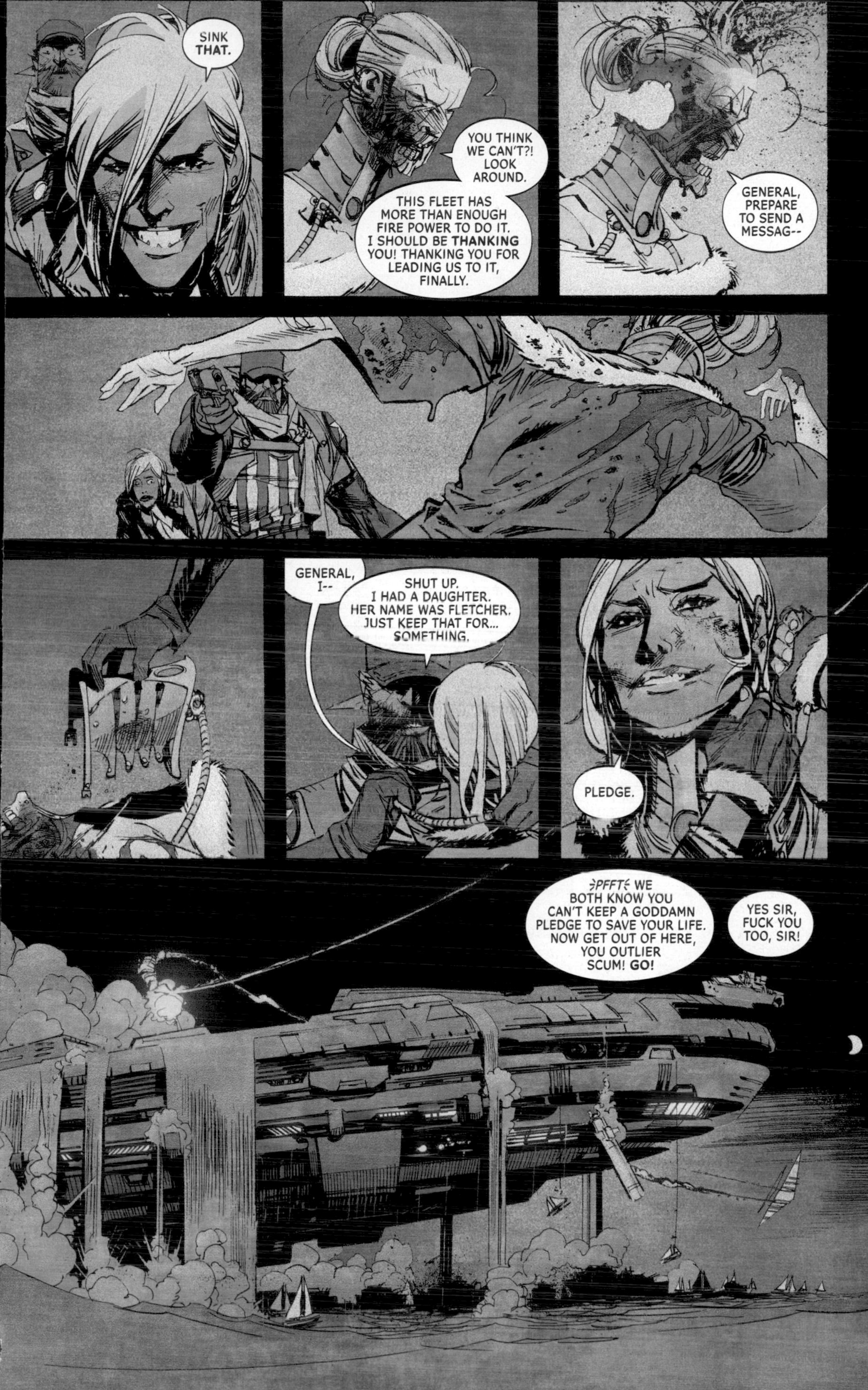
SINK **THAT.**
YOU THINK WE CAN'T?! LOOK AROUND.
THIS FLEET HAS MORE THAN ENOUGH FIRE POWER TO DO IT. I SHOULD BE **THANKING** YOU! THANKING YOU FOR LEADING US TO IT, FINALLY.
GENERAL, PREPARE TO SEND A MESSAG--
GENERAL, I--
SHUT UP. I HAD A DAUGHTER. HER NAME WAS FLETCHER. JUST KEEP THAT FOR... SOMETHING.
PLEDGE.
PFFT WE BOTH KNOW YOU CAN'T KEEP A GODDAMN PLEDGE TO SAVE YOUR LIFE. NOW GET OUT OF HERE, YOU OUTLIER SCUM! **GO!**
YES SIR, FUCK YOU TOO, SIR!

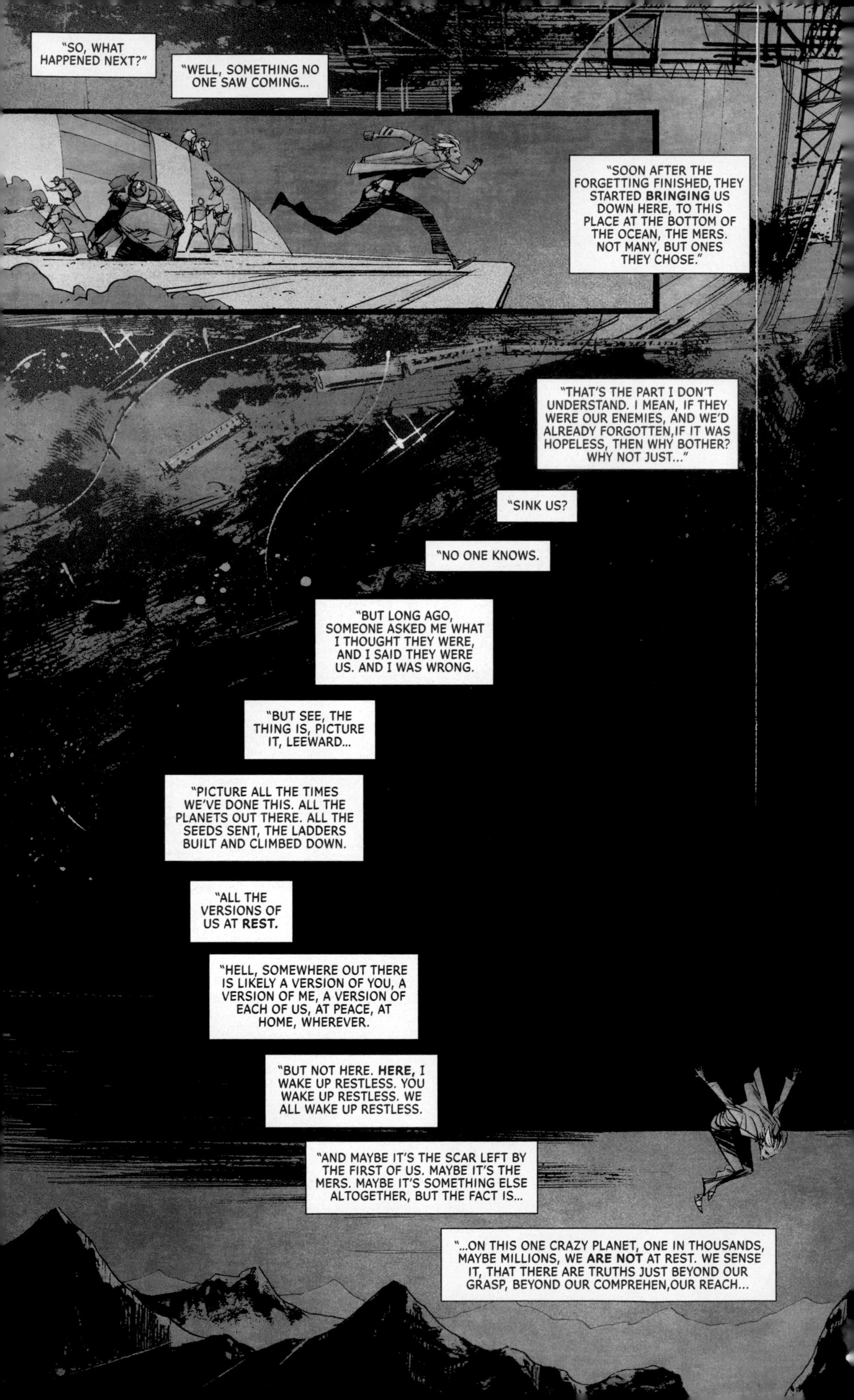
"SO, WHAT HAPPENED NEXT?"
"WELL, SOMETHING NO ONE SAW COMING...
"SOON AFTER THE FORGETTING FINISHED, THEY STARTED **BRINGING** US DOWN HERE, TO THIS PLACE AT THE BOTTOM OF THE OCEAN, THE MERS. NOT MANY, BUT ONES THEY CHOSE."
"THAT'S THE PART I DON'T UNDERSTAND. I MEAN, IF THEY WERE OUR ENEMIES, AND WE'D ALREADY FORGOTTEN,IF IT WAS HOPELESS, THEN WHY BOTHER? WHY NOT JUST..."
"SINK US?
"NO ONE KNOWS.
"BUT LONG AGO, SOMEONE ASKED ME WHAT I THOUGHT THEY WERE, AND I SAID THEY WERE US. AND I WAS WRONG.
"BUT SEE, THE THING IS, PICTURE IT, LEEWARD...
"PICTURE ALL THE TIMES WE'VE DONE THIS. ALL THE PLANETS OUT THERE. ALL THE SEEDS SENT, THE LADDERS BUILT AND CLIMBED DOWN.
"ALL THE VERSIONS OF US AT **REST.**
"HELL, SOMEWHERE OUT THERE IS LIKELY A VERSION OF YOU, A VERSION OF ME, A VERSION OF EACH OF US, AT PEACE, AT HOME, WHEREVER.
"BUT NOT HERE. **HERE,** I WAKE UP RESTLESS. YOU WAKE UP RESTLESS. WE ALL WAKE UP RESTLESS.
"AND MAYBE IT'S THE SCAR LEFT BY THE FIRST OF US. MAYBE IT'S THE MERS. MAYBE IT'S SOMETHING ELSE ALTOGETHER, BUT THE FACT IS...
"...ON THIS ONE CRAZY PLANET, ONE IN THOUSANDS, MAYBE MILLIONS, WE **ARE NOT** AT REST. WE SENSE IT, THAT THERE ARE TRUTHS JUST BEYOND OUR GRASP, BEYOND OUR COMPREHEN,OUR REACH...

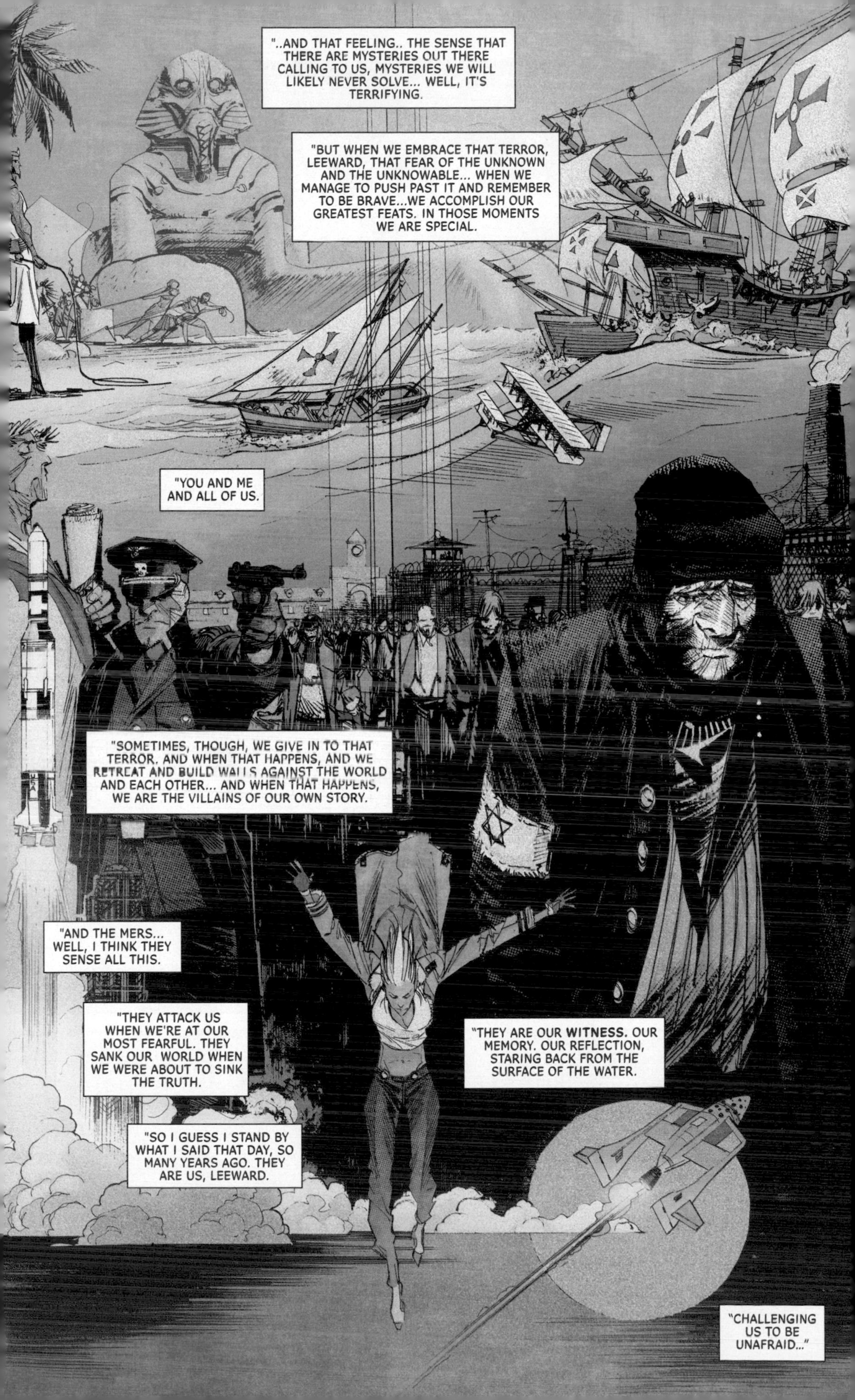
"..AND THAT FEELING.. THE SENSE THAT THERE ARE MYSTERIES OUT THERE CALLING TO US, MYSTERIES WE WILL LIKELY NEVER SOLVE... WELL, IT'S TERRIFYING.
"BUT WHEN WE EMBRACE THAT TERROR, LEEWARD, THAT FEAR OF THE UNKNOWN AND THE UNKNOWABLE... WHEN WE MANAGE TO PUSH PAST IT AND REMEMBER TO BE BRAVE...WE ACCOMPLISH OUR GREATEST FEATS. IN THOSE MOMENTS WE ARE SPECIAL.
"YOU AND ME AND ALL OF US.
"SOMETIMES, THOUGH, WE GIVE IN TO THAT TERROR. AND WHEN THAT HAPPENS, AND WE RETREAT AND BUILD WALLS AGAINST THE WORLD AND EACH OTHER... AND WHEN THAT HAPPENS, WE ARE THE VILLAINS OF OUR OWN STORY.
"AND THE MERS... WELL, I THINK THEY SENSE ALL THIS.
"THEY ATTACK US WHEN WE'RE AT OUR MOST FEARFUL. THEY SANK OUR WORLD WHEN WE WERE ABOUT TO SINK THE TRUTH.
"THEY ARE OUR **WITNESS.** OUR MEMORY. OUR REFLECTION, STARING BACK FROM THE SURFACE OF THE WATER.
"SO I GUESS I STAND BY WHAT I SAID THAT DAY, SO MANY YEARS AGO. THEY ARE US, LEEWARD.
"CHALLENGING US TO BE UNAFRAID..."

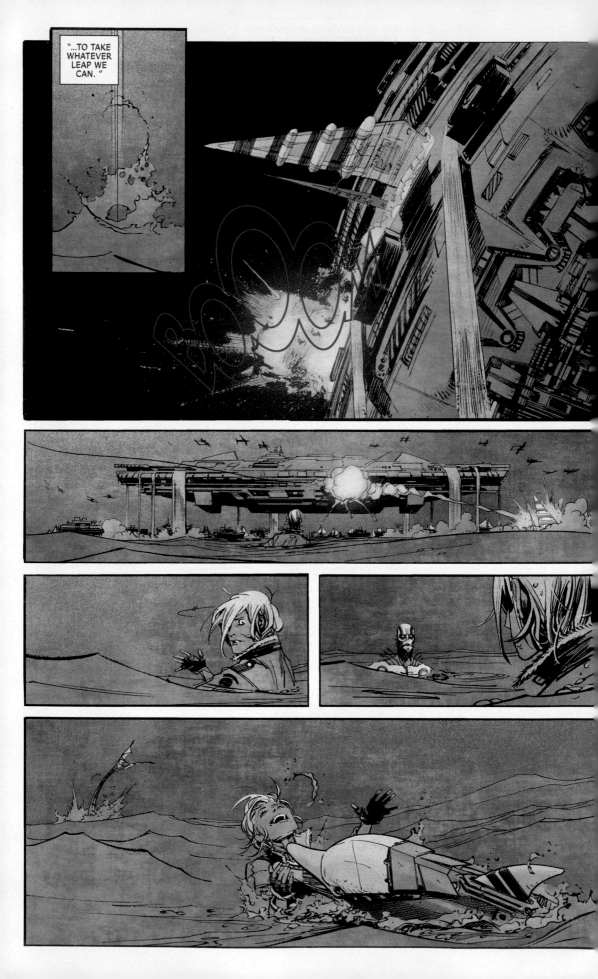

"...TO TAKE WHATEVER LEAP WE CAN."

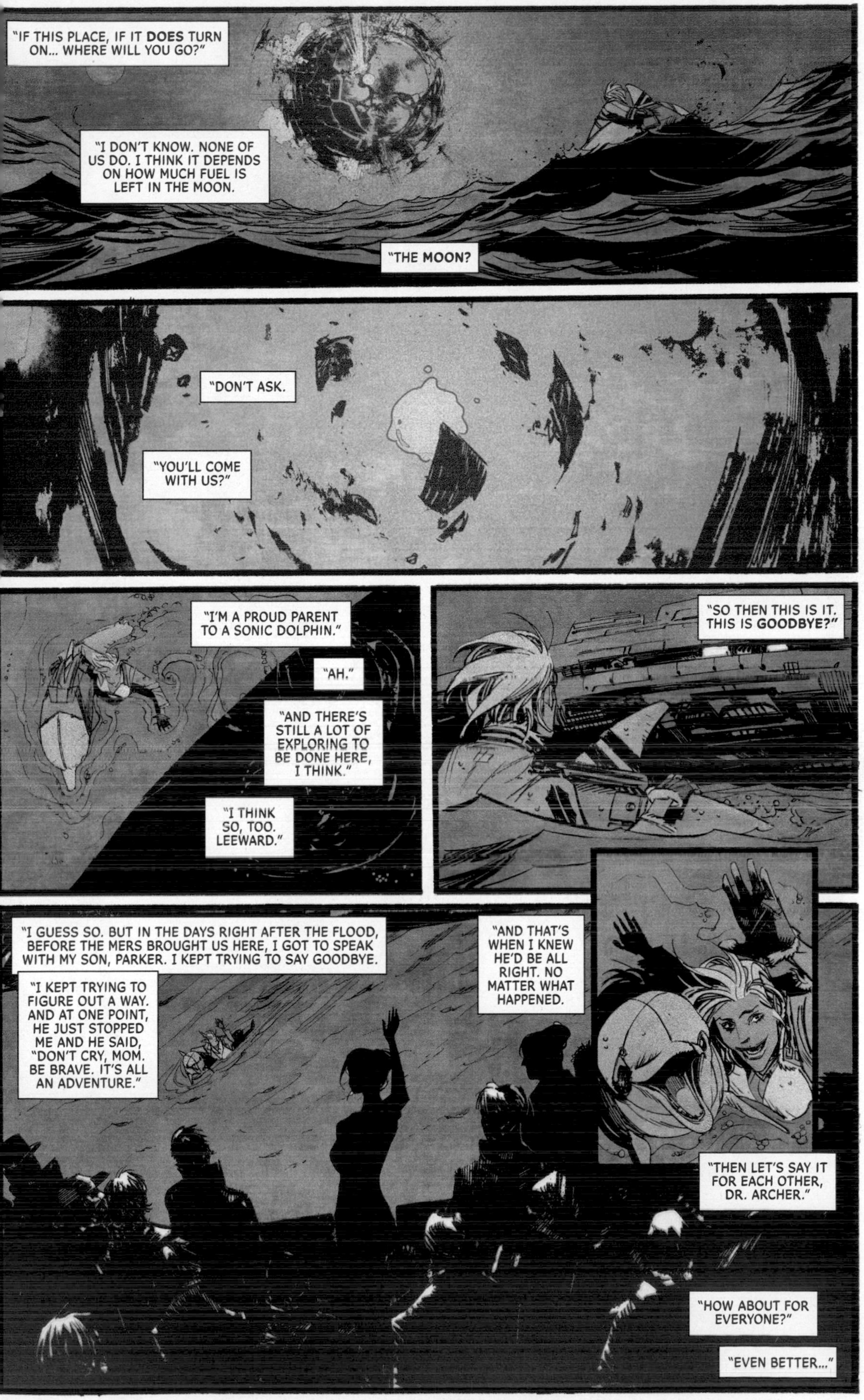
"IF THIS PLACE, IF IT DOES TURN ON... WHERE WILL YOU GO?"
"I DON'T KNOW. NONE OF US DO. I THINK IT DEPENDS ON HOW MUCH FUEL IS LEFT IN THE MOON.
"THE MOON?
"DON'T ASK.
"YOU'LL COME WITH US?"
"I'M A PROUD PARENT TO A SONIC DOLPHIN."
"AH."
"AND THERE'S STILL A LOT OF EXPLORING TO BE DONE HERE, I THINK."
"I THINK SO, TOO. LEEWARD."
"SO THEN THIS IS IT. THIS IS GOODBYE?"
"I GUESS SO. BUT IN THE DAYS RIGHT AFTER THE FLOOD, BEFORE THE MERS BROUGHT US HERE, I GOT TO SPEAK WITH MY SON, PARKER. I KEPT TRYING TO SAY GOODBYE.
"I KEPT TRYING TO FIGURE OUT A WAY. AND AT ONE POINT, HE JUST STOPPED ME AND HE SAID, "DON'T CRY, MOM. BE BRAVE. IT'S ALL AN ADVENTURE."
"AND THAT'S WHEN I KNEW HE'D BE ALL RIGHT. NO MATTER WHAT HAPPENED.
"THEN LET'S SAY IT FOR EACH OTHER, DR. ARCHER."
"HOW ABOUT FOR EVERYONE?"
"EVEN BETTER..."

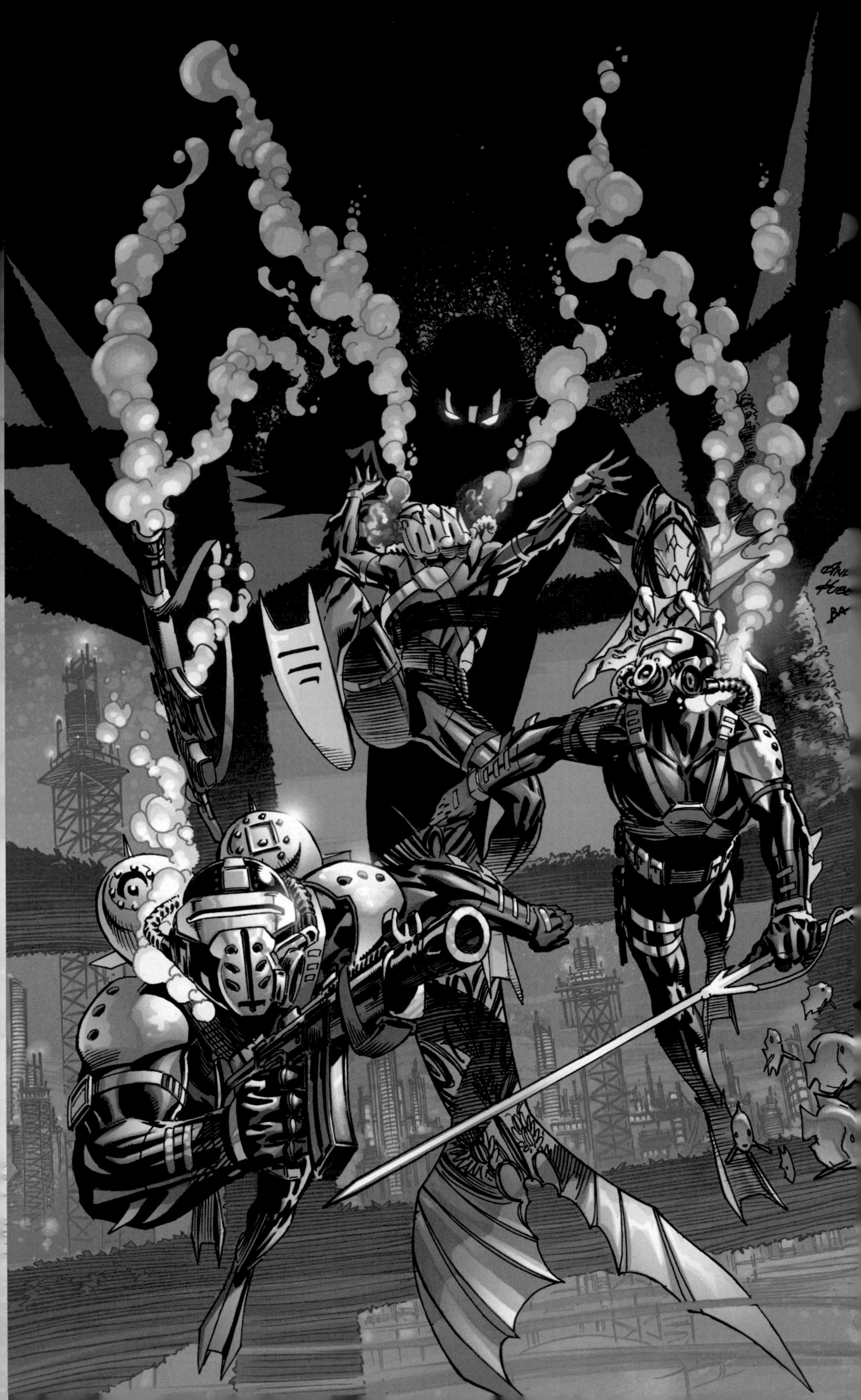

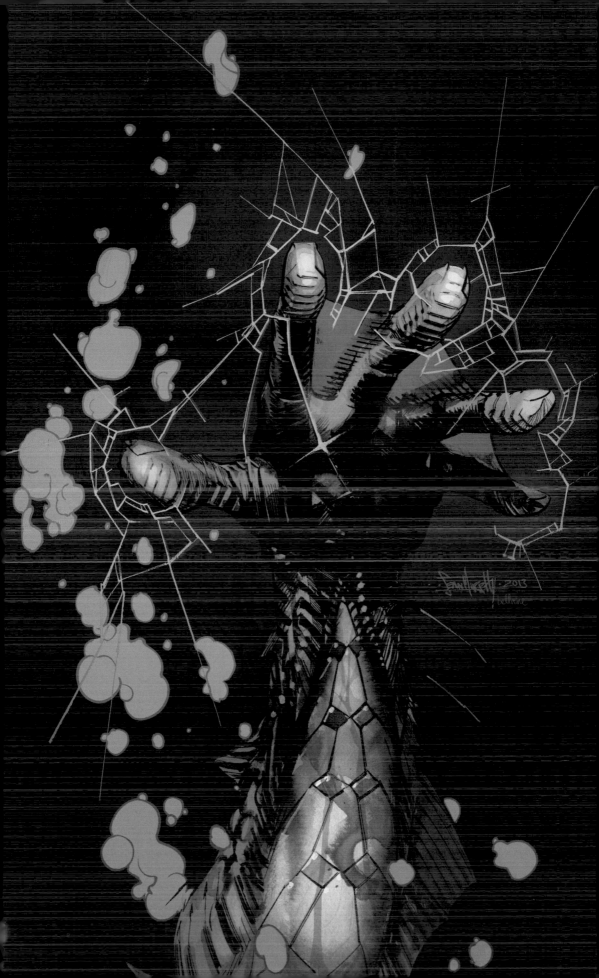

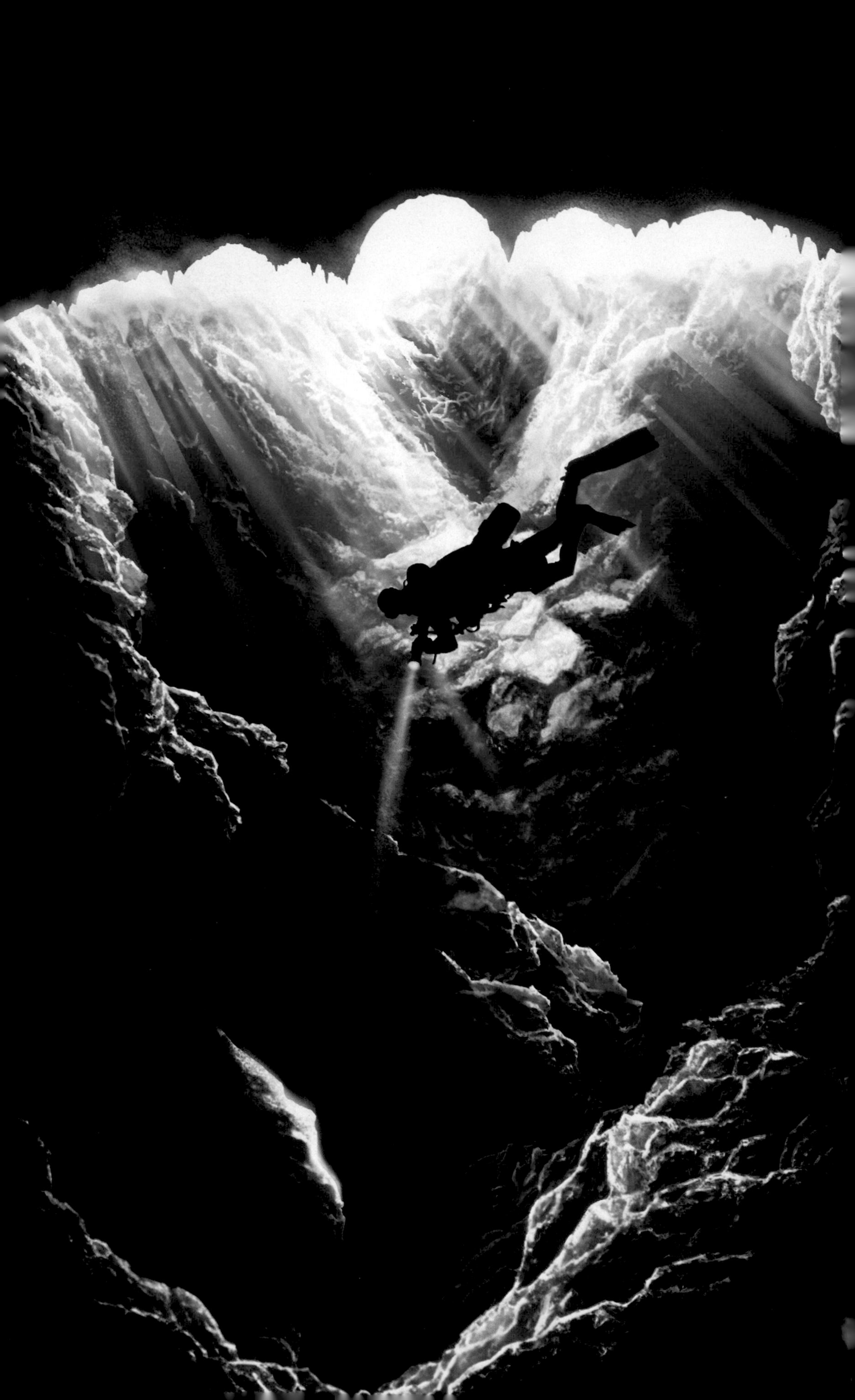

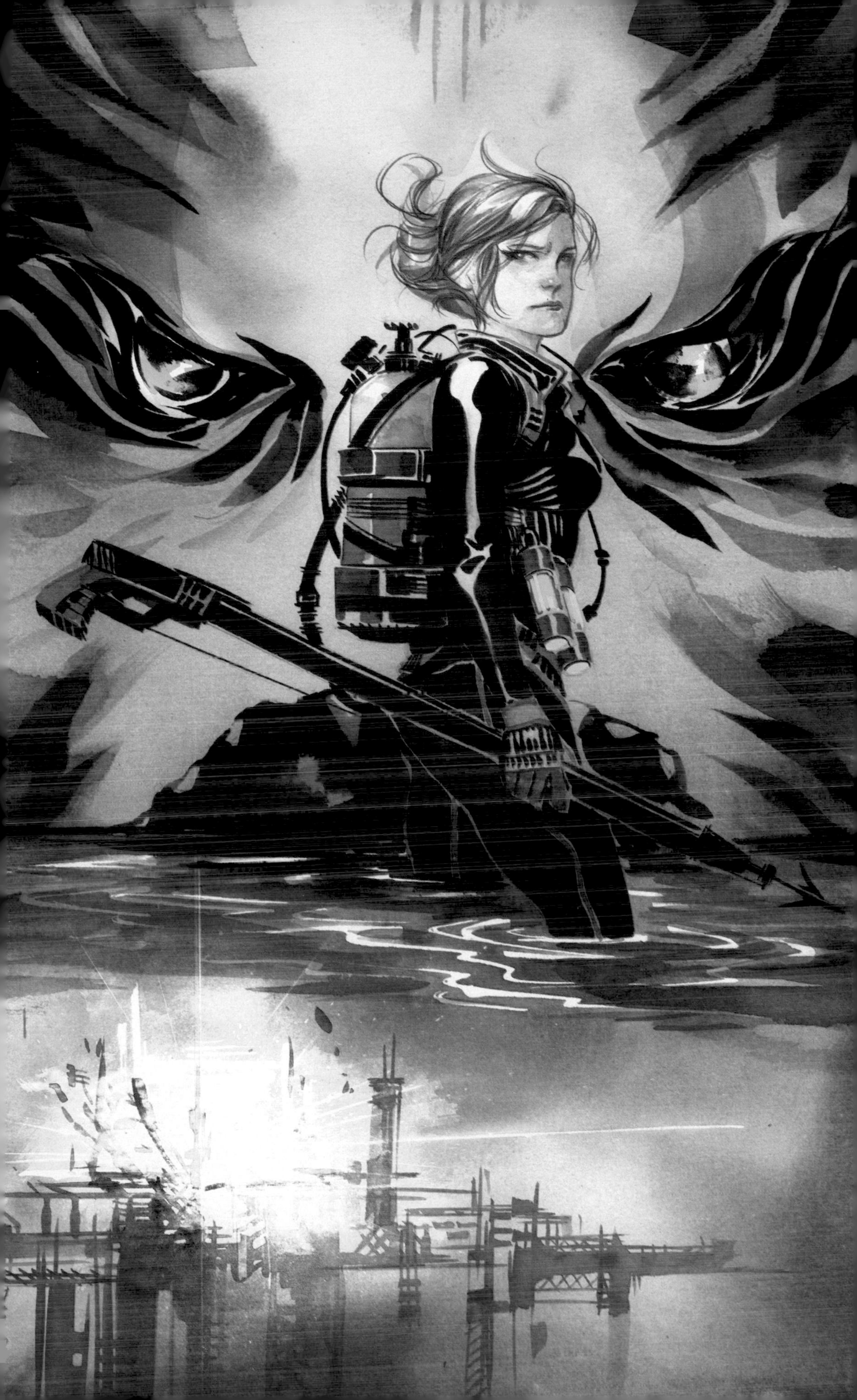

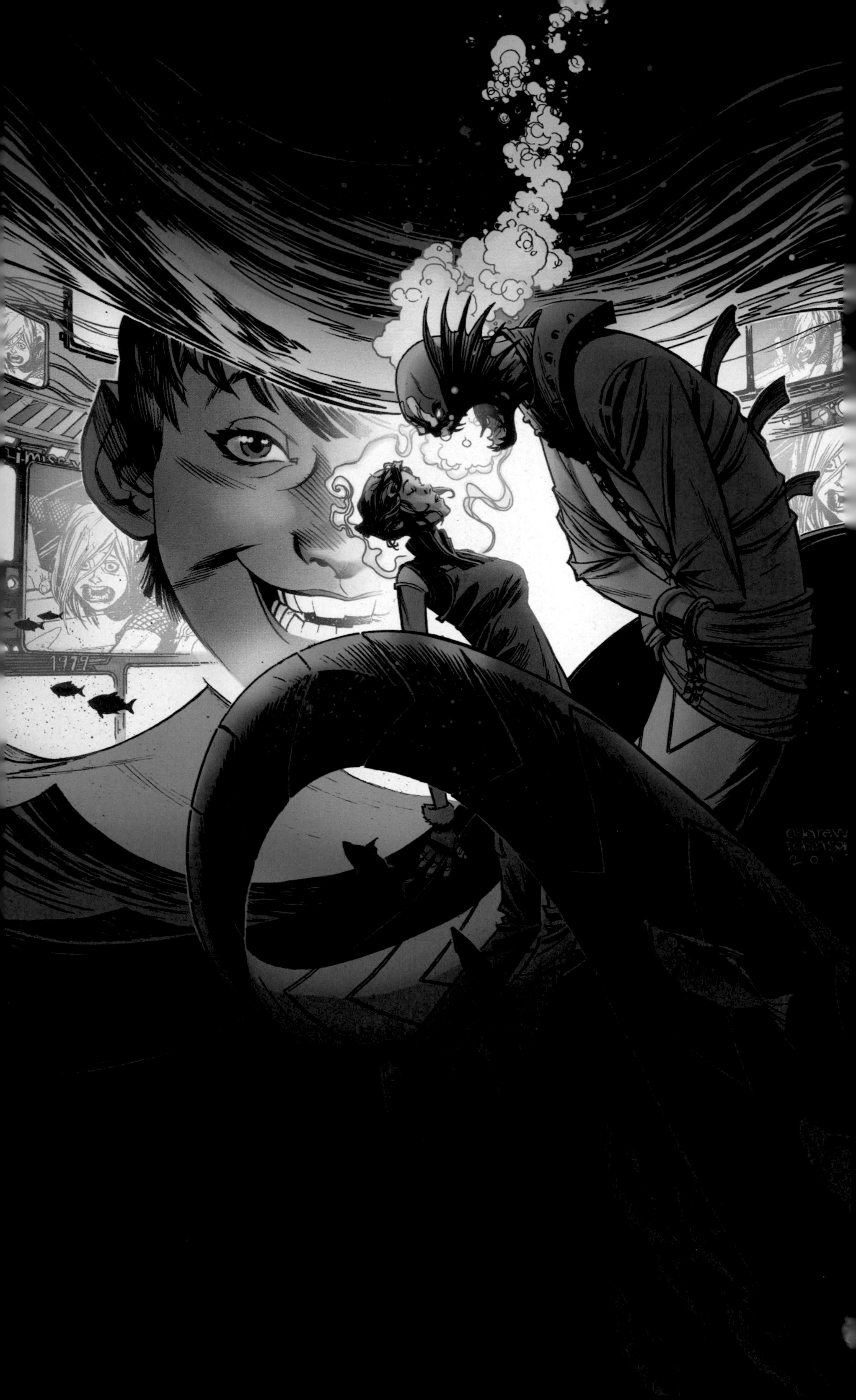
1979

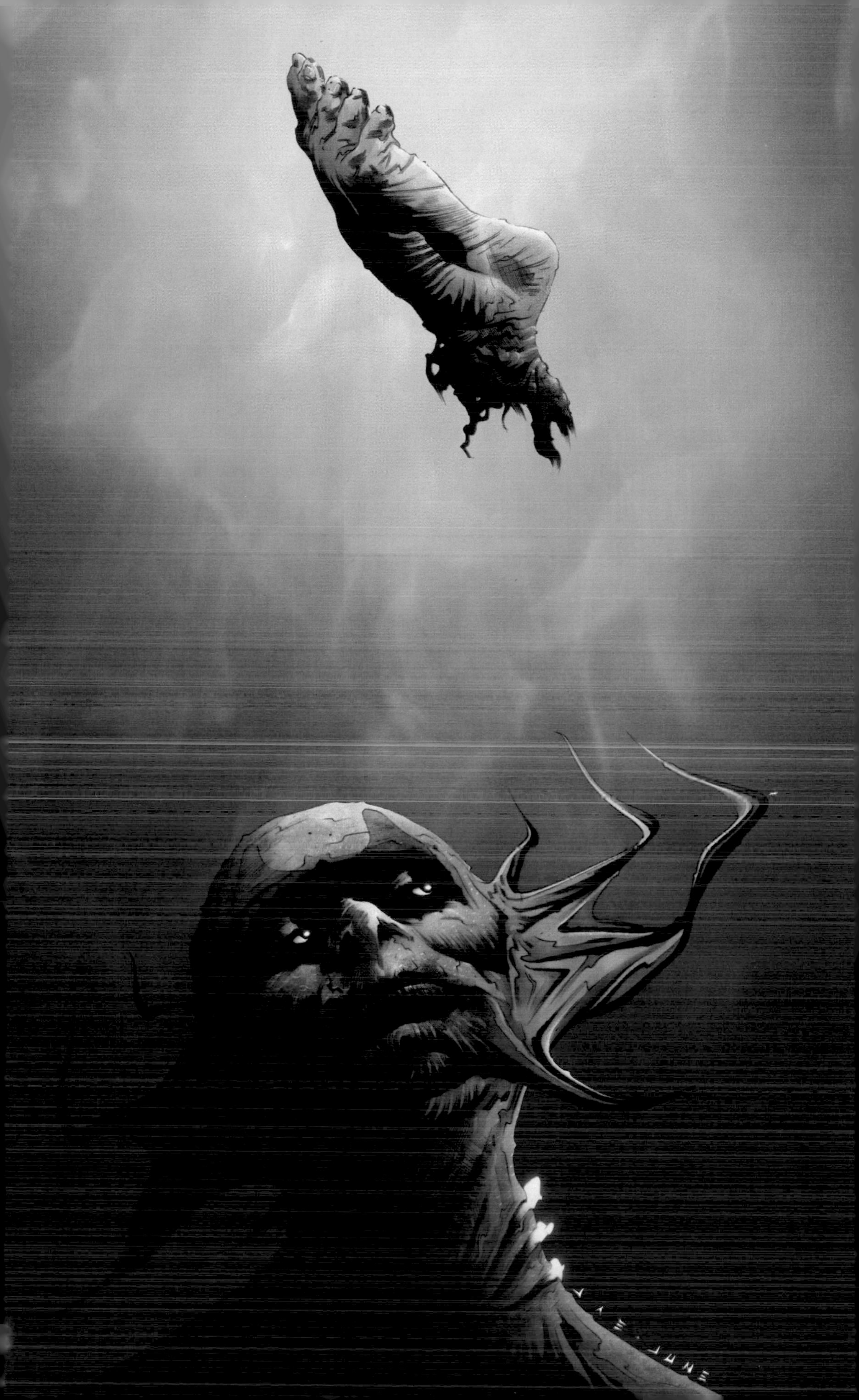

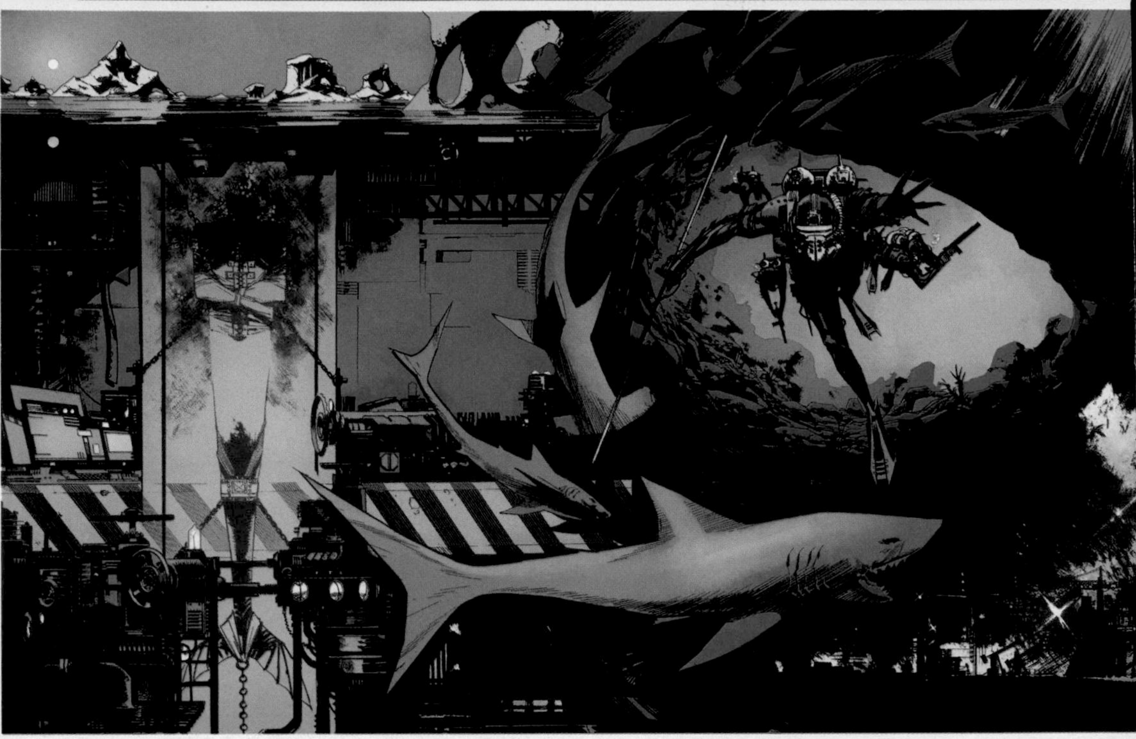

The Wake 1-5 Connecting Covers

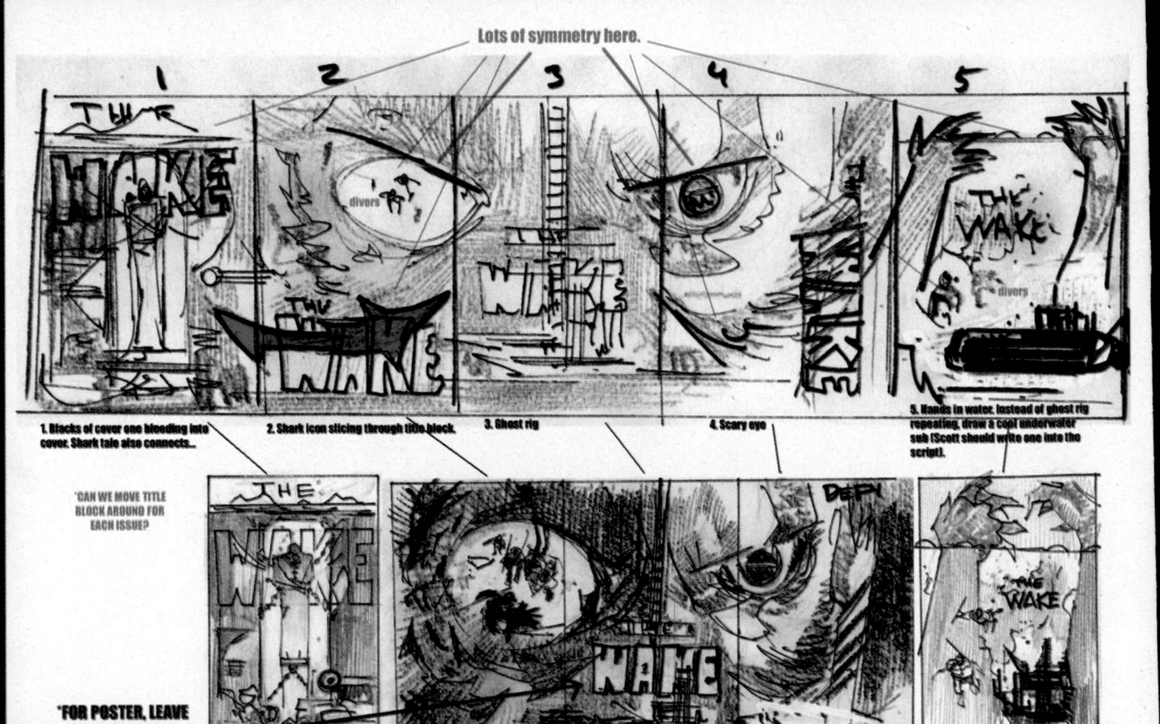

Lots of symmetry here.
1
2
3
4
5
divers
divers
1. Blacks of cover one bleeding into cover. Shark tale also connects...
2. Shark icon slicing through title block.
3. Ghost rig
4. Scary eye
5. Hands in water. Instead of ghost rig repeating, draw a cool underwater sub (Scott should write one into the script).
*CAN WE MOVE TITLE BLOCK AROUND FOR EACH ISSUE?
*FOR POSTER, LEAVE ONLY THE MIDDLE TITLE BLOCK.

Connecting Covers Sketch

We knew we had a big, epic series and Sean wanted to do a series of connecting covers to show the scope of this story.

Internally we called it the "Bond Poster" because it looked like a big, detailed illustrated poster for a James Bond poster in the '60s.

THE WAKE
Sketch Book

Sean went through a variety of looks for the head of the creature before we settled on the final design — a fast, slick and scary creature.

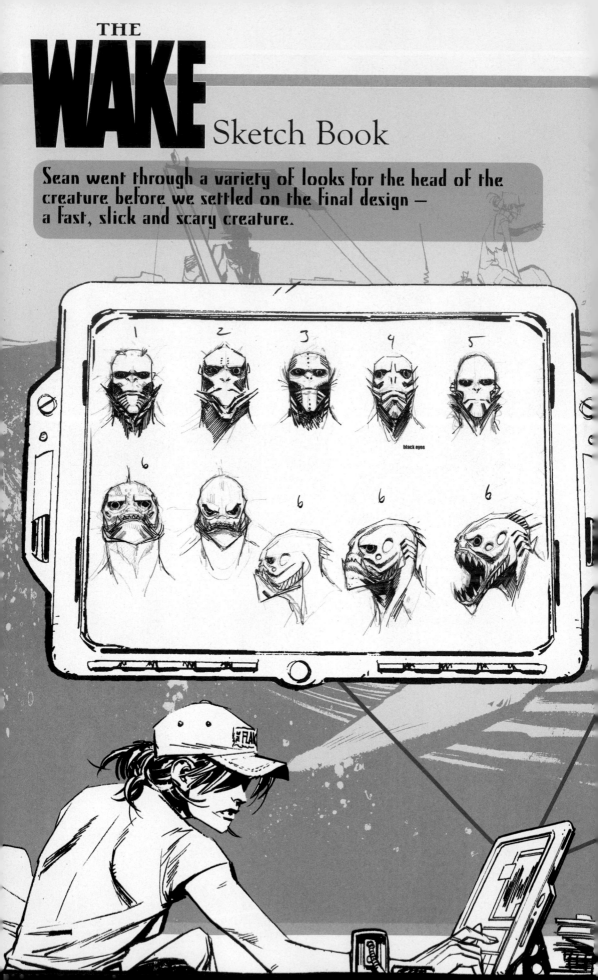

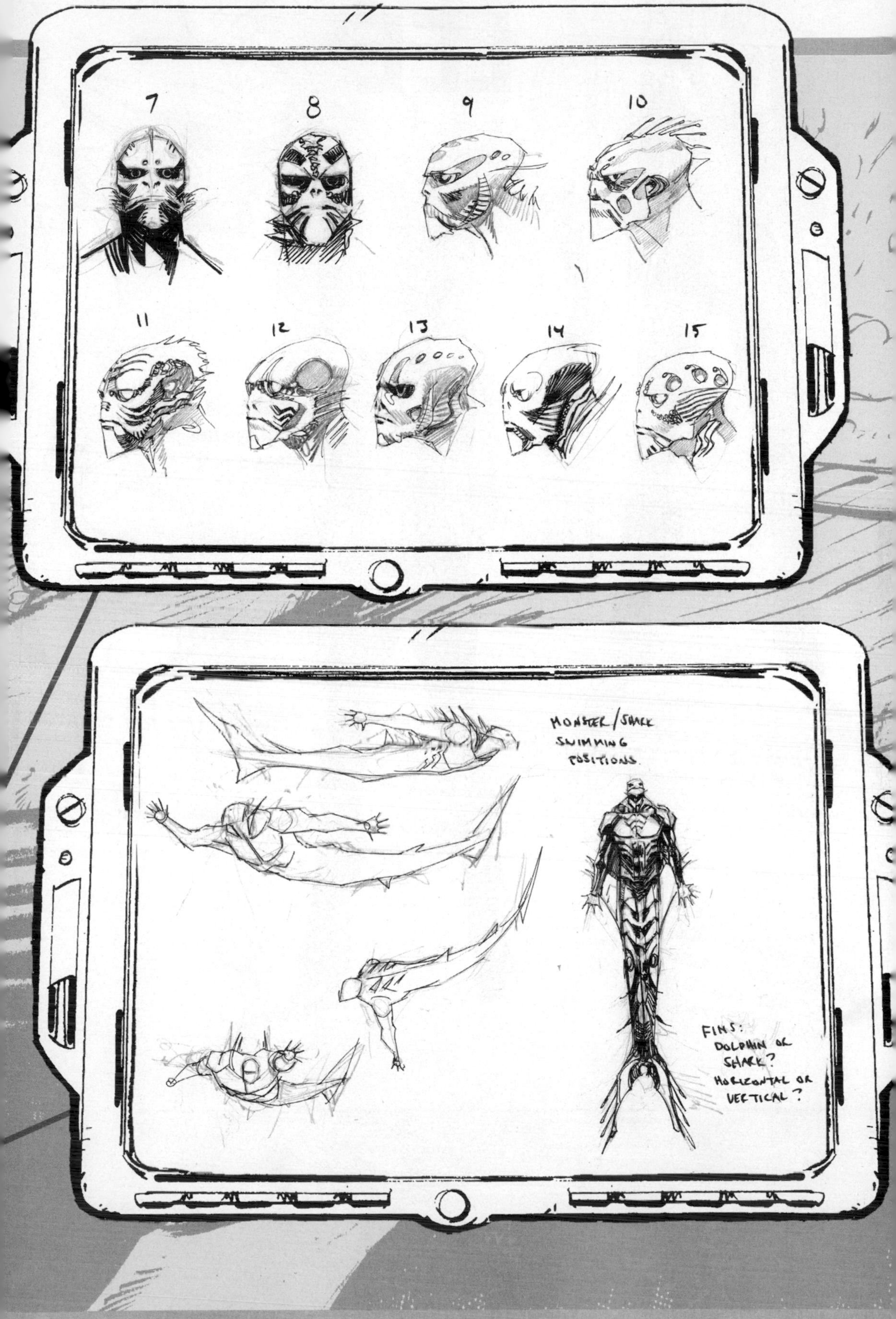

7
8
9
10
11
12
13
14
15
MONSTER/SHARK
SWIMMING
POSITIONS.
FINS:
DOLPHIN OR
SHARK?
HORIZONTAL OR
VERTICAL?

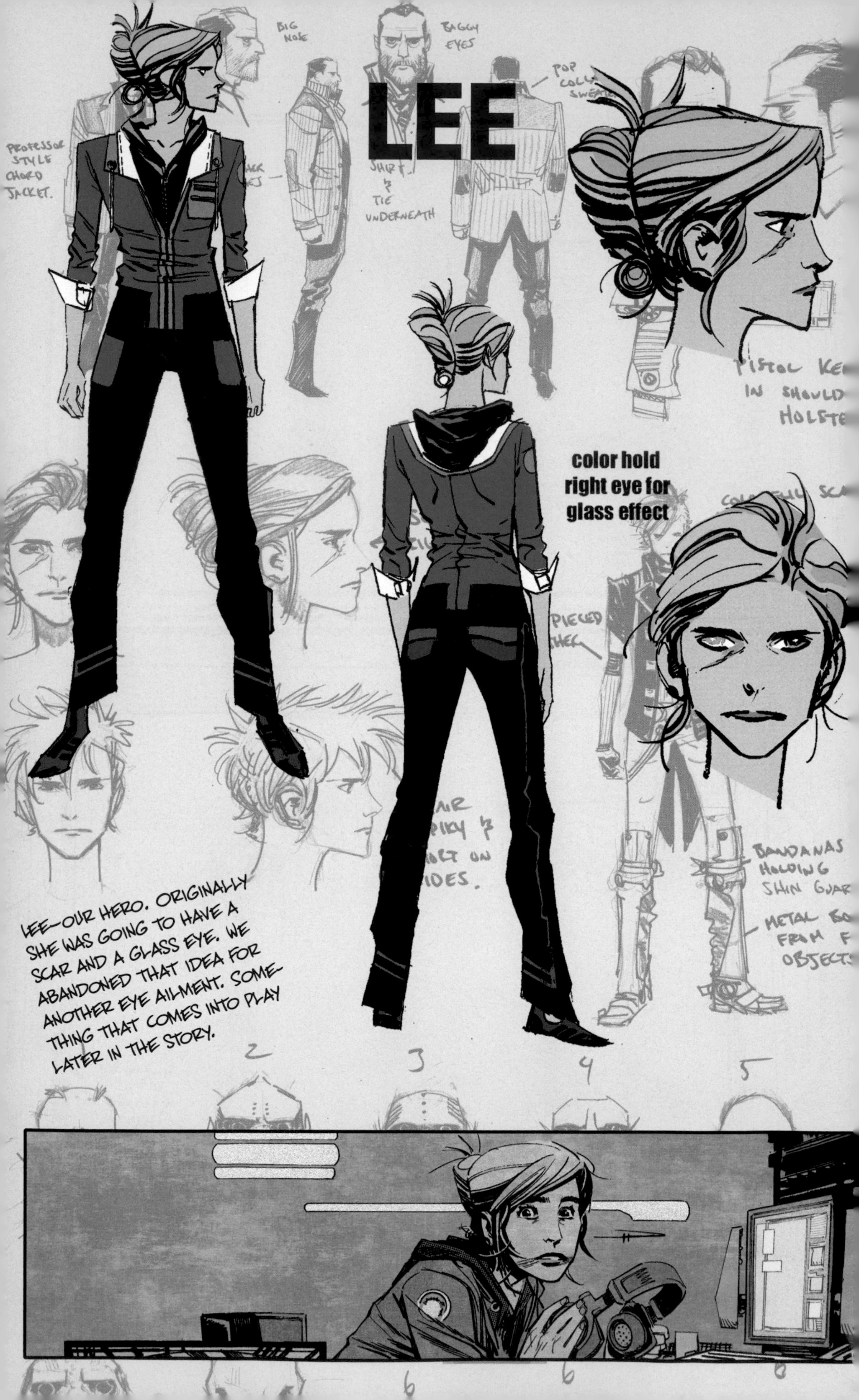
LEE
BIG NOSE
BAGGY EYES
PROFESSOR STYLE CHORD JACKET.
SHIRT & TIE UNDERNEATH
color hold right eye for glass effect
LEE—OUR HERO. ORIGINALLY SHE WAS GOING TO HAVE A SCAR AND A GLASS EYE. WE ABANDONED THAT IDEA FOR ANOTHER EYE AILMENT. SOMETHING THAT COMES INTO PLAY LATER IN THE STORY.

LEEWARD

BIG NOSE

BAGGY EYES

POP COLLAR SWEATER

SHIRT & TIE UNDERNEATH

PISTOL KEPT IN SHOULDER HOLSTER

SCARF

PIECED TOGETHER

BANDANAS HOLDING SHIN GUARDS

METAL BOOTS FROM FOUND OBJECTS

OUR MYSTERY GIRL FROM THE FUTURE. HOW DOES HER STORY RELATE TO LEE? WHAT DOES THIS HAVE TO DO WITH THE CREATURE? WHERE'D SHE GET THAT COOL DOLPHIN?

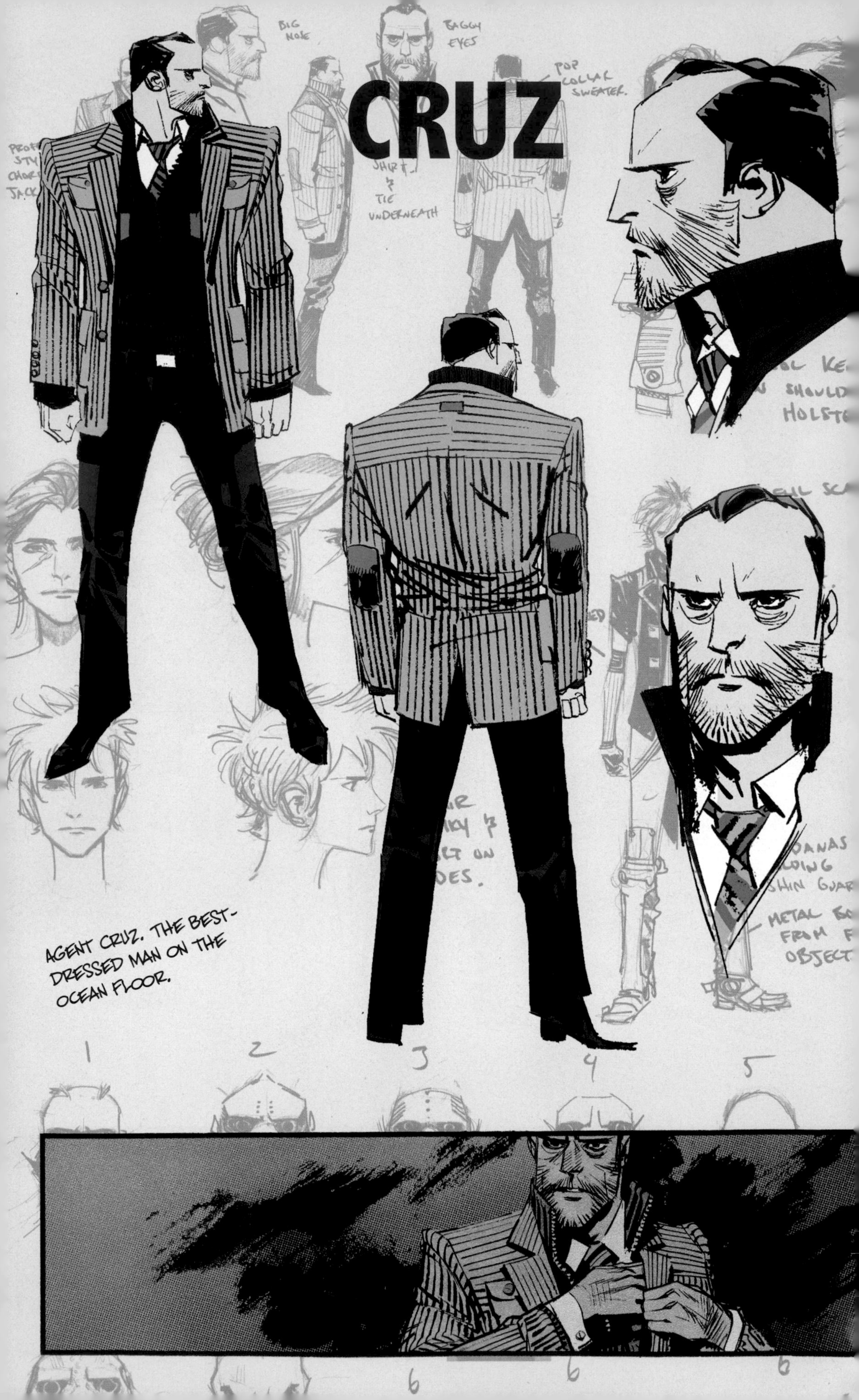
CRUZ
BIG NOSE
BAGGY EYES
POP COLLAR SWEATER.
SHIRT & TIE UNDERNEATH
AGENT CRUZ. THE BEST-DRESSED MAN ON THE OCEAN FLOOR.
1
2
3
4
5
6
6
6

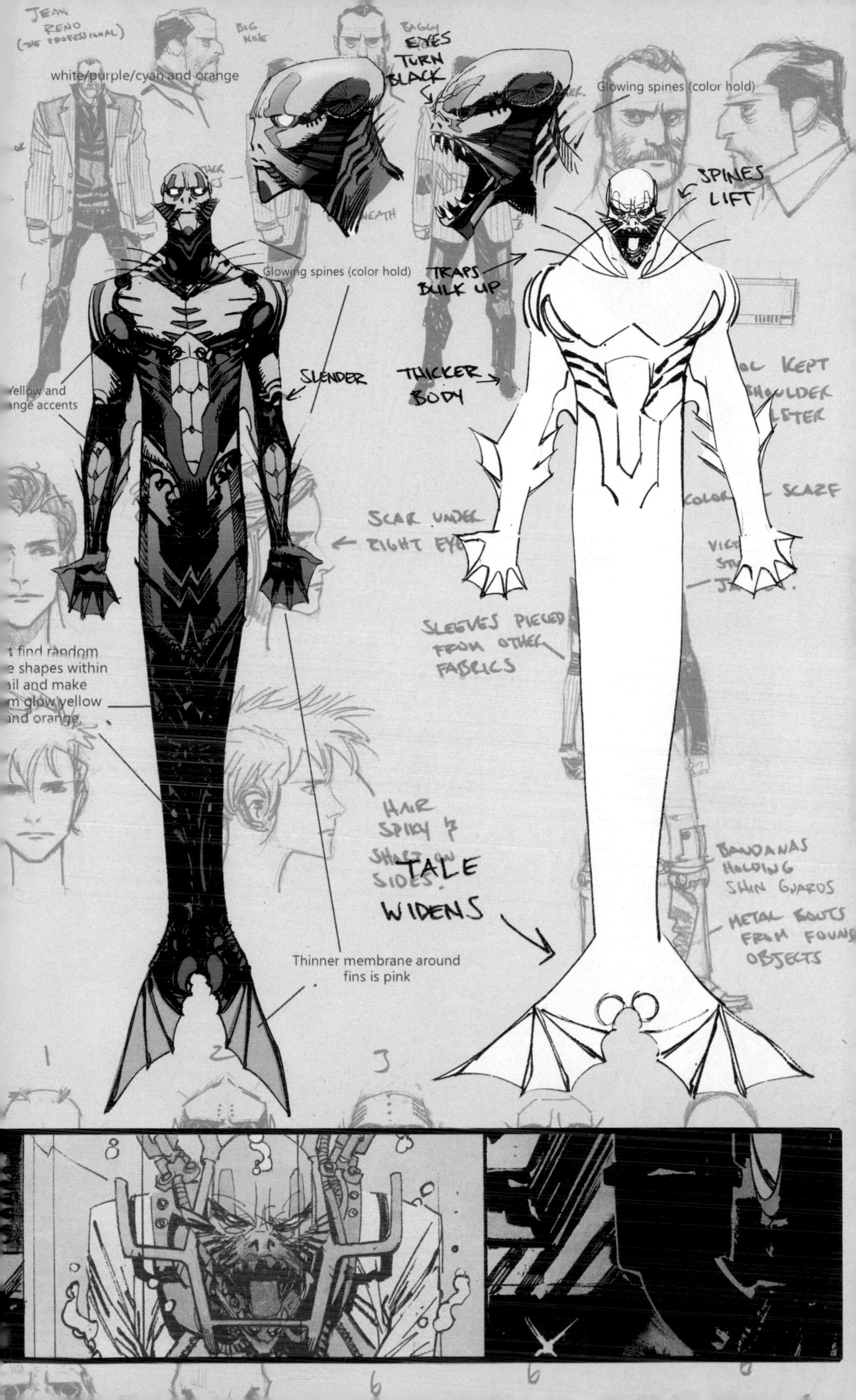
JEAN RENO (THE PROFESSIONAL)
BIG NOSE
BAGGY EYES
white/purple/cyan and orange
EYES TURN BLACK
Glowing spines (color hold)
SPINES LIFT
Glowing spines (color hold)
TRAPS BULK UP
SLENDER
THICKER BODY
Yellow and
ange accents
SCAR UNDER RIGHT EYE
SLEEVES PIECED FROM OTHER FABRICS
t find random
e shapes within
ail and make
m glow yellow
and orange.
HAIR SPIKY & SHORT ON SIDES.
TALE WIDENS
BANDANAS HOLDING SHIN GUARDS
Thinner membrane around fins is pink

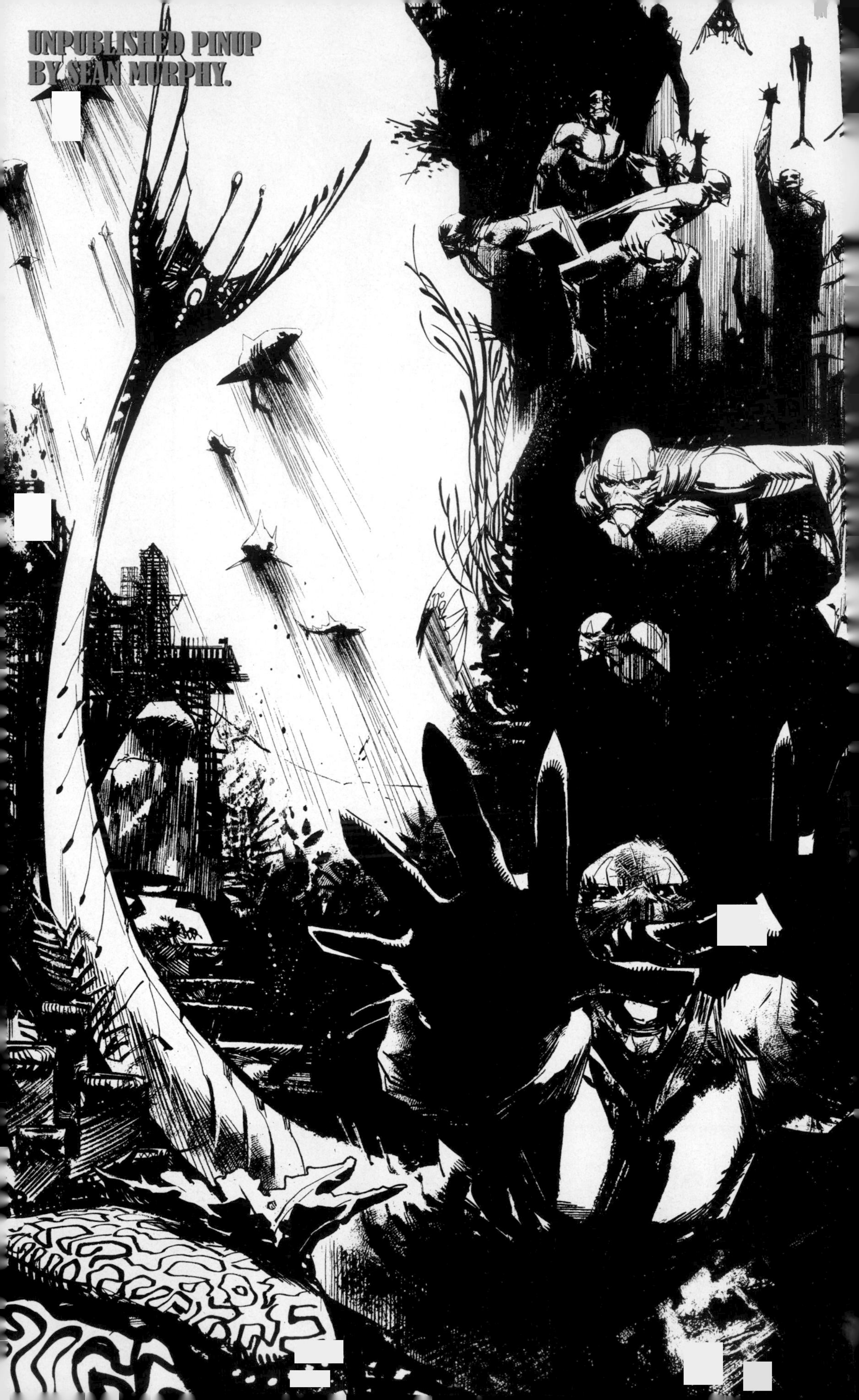

UNPUBLISHED PINUP
BY SEAN MURPHY.

Colors By Matt Hollingsworth

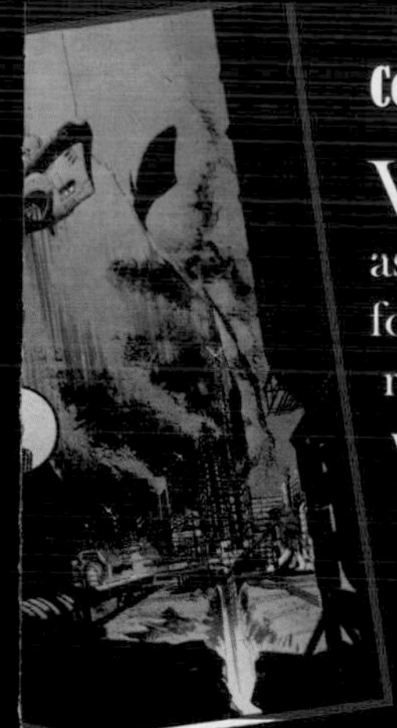

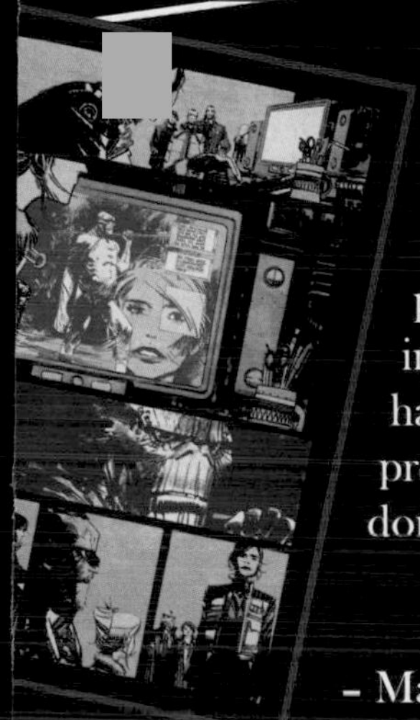

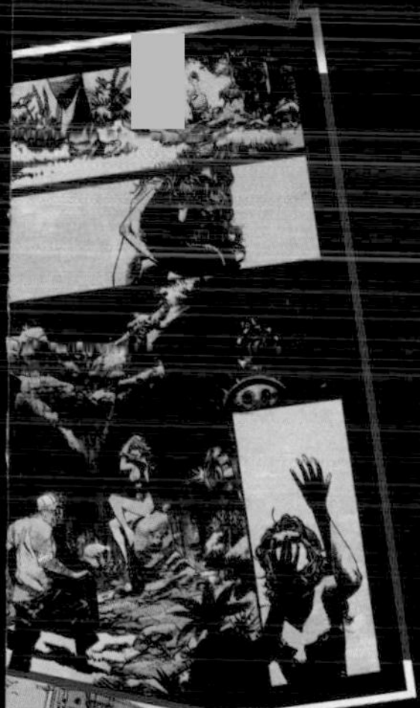

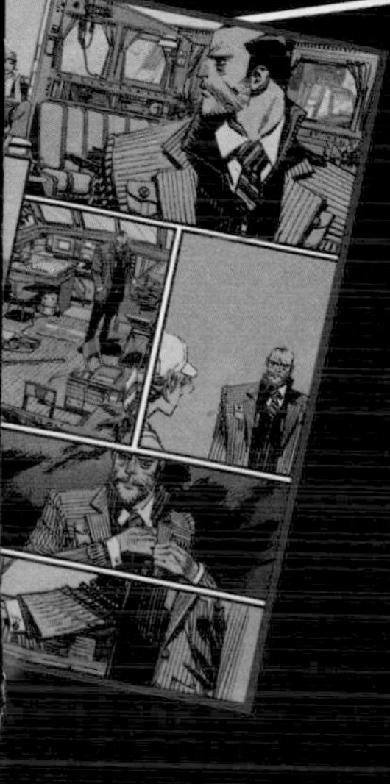

When I first started talking with Sean about working on The Wake, he asked me if I liked Japanese woodblock prints and if I'd be willing to go for a similar look on the book. He sent me links to various pieces by Hiroshi Yoshida, which I loved. I looked and found more and more of his work and used it as inspiration. I would open a few pieces on my second monitor and leave them up while working. I wasn't copying them or their palettes, just drawing inspiration from some of Yoshida's amazing work. While I can't claim to have produced anything approaching the level of genius that Yoshida had, I'm glad that Sean turned me on to his work.

Another part of my approach on the book is that I color the entire book at one time. I keep all of the pages open and go back and forth on them, looking at the entire book and how it's fitting together as an overall design. It's important to me that the book works as a unified piece of storytelling rather than just having a bunch of pretty pieces that don't fit together.

- Matt

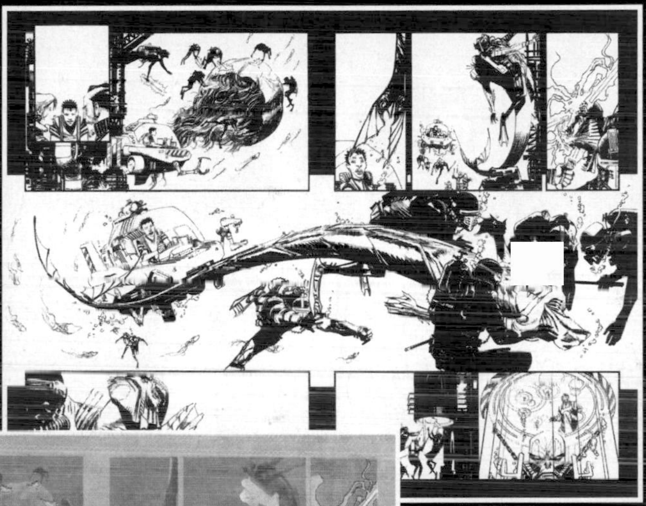

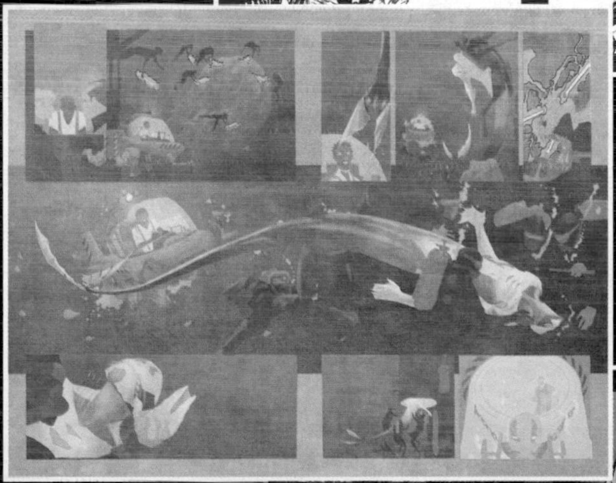

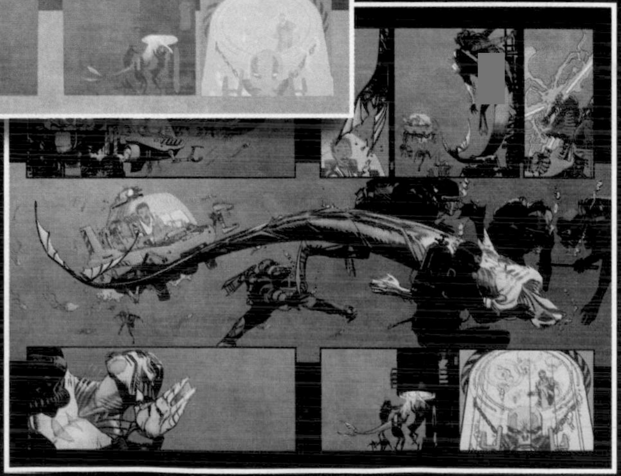

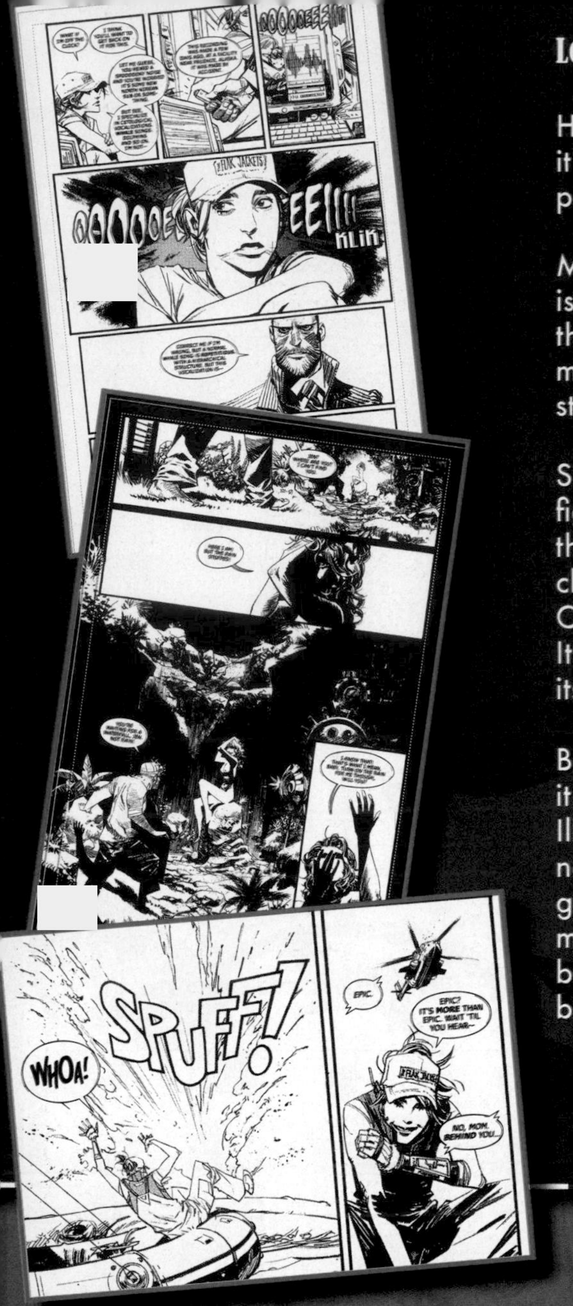

SPUFF!
WHOA!
EPIC.
EPIC? IT'S MORE THAN EPIC. WAIT 'TIL YOU HEAR—
NO, MOM. BEHIND YOU.

Letters by Jared K. Fletcher

Here would be my "process" if you could call it that. I always feel like my process is a damn process unto itself...

My entire approach to lettering comics like this is to try to make everything fit within the style c the artist. My style is that I have many styles. C maybe no style. But I never teach the Wu-Tang style.

Since Sean's line is so thin, and a lot of the figures are on the taller side, I wanted a font that could match those qualities. Something clean with nice smooth lines. So I'm using a Comiccraft font called Legendary Legerdemair It's crisp and doesn't draw too much attention itself.

But the art also has a brush quality to parts of it. So I built a custom digital brush in Adobe Illustrator to stroke the word balloons with. It's normally just a flat uniform line weight. But this gives it some subtle variation to the lines that make up the balloons and help them better blend in with the art style. It takes a lot longer but I think it's been worth it so far.

The Mermaid balloons

Since the guy is seeing essentially a mirage of the woman, I wanted the balloons to be more of a mirage as well. I kept the font the same because he is still hearing a human voice. A change in that makes you think it's a creature he is talking to. So instead I changed the balloon shapes to tip it visually that this isn't quite what it appears to be. Now that I am working on a cintiq, I actually drew out all these balloons freehand with that. I'm using these digital tools with an analog method to try to get as much out of both as I can.

–J

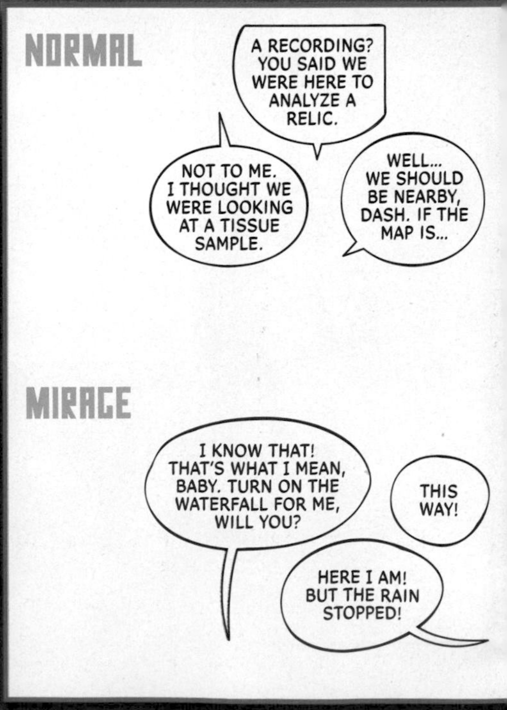

NORMAL
A RECORDING? YOU SAID WE WERE HERE TO ANALYZE A RELIC.
NOT TO ME. I THOUGHT WE WERE LOOKING AT A TISSUE SAMPLE.
WELL... WE SHOULD BE NEARBY, DASH. IF THE MAP IS...
MIRAGE
I KNOW THAT! THAT'S WHAT I MEAN, BABY. TURN ON THE WATERFALL FOR ME, WILL YOU?
THIS WAY!
HERE I AM! BUT THE RAIN STOPPED!

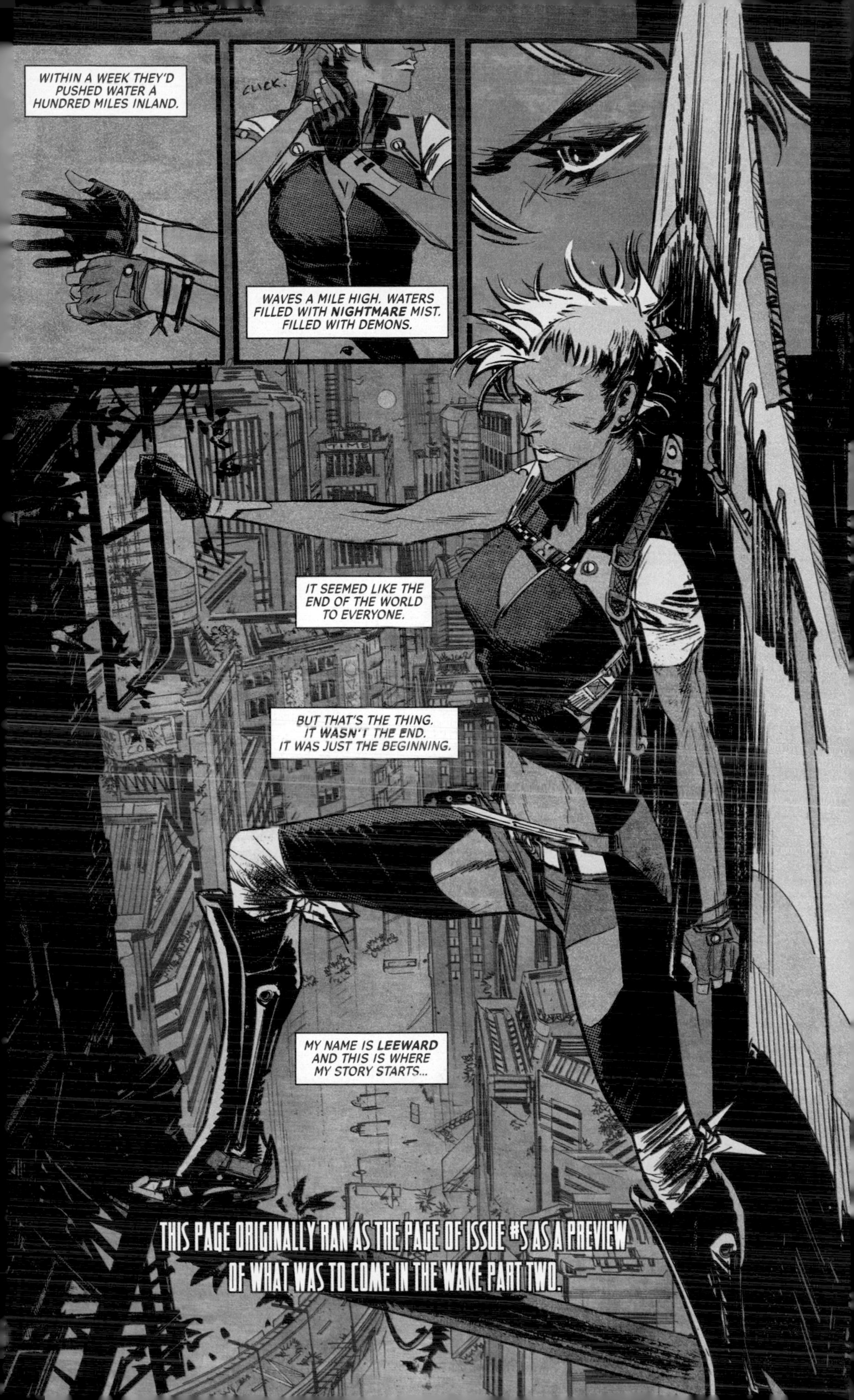
WITHIN A WEEK THEY'D PUSHED WATER A HUNDRED MILES INLAND.
CLICK.
WAVES A MILE HIGH. WATERS FILLED WITH **NIGHTMARE** MIST. FILLED WITH DEMONS.
TIME
IT SEEMED LIKE THE END OF THE WORLD TO EVERYONE.
BUT THAT'S THE THING. IT *WASN'T* THE END. IT WAS JUST THE BEGINNING.
MY NAME IS **LEEWARD** AND THIS IS WHERE MY STORY STARTS...

THIS PAGE ORIGINALLY RAN AS THE PAGE OF ISSUE #5 AS A PREVIEW OF WHAT WAS TO COME IN THE WAKE PART TWO.

SCOTT SNYDER

Scott Snyder has written comics for both DC and Marvel, including the best-selling series BATMAN and SWAMP THING, and is the author of the story collection *Voodoo Heart*. He teaches writing at Sarah Lawrence College and Columbia University. He lives on Long Island with his wife, Jeanie, and his sons Jack and Emmett. He is a dedicated and un-ironic fan of Elvis Presley.

SEAN MURPHY

After breaking into the industry at a young age, Sean Murphy made a name for himself in the world of indie comics before joining up with DC. In his tenure, he has worked on such titles as BATMAN/SCARECROW: YEAR ONE, TEEN TITANS, HELLBLAZER, JOE THE BARBARIAN and the miniseries AMERICAN VAMPIRE: SURVIVAL OF THE FITTEST. Sean also wrote and illustrated the original graphic novel *Off Road*, as well as his popular miniseries, PUNK ROCK JESUS.

MATT HOLLINGSWORTH

Matt Hollingsworth has been coloring comics since 1991. In that time, he's worked on such books as *Preacher*, Hellboy, Daredevil, *Hellblazer*, Death, *The Filth*, Catwoman, *Gotham Central*, Alias, Thor and Hawkeye. He also worked as a texture painter and digital artist on a number of feature films during a two-year stint at Stan Winston Studio, Rhythm and Hues and Sony Pictures Imageworks. He'd like to thank Hiroshi Yoshida, Moebius and Vincent van Gogh for continuing to inspire him. He moved to Croatia in 2006 where he continues to live with his wife Branka and their son Liam.